THE 7 QUALITIES OF TOMORROW'S TOP LEADERS

ANDREAS VON DER HEYDT

For my beautiful girls
Bianca, Jule, and Felicity

ACCLAIM FOR THE 7 QUALITIES OF TOMORROW'S TOP LEADERS

"Andreas von der Heydt has written a very informative and insightful book rooted in his experience at Amazon, L'Oréal and as an executive coach and LinkedIn influencer. A quick read that offers deep and meaningful insight."

—*Jeff Stibel, Chairman, President and CEO,*
Dun & Bradstreet Credibility

"*The 7 Qualities of Tomorrow's Top Leaders* is incredibly engaging, highly relevant, and extremely broad and deep with regards to the topics it covers. Written in a clear and well-structured manner. A must-read for seasoned managers and young entrepreneurs alike."

—*Frédéric Rozé, President & CEO, L'Oréal USA*

"The theme of the book is perfect in terms of timing and pushing the thinking on how to develop the leaders of the future. Innovation and progress are more than ever driven by people. Finding the right attributes and then developing future leaders is the most important task. The chapters and the presented approaches are very well laid out, are comprehensive and extremely thought-provoking."

—*Wolfgang Baier, Group CEO, Singapore Post*

"Andreas von der Heydt is known for his practical and insightful advice on how to be an effective leader. His eclectic views include everything from how to stay calm and perform under pressure to what makes a winning world cup football team. *The 7 Qualities of Tomorrow's Top Leaders* bridges the gap between personal and leadership development. It contains an abundance of useful how-to tips that spring from years of real experience."

—*Jeff DeGraff, Professor, Ross School of Business, University of Michigan*

"A lot has been written about leadership, but no one has so eloquently and accessibly summed up the keys to leadership as we move forward in the emerging Purpose Economy as Andreas von der Heydt."

—Aaron Hurst, CEO & Co-Founder of Imperative,
Founder of Taproot Foundation

"Andreas von der Heydt has distilled volumes of information about management and leadership into the most essential elements that leaders of today and tomorrow can apply to inspire others and outperform. His wisdom is both thoroughly current with regard to realities of organizations and competition today, and timeless as to how people are motivated to achieve great things."

—James M. Citrin, Author, The Career Playbook

"Great future leaders are those that will invest to have the best team, those that will create a strong environment of team work, those that will allow all members to give more to the company and brand, and those who know that the human touch makes the difference. This is one of the core messages of *The 7 Qualities of Tomorrow's Top Leaders*. Substantiated with many relevant examples and practical advices."

—Volfango Bondi, General Manager Europe, Puma

"Andreas von der Heydt wrote a very relevant book. It shows the path for future leaders. You better start the journey today. No time to be wasted."

—Raanan Cohen, Co Founder and CEO, Bringg

"Disruption not only applies to business models, but also to the act and practice of leadership itself. Andreas von der Heydt introduces disruptive leadership – new tools, new rules, and new role models."

—Nicholas Russell, CEO, We Are Pop Up / Ephemeral Labs Limited

"Andreas von der Heydt did a great job in presenting and explaining the *new* leadership needs via a *context triangle* including his impressive experience, a company's future needs and the much needed business impact. *The 7 Qualities of Tomorrow's Top Leaders* is an exceptional book and beautiful learning experience. Andreas perfectly translates his passion into fabulous insights."

—Dr. Dag Piper, Head of Sensory & Consumer Science, Mars

"Quality #8: The leaders of tomorrow read books like these. For the other 7, read the book! You won't be disappointed as anyone who has read Andreas' writings will tell you."

—Lakshmanan (Lux) Narayan, CEO & Co Founder, Unmetric

"*The 7 Qualities of Tomorrow's Top Leaders* postulates that a successful future leader is not any longer a hero, but a balanced leader that also admits mistakes and weaknesses. Andreas' pledge for head and heart leadership underlines that tomorrow's best leaders will strive to achieve both impactful results and sustainable social cohesion in order to build great teams. His book is a realistic-optimistic long-term view on leadership. A true must-read with many helpful advices, examples, and proposed actions."

—Francois Volpi, Vice President Human Resources EMEA &
Americas, Rio Tinto

"The notion to Inspire, Lead & Execute, Explore, Grow, Develop,

—Attila Akat, CEO, Team Creatif USA

"As an avid follower of Andreas von der Heydt I have always found his work highly intriguing. *The 7 Qualities of Tomorrow's Top Leaders* offers a thoughtful journey into the vast field of leadership. Andreas makes leadership theory meaningful and tangible. A true source of inspiration."

—Markus T. Ense, Vice President EMEA, Amer Sports

"An executive book that covers key attributes of a true leader for today's and tomorrow's business environment. An impressive collection of practical experiences and inspirational insights. The new road map that guides future leaders to what they need to develop to become successful leaders."

—Deia Bayoumi, Vice President Electrical / Electronic
Manufacturing, ABB

"There's a great difference between leadership and management. Andreas von der Heydt teaches us what it takes to lead, to inspire teams and to innovate. His 7 qualities of future leaders changes everything about how we should work and lead."

—Brian Solis, Principal Analyst Altimeter Group,
Best-selling author, Leader

CONTENTS

FOREWORD

I F MAKING PROFESSIONAL mistakes were a sport I would be a champion. I've made most of the common mistake, like forgetting to manage up. I've ignored the need to build solid relationships across functional areas. I've failed to read the mood of meeting rooms and pushed a point too long, too hard, and too far. I've assumed that what was said was what was actually meant.

You probably have, at least once, made the same types of mistakes.
Yet I've ranged a lot farther afield with my career missteps. I once ate my lunch during an internal job interview. (In my defense, I was hungry.) I insulted a boss's wife at an office party. (In my defense, she deserved it.) I decided dress codes applied to everyone not named Jeff. (In my defense, I really didn't like wearing khakis.)

Too often I thought the rules didn't apply to me... and I wasn't at all smart about noticing when the time was right to break a rule – for all the right reasons. So while I was a solid performer and stood out for a number of great reasons, I also stood out for a number of negative reasons – and that definitely impacted my early career success. I did learn from all my mistakes. But those lessons were painful and set my career back months and even years.

If experience is the best teacher, Andreas's book is the second best teacher. He's not only been there and done that (a particularly American phrase), but he's thought about what he's done – and he's thought about how to do it even better. He's collected a series of posts that provide outstanding nuts and bolts tips leavened with a big dose of humanity, caring, and empathy.

Most importantly, he shares tremendous insights on the most vital career skill set of all: working for, with, and through other people to achieve professional and personal success. No one does anything worthwhile alone, and Andreas not only embraces that fact, he shows how it's done – and done exceptionally well.

It's okay to make mistakes. We've all made them, and we'll all continue to make them. No mistake is every fatal as long as we learn and grow from the experience. So it's okay to make mistakes.

What's not okay is to ignore ways to learn and grow by listening to smart, experienced, and insightful people. Andreas is one of those people – and in the following pages he'll help you not only avoid making a few career missteps, more importantly *The 7 Qualities Of Tomorrow's Top Leaders* will provide you with some tools that will help you achieve your professional and personal goals.

So turn the page and take notes, make plans, set your goals a little higher... and remember not to eat your lunch during a job interview. Trust me; it won't go well.

Jeff Haden, Inc. Magazine Contributing Editor,
Speaker, LinkedIn Influencer

INTRODUCTION

WHEN I WAS asked in late summer 2012 if I would like to attend a brand new program at LinkedIn by becoming one of their first 50 global LinkedIn Influencers, my interest was captured from the very beginning. Mainly because it gave me the beautiful opportunity to pursue one of my passions and to write blog articles on LinkedIn about any topic and share and discuss them with millions of business professionals, students, and academics from all over the world.

Since then, I've published 100 articles which have been read by more than 3 million people, commented on several thousand times, and liked by tens of thousands. Many of them sent mails of appreciation, others challenged my thoughts and concepts, and some even proposed specific topics for my upcoming blog articles. It came with big surprise - and even bigger joy - when an increasing number of readers asked why I would not bring all of my articles together into a book so it could serve them as a single point of consolidated reference. The more often I was asked, the more realistic the thought became.

Finally – and certainly stimulated by the natural milestone of having written 100 articles - I've finally categorized the articles into what I believe are the 7 crucial qualities and characteristics of great future leaders. In addition, I put all articles into a specific order, wrote the intro texts for each of the 7 chapters, and got everything proofread by the magnificent Helen Gadie, who was a highly capable and professional help. Last but not least, I had to come up with (hopefully) a good book title and an eye-catching cover (many thanks Mila!). Not to mention having to learn how to publish an ebook on Kindle Direct Publishing.

Anyway, here is the final piece! I sincerely hope you will enjoy it and that it might also help you to rethink, to reflect, to grow, and to succeed in your very own personal way. It certainly helped – and still helps - me a lot to continue learning on my journey to become a better future leader.

I would be very pleased to hear your feedback and thoughts on the book. Please comment on Amazon, or on any other platform where you bought the book, or simply mail to: avonderheydt@consumergoodsclub.com. Thank you very much!

Andreas von der Heydt

Chapter 1

INSPIRE!

TOMORROW'S TOP LEADERS truly think bold and big. They challenge themselves and their teams to live their dreams. They trust in their skills and capabilities, search for the big picture, and enjoy looking beyond it. They think, feel, behave, and act positively. They surround themselves with like-minded believers, positive shapers, and creative makers. They have understood that you are what you eat, i.e. you are affected by the company you keep.

They use the power of questioning (e.g. tons of Why and Why Not questions) to overcome fear of failure, bringing more alteration to their lives, and helping to uncover what one really wants to do with their life to assist in triggering improvements and innovations.

Although these leaders also analyze mistakes and failures of the past, they are much more focused on developing future visions by thinking outside of the box. And afterwards, they spend a lot of time explaining their visions to their teams to get their buy-in and support.

Finally, great future leaders know how to deliver mind-changing and inspirational presentations and speeches. They include impactful and often emotional stories to make their points, they respect their audience by talking to them and involving them, and they keep their message simple and concise.

1. THE MAGIC OF THINKING BIG

In order to achieve big goals we need to be willing to think big. Theoretically we all can do it. In reality, however, we often constrain ourselves, we have doubts in our skills and capabilities, and we might lack self-belief and confidence. As a result we do not see the big picture.

How to get rid of our self-imposed limitations? How to give ourselves a try? Below are my best strategies for you to become a Big Thinker and to experience its magic:

Live your dreams. If you can dream and imagine it, you can do it.

Allocate enough time to dream and to think. Sounds (too) obvious? Well, are you doing it?

Believe in you and your ideas. Then others will copy and follow you.

Think, feel, behave, and act positively. That will trigger a positive spiral of self-confidence and create a can-do-attitude.

Be bold and brave. Be daring and encourage yourself and others to fail.

Get on your feet again after each failure. Be proud of you. Analyze the reasons of the setbacks. Then look ahead, keep going and try it again, and again.

Delete the word "problem" from your vocabulary and replace it with "solution."

Think outside of the box. Think colors instead of numbers.

Surround yourself with like-minded believers, positive shapers, and creative makers. You are what you eat, i.e. you are affected by the company you keep.

Treat others with respect. Then they will support and respect you. This will strengthen your self-confidence, and – as a result – will stimulate your creativity and boldness.

Be prepared to be misunderstood (for a long time). Don't question yourself too often. Instead, try to explain your vision and don't stray from your path, if you're fully convinced. Stay focused.

Break down your vision into ambitious goals. Have them supported by a doable action plan. Take possible setbacks into account for your planning. They will naturally occur.

2. SIX SUCCESS QUESTIONS YOU MUST ASK

Progress and innovation - and ultimately success - are significantly influenced by questions which have been asked. Either asked out of necessity or out of general curiosity.

Unfortunately, many of us have forgotten how to ask questions. Others have become too lazy to ask them. And again others might not have many opportunities to raise questions or are afraid of doing so. Why?

Let's face it: Our education systems, way of life, and even the business world is not geared toward questions. Moreover, we often tend to address topics in a superficial manner by asking questions which rather test and reward knowledge (mostly using closed questions) than stimulating inquisitiveness (applying open questions, for example).

To flip that, I suggest applying the following set of powerful questions both in personal and professional settings:

The *WHY?* Question

This should be the very first question to be asked. It encourages you to step back. It makes you think about the deeper purpose, the vision, and the need for change. Restless and successful companies, often also start-ups, are true Why Question Masters. Examples:

"Why am I doing that?"
"Why have they chosen this color?"
"Why are we doing it this way?"
"Why are we in this business?"

The *WHY NOT?* Question

It's more than just the opposite of the "Why?" question. It is about overcoming resistance. Your own inner one and/or objections from others who challenge your thinking and ideas. Examples:

"Why am I not stopping it right now?"
"Why are we not selling dog food instead of cars?"
"Why might our customers not like this offer?"

The *What If?* and *What If Not?* Questions

These questions take us further in the decision making process. They make our ideas more real and bring them closer to a possible implementation. They also help us to find out which answer and solution is the most adequate one. And which ones might not be suitable at all. Examples:

"What if we were to do it like x or y?"
"What if money were no issue?"
"What if I did not run this project?"
"What if our company were not to compete in this market segment?"

The *What Else?* Question

This is a crucial question which is frequently and easily forgotten. Still, it's key as it motivates us to change our perspective even more drastically. It assists in continuing to ponder on different options and on possible alternatives. It stimulates us to think in bolder terms and to further peel the onion. Examples:

"What else can we do?"
"What else would Warren Buffet do?"
"What else can product X deliver?"
"What else do our customers expect?"

The *How?* Question

This is the second to last question. Usually it's also the most difficult one as it bridges the creative and strategic thinking and questioning process with more operational aspects, questions, and tasks. Examples:

"How I can I improve my life by doing this?"
"How can we best launch the product?"
"How would Peter or Sarah do it? How would company X do it? How would they do it in another industry?"

The *Who?* and *When?/ By When?* Questions

Finally, and to ensure implementation of our answers, ideas, and concepts, we need to raise these two sets of closed questions (note: do not ask any closed question any earlier than at this stage of the evaluation process). Examples:

"Who will take care of such customer complaints?"
"When can we deliver it?"
"By when will Fred have changed the material?"

Regrettably, asking the right questions is typically not taught in schools or MBA programs. Using questioning in your daily life, i.e. using the right questions to overcome fear of failure, bringing more alteration to your life, and helping you uncover what you really want to do with your life is very powerful and assists in triggering improvements and innovations.

Today's speedy business world often considers asking questions as a waste of time and a distraction from executing. I'm a general supporter of the "just do it and bias for action" mentality. At the same time, I believe in thinking, analyzing, reviewing and drafting a thorough strategy.

And to do that in a solid and comprehensive manner, we firstly need to ask the right questions. Or, in other words:

"He who asks a question is a fool for five minutes; he who does not ask a question remains a fool forever." (Chinese Proverb)

Final note: I'd like to recommend you to read the inspiring book 'A More Beautiful Question' by Warren Berger. Warren superbly categorizes - by giving excellent background and latest research information – the creative questioning process into the Why - What If - How stages.

3. STOP MAKING RESOLUTIONS - DEVELOP YOUR VISION INSTEAD!

Late December 2012 I arrived with my family in New York City to celebrate New Year's Eve and to spend some enjoyable, relaxing and at the same time exciting days - days full of family togetherness, of stimulation and in parallel packed with thought-provoking ideas and some madness.

A contradiction? Possibly. Depending on one's point of view and expectations. And there's nothing wrong with that of course. I fully respect that for many people these two angles do not go well together. Personally, I need such "mixed" and somehow "confronting" moments. Such inter-linked situations of calmness on the one side and inhaling new impressions on the other side. That keeps my brain firing and generating new synopses. And more importantly, it makes me start dreaming and coming up with bold, brand-new thoughts. Thoughts beyond traditionally self-imposed limitations: True and inspiring visions! And where better to dream and visionize than in the city that never sleeps?

According to Wikipedia, dreams are defined as "successions of images, ideas, emotions, and sensations that occur involuntarily in the mind during certain stages of sleep." That's at least the more academic definition. Not exactly what I'm referring to here. The "dreams" I'm pursuing whilst trying to do some elegant ice skating moves at the Trump – Wollman rink in Central Park, or whilst enjoying the breath-taking view from the 102nd floor of the Empire State building at night, or when admiring the beautifully decorated shop windows at Bergdorf Goodman on 5th Avenue, or when watching the splendid Mamma Mia musical at Broadway's Winter Garden theater, or whilst inhaling the hype and vibrations at 5th Avenue's huge Uniqlo store, are very different. They're much more like having visions. Yes, that's it. Such special moments strongly resemble "a long-term view and concentration on the future. It can be emotive and it is a source of inspiration."

And now, as we are already one week into January and as we have just bid farewell to another year, the time has come when we are conditioned to turn our thoughts towards making these (in)famous New Year's resolutions: "I need to work out more this year"; "I need to quit smoking"; "I need to spend more time with friends", etc., etc. You certainly know all about it and about your own personal New Year resolutions, don't you? Such resolutions are mostly about what we should stop in the future or what we should start doing soon in order to become more effective and to become a "better" person. Whatever that might mean. And that's the reason I'm not such a big fan of them.

What I'm saying is: Forget about making any resolutions. Don't waste your energy and efforts on doing so. Instead, you should immediately start developing your professional and personal vision for this magnificent new year. What is it you'd really love to achieve? What is it you've always wanted to do? What is it that would make you happy and would give you the unique feeling of fulfilment?

Yes, open up your thinking horizon! C'mon, start dreaming! Now! Follow your desires and wishes, and think about how you would like to realize your hopes and wishes. That means, once you have come up with your vision, translate it into specific objectives. And only once you have done that, think about concrete action steps to attain such goals. And at the very end, and not before that, you can develop a couple of New Year's resolutions... if you really think you can't live and make it without them... which you can, you brave women and men out there!

So, let's start every year in a pro-active, creative and outrageous thinking way. Do not kick it off by contemplating what might be wrong and what you might need to stop doing in the future. Instead, dare to be bold and dare to dream!

4. WHAT THE BEST BRANDS WILL DO IN 2015

2014 is over and smart marketers know that they need to get ahead of the trends and anticipate relevant new products and services. If not, they will be devoured by their competitors.

Some of my marketing and brand forecasts heading into 2014, such as the sharp growth of the shared economy, came true sooner than expected: Airbnb is now valued at more than $13 billion (vs. Hyatt Hotels $9 billion) and Uber more than $18 billion. Other predictions, such as top brands' push for being best in retail or the digital transformation, are under way and gain momentum by the day.

Now, let's jointly look at what I think can be some of the most important focus areas of top brands in 2015:

Being Best in Focusing

Whenever I speak with chief marketing officers and marketing directors it becomes quickly obvious that many struggle with how to tackle digital marketing, how to develop a holistic content marketing strategy, and how to implement the tons of new ideas. As a consequence, in 2015 the best marketers will clean up the house and focus on selected big bets. Major projects and concepts which fit best with their brand's DNA and core values. Going "Back to Basics" will be a key trend in 2015: To re-evaluate the target audience, determine what works and what doesn't, re-prioritize and be smart about resource allocation and investment.

Being Best in Shifting Marketing Investments into Mobile and Digital

In its most recent ad spending report, Zenith Optimedia reduced their 2015 marketing spend forecast by 0.4 points to a +5.3% growth; anticipating weaker growth for traditional media and for Europe and Japan. Strong digital media growth will be mostly fuelled by mobile advertising which is expected to grow by an average of 51% a year between 2013 and 2016.

Being Best at Justifying Marketing ROI

Also in 2015, brands will have to challenge themselves on how to measure marketing ROI, how to maximize marketing impact in consumer and business-to-business settings, how to adopt best practices for customer lifecycle management, and how to implement state-of-the-art segmentation techniques. More than ever the challenge will be to measure the ROI of their investment in content marketing. Yesterday it was about fans and likes. Today it's about social reach and page views. And in 2015 it will be about attention, engagement, desire, and how these affect the company's sales and reputation. Leading brands will have the right software tools in place to plan and to track. You might want to check out Wingify's A/B testing platform – called Visual Website Optimizer - which is for people even if they don't have HTML or coding experience (like me).

Being Best at Meeting the Audience

Top brands constantly analyze the communities and geographies where their audience is. In most Western countries you would need to be on Facebook, Twitter, and Instagram. Depending on your business, you would also need to be on LinkedIn (a must channel for B2B marketing), Pinterest, and YouTube. In other countries like China, sites and services like Sina Weibo, RenRen, or Pengyou should be covered. And yes, don't worry too much about Google+ in 2015. In summary, don't rush into every new social network. Instead, find the right ones for you, i.e. evaluate carefully where your current and potential customers are and might go to.

Therefore smart marketers will make sure to be in all relevant interest-based networks (as opposed to Facebook-style people-based networks). Depending on your product, consider sites for cat lovers, for cooks and food lovers, or sites like Fitocrazy for fitness junkies. You could even build your own social network (possibly in cooperation with other companies), by using Tint, for example, which is a self-service platform that allows organizations to create social hubs in minutes. Tint aggregates, curates, and displays any social media feeds anywhere. According to Mary Meeker and her famous Internet Trend Reports, the 4 Ps have been supplemented by the 3Cs: Content, community, commerce.

The following rising social media sites and apps every top marketer should watch: Ello (the hipster social network which promised to never sell user data, currently still in Beta and invite-only), Yik Yak (exchanges fully anonymous posts with people who are physically nearby), Whisper,

Bubbly, Heard, and WeChat. To find out more on how to grow your brand and your business via social media, go ahead and read the social media industry report.

Being Best at Saving Customers' Time and responding ASAP

Top brands and companies will offer more "order ahead" functionalities and superefficient services allowing their customers to save time. In hotels, many guests want to skip the front desk. Therefore an increasing number of hotels will introduce a digital check in allowing their guests to use their smartphone as the room key. Hyatt, Hilton, and Starwood hotels are already testing some of these services. Another example is Starbucks, which announced that it will introduce for the first time Mobile Order and Pay in stores in 2015. This will enable customers to place orders in advance of their visit and pick them up at their selected Starbucks location. Imagine not having to wait in-line any longer than 15 minutes for your Caramel Machiatto!

Social media created a consumer with short-term thinking. And best marketers – with lots of data at their hands – are capable of faster adaption, shorter lead times, and real-time communication. Marketing champions will answer within an hour and not within a week or a day. In Edelman's Brandshare study of 15,000 people worldwide, the number one most important behavior indicated was a brand's ability to respond quickly to concerns and complaints; with 78% of consumers saying it's important but only 17% feeling brands do this well. The gap is particularly pronounced in the areas people value most – responsiveness, involvement and conviction.

Being Best at addressing new Consumers entering the Marketplace

The Millennial generation - aka Generation Y and with most researchers using birth years ranging from the early 1980s to the mid-1990s – according to a 2014 report by The Boston Consulting Group (BCG) chooses brands that are better aligned with their own morals and values. And because Millennials are social media and mobile users, the impact of their brand choices and feedback is greatly amplified and accelerated.

Then there is Gen Z. A name used for the cohort of people born after the Millennial Generation, i.e. born roughly between 1995 and 2010. They carry a large influence and buying power. Gen Z demands complete personalization, expects instantaneous validation, and looks for affirmation from their peers. For example, national retailer Claire's Inc. developed their Best Friends Forever

(BFF) jewelry offerings, grew their social media databases, and engaged their "tween" girl target by appealing to Gen Z's sense of creativity and individuality. Read the whole case study here.

Being Best at generating Engagement and creating Emotional Bonding

An excellent example is Nike's Find Your Greatness campaign which touches all of us because it's such a positive, inclusive message. One of the campaign's best commercials is The Jogger, featuring 12-year-old Nathan from London, Ohio who tells us that greatness is not beyond his reach, nor is it for any of us. It's a memorable ad which resonates with consumers as it delivers a personally meaningful message. It links back to the brand's values and at the same time represents beliefs which go beyond the brand and its products.

Top brands will use tools like Digital Platform GPS which can optimize placements and resolve issues related to native advertising and shorter consumer attention spans. Metrics will move away from counting the number of views, sharing, and likes, toward real engagement. Brand consultancies like Brandkeys have developed specialized systems that provide brands with predictive and strategic findings that can increase ROI, sales and profitability.

Also, the ability to craft visual stories that inspire emotion and spark the movement will help companies get noticed and amplify their message. For example via Visual Storytelling. If you're looking for a book that will give you inspiration for creating a visually based marketing campaign using a wide variety of social media platforms, then I recommend the book The Power of Visual Storytelling by E. Walter and J. Gioglio.

Being Best at practicing a human and transparent Communication Style

Leading brands will interact with their audience with respect and not just post and think that's it. They exchange with their customers in a consistent and regular manner, and quickly and clearly answer their questions. These brands will give an accurate and real-time picture of what they are doing in the interest of the consumer, at any given time. They define content marketing as not being advertising. They focus on building relationships in a simple and straightforward manner.

Taking the Classroom to the Streets is an excellent example for such a campaign, even executed with a small budget. I also see more and more companies applying human and humorous elements. A good laugh or the vulnerability of silliness is a convincing way to earn trust and loyalty. Wren, a small L.A. clothing label, with "First Kiss", did a three-and-a-half-minute video showing strangers being asked to kiss on camera. Showing deep emotions and human vulnerability it was – and even if you did not like it – affecting, fascinating, and touching. And by the way, it got 5 million views in its first day, and has close to 100 million to date.

Another good example: In honor of Earth Day on April 22, NASA has invited everyone to take part in a Global Selfie and submit a photo via Twitter, Facebook, Instagram, Flickr, and Google+. Finally an image was built using 36,422 individual photos.

Being Best at caring in a sincere Manner

Most of today's consumers do not express their protests in the streets anymore. They're voting for or against a brand at the check-out of both offline and online stores. In other words: Top brands will supplement their big and often anonymous Corporate Social Responsibility projects with more localized, individualized, and personalized initiatives. Marketers will need to keep adding "purpose" to their brands and products. In 2015, consumers want to balance consumption with ethical concerns more than ever. Initiatives like Small Business Saturday or Giving Tuesday as a natural corrective to Black Friday and Cyber Monday will gain further momentum.

Top brands will need to find a way to get involved now and not to be left out. They will need to support people to find their individual strengths, skills, and ways to improve their behavior and way of life, either by offering special services and trainings which go beyond the pure product or by granting personalized incentives or rewards that motivate customers to continue with their efforts. A good example is the Headspace meditation app. As a user you can map your journey, track your progress, and get rewards as you go. You can even buddy up with friends and motivate each other along the way. Foodtweek is another superb example for combining business with supporting relevant causes. Every calorie you trim with Foodtweek will be donated to a local food bank and becomes a nutritious calorie for a hungry family.

Being Best at applying new Marketing Technologies

Too many companies think in terms of digital marketing. Instead, they should be thinking in terms of marketing in a digital world. The best marketers in 2015 will consider themselves also as marketing technologists - as someone with heavy digital acumen and a passion for technology, data, and analytics. Without doubt, 2015 will be the year digital measurement finally comes of age. Smart brands have already formalized their efforts across organizations as well as marketing and IT departments. You might want to check out the following course about strategic data-driven marketing. For additional good courses to acquire data science degrees for a fraction of the cost of business schools, have a look at these excellent MOOC (Massive Open Online Courses) courses.

Another very useful source of information can be found here. Companies like Google are also offering some helpful seminars and tools with its Analytics Academy or its Analytics Premium tool. The very best brands, however, will go beyond analytics in 2015 as they've understood that analyzing is only a descriptive exercise. Benchmarking is fundamental to understanding what's happening today.

But to outperform your competitors you need something that will help you produce the right content moving forward. These brands will use social media analytics and competitive intelligence platforms like Unmetric, which are able to compile data in minutes, analyze marketing efforts and compare them against the competitors that matter. Armed with this information and specific data-driven creativity tools, such marketers will be able to plan and create content that will set their brands apart. As a top-notch marketer you should also know Kenshoo, which offers one of the most advanced predictive marketing softwares encompassing campaign creation, audience targeting, bidding and budgeting, measurement, training and support.

Being Best at marketing new Consumer Technology

Visual communication will be a main trend in 2015. Just think Instagram or YouTube for videos. However (and what a surprise), YouTube is not the only traffic-generating place where you can upload your videos. I recommend the following ones to upload and distribute your video content: Vimeo (fast growing!), Flickr (not only for still images), Break, Dailymotion, and Vine.

Another trend is the further rise of messaging apps. The most popular ones are: WhatsApp (still the dominant leader), Slack (very popular among young businesses), Snapchat (although there were privacy concerns), Kik (popular among teens), and Japanese Line (popular among celebs, allowing voice calls over the internet, etc.).

Video blogs and videos will continue to gain significantly more shares versus print and text blogs. Already today, more than 5,000 companies use Brightcove to publish and distribute online videos to websites, social networks, smartphones and tablets.

Simple, clean, and single-purpose apps which are easy and fast to use will be another major trend to watch for in 2015. Even Facebook looks to further unbundle its experience into single-use applications like messaging, photography, contact management, location services, etc. Foursquare has already broken itself up by having launched Swarm some months ago. Other multi-brand and multi-product companies should seriously think about how best to develop unique apps for each of them. Saying that, marketers must carefully review their core user base and analyze their behaviors, needs, and wants. And only then define their (mobile) app and content strategy: single-use app, multi-purpose apps, and/or hybrid apps.

Artificial Intelligence (AI), virtual reality, and wearables represent another three key technologies in 2015 for top brands to follow and possibly shape. In regards to AI, many leading brands – and not only the usual suspects like Google, Amazon, Facebook, etc. - will take their first serious steps with machine learning and will invest in robotics. With giant eyes and a childlike face, Softbank's Pepper humanoid robot that can read and react to human emotions will help to sell Nescafe coffee in Japan. Also, other companies in the hospitality industry, for example, will use cutting-edge technology to create unique guest experiences by offering drone delivery service like at the Casa Madrona hotel in Sausalito or the robot A.L.O. as a concierge at the Aloft Hotel in Cupertino, California.

Even if in 2015 AI might be embraced only by the very elite of the top brands, progressive marketers should already now think about using tools which are powered by AI, such as e.g. Conversica which is one of the very few automated software solutions that can contact, engage, nurture, qualify and follow-up with leads without the need for human interaction.

With developments such as a cardboard DIY headset from Google and the Samsung Gear VR coming soon, I expect that virtual reality will get closer to the mainstream in 2015 than ever before.

Finally, wearables like fitness trackers (e.g. those from Jawbone and Fitbit), fitness-tracker and smartwatch hybrids like the Gear Fit and Microsoft Band, smartwatches like Samsung Gear S, Motorola Moto 360, Pebble, or the soon to come iWatch of Apple collect data and zap it off wirelessly to the Internet and all major social networks. Regardless if it's a good thing or not, it will happen, and as a marketer you better know what to do about it.

Being Best at offering easy mobile Payment Solutions

With Apple, Amazon, Google, Facebook, Twitter, and many more working on it, the mobile wallet will get significant traction in 2015. In addition, there are other powerful new kids on the block which top marketers need to have on their radar; like Venmo, SinglePoint, Square or Level Up.

Although at this stage the endgame isn't exactly clear, for sure we will also see major social networks trying more aggressively to handle financial transactions in 2015. Click here to get the latest mobile payment influencer study.

Being Best at embracing the Sharing Economy

All leading and ambitious brands will need to be part of it. Full stop. Even, if it's only to try it and to learn from their experiences to further develop their main products and offerings. The sharing economy has arrived in a big way and is here to stay. The internet of things will also become the internet of sharing things. Although in some countries some old-fashioned and backward looking politicians and lobbyists try to stop some Peer-to-Peer sites with sometimes obscure legal means, by now most of us have taken an Uber ride or stayed at an Airbnb place.

In 2015 the sharing economy will enter the next level. First, existing players will diversify their offers. Ride-sharing services, like Lyft, launched Lyft Line mid-2014. Currently available in three US cities, users can share a ride with others going the same way, and pay up to 60% less. There will be a national roll out during 2015.

Second, third party companies like Breeze – only founded in 2014 and backed by Marc Cuban – will build an ecosystem around existing sharing economy companies. Breeze offers customers flexible access to vehicles they can use to support jobs as drivers for Uber, Lyft, etc. Denver-based Evolve is doing something similar by offering marketing and booking services for homeowners and offering travelers a simple booking experience.

Third, the sharing economy will spread into all areas of life. Think of companies like Simplist, which helps you find experts across all of your networks. And fourth, it is expected that membership and subscription models will continue to grow in 2015 such as book subscription services like Kindle Unlimited, Scribd, Oyster or video streaming services like Netflix, Amazon Instant Video, Google Play, etc. To get more info, data, case studies, etc. on the pulse of Mesh and the sharing economy, click here.

Being Best at Data Security

Remember Target, Home Depot, eBay, Sony... All of them – and many more companies – were hacked. Customer data is a key asset for both companies and their customers. Unfortunately, still too many companies are treating customer data with woefully inadequate protections. As "The Internet of All Things" matures, consumers will expect greater security. The time is now to apply a strict security strategy and to have contingency plans in place. Moreover, there is a severe need to cooperate with specialized companies like Security Scorecard which provide insights into the security posture and key risks of a company and its business partners to proactively tackle cybercriminals.

Being Best at Setting up own in-house Incubator and Accelerator Programs

Already in 2010 Pepsi launched PepsiCo10, an incubator program that matches technology, media and communications entrepreneurs with PepsiCo brands for pilot programs. Other leading brands like Coca-Cola, Disney, Siemens, etc. followed.

In the majority of cases, however, these models use the traditional principle that the sponsoring company provides expertise and guidance and allows the emerging new venture to create and develop its own brands and products.

In 2015, however, top brands will start to run in-house incubators of "start-ups" to assist with the development of new products and services which are at the core of their businesses; instead of just considering a "start-up" as an opportunity to develop new technologies or improve processes. Also, small companies which are tied down by a shoestring budget can use sophisticated software programs and services like HubSpot's Jumpstart to build or expand their online business in an incubator-style. Jumpstart gives you 30+ marketing tools starting at €64 per month.

Being Best at Internal Communications

In 2015, top brands and companies will focus more than ever on internal communications as a marketing asset. They will communicate frequently and broadly with all key stakeholders to explain the brand's vision, ambitions, and strategy. The more innovative, dynamic, and disruptive they are, the more they need to get employees, suppliers, and partners involved and engaged. The very best brands will create brand ambassador programs centered around their own employees or customers. By assessing a company's core values and cultivating a workforce that lives up to those values, these brands create a culture that promotes loyalty, strong customer service, and fun. One of my favorite examples is Zappos, which is magnificent at giving its employees freedom to develop and to act as an ambassador by talking on behalf of Zappos in front of customers, key vendors or industry events, for example.

Being Best at building A Brand Ecosystem

In the age of mobile content consumption people no longer simply "listen" and "read." They "monitor" and "scan." They make a decision in the blink of an eye as to how valuable a piece of content is, how much time they should give to it, and ultimately whether they buy a product or not. As a result, an organization must craft user experiences that befit the environment in which readers will discover, read, and share. Best brands will continue to create a common brand experience across the digital experience on- and offline by building a meaningful community, i.e. an ecosystem around the brand and crafting the right pathway to the product or service that a specific user needs and wants. A good example is the MINI - Chase The Paceman campaign which ran in the UK this year.

Being Best at morphing Departments

The markets are turning more complex. Top companies and brands will push hard to continue overcoming functional borders within their organizations. They will break up traditional silos and insist on bringing people together from various departments. They will morph the marketing and sales function into one as both are the critical customer-facing departments. The CMO will have to apply a holistic and integrating mindset and convince her teams, peers, and CEO for support of such an approach, all in order to improve and exceed at serving the customers. As expressed by Doug Warner from the opposite perspective: "In the world of Internet Customer Service, it's important to remember your competitor is only one mouse click away."

Being Best at keeping and recruiting top Talents

Big corporations will face more trouble than ever retaining and finding top marketing talents. Increasingly, those will reject corporate treadmill careers and instead prefer becoming their own and independent boss via freelancing, partnering with creative boutique agencies, or working for crowdsource brand-building platforms like Colossal Spark or eyeka.

Final Thoughts

In the end it's still the brand that matters. Also in 2015, and facing a more competitive environment than ever with highly demanding and sophisticated consumers, brands will need to continue to differentiate themselves and to clearly stand for something relevant, emotional, and meaningful to consumers.

There is no reason to wait only for top brands to make this happen. Neither now nor in 2015. Every marketer can take over ownership, pay attention to what looms ahead, plan her moves in advance, put herself into the driver seat, and make it happen.

5. WHAT THE BEST BRANDS WILL DO IN 2014

The pace of change, disruption, and fragmentation in many industries can sometimes overwhelm even the savviest and experienced of us. There is a very solid level of know-how and experience required to successfully drive marketing and brand strategies and to execute in excellence. Even more so in the future.

Let's have a look at what I think the main focus areas and aspirations of successful brands will be in 2014.

Being Best in Product and Services Development and Delivery

At the heart of successful marketing and branding is – and also in 2014 and beyond will be – a great product and/or service creation and delivery. Successful brands, products, and services will have a higher level of personalization in order to become more relevant and meaningful to consumers. Besides rational features like quality, price, customer services, etc., the brand decision process will become more emotionally-driven. Strong brands will identify and communicate appropriate emotional values to differentiate themselves and to establish close bonds with consumers and customers. More than ever, and to actively engage today's high-expectation consumers, brands will need to be more focused to develop products and offers which grow the whole category they're operating in and not only their own products.

Being Best in Collaboration

In 2014, organizations and marketing managers need to quickly position themselves in this new open and more collaborative economy. An economy characterized by speedy change and permanent disruption. On the one hand, brands from different industries will work more closely together, from R&D to joint marketing initiatives. On the other hand, the phenomenon of consumers co-creating content and products and sharing ideas will continue to grow. For instance, Airbnb topped 10 million guest stays since its launch and now has 500k properties listed worldwide.

Being Best in Retail

Brands, being confronted with showrooming, e-commerce and cost-conscious, always connected consumers, need to make retail more relevant to consumers and customers by combining off- and online elements into one single multi-channel distribution strategy.

They need to deliver direct brand-to-customer interaction with the help of innovative technology (e.g. touchscreens, sensors, interactive cameras, Wi-Fi- and 4G-connectivity, LCD screens, etc.) by providing opportunities to experience products (see, feel, touch, smell, hear, taste) before and during the purchasing process, by providing easy-to-understand and stimulating product presentations and merchandising solutions, by offering expert staff, consultation facilities, samples, etc. Good examples are Nike, Wal-Mart, and Ikea.

Being Best in Communication

Content is king. That's nothing new anymore. Still, many brands seem to confuse quantity and quality, since there exist so many exciting communication channels and platforms. Just writing up keyword rich blog posts and articles don't cut it anymore. Brands have to say something meaningful and insightful to customers while entertaining them at the same time. There is a great need and opportunity to develop unique brand experiences that engage consumers deeply and comprehensively, that stimulates word of mouth, and that generates a lot of user-generated content. Further, business impact will come from very targeted niche communities from co-operations with credible and influential brand advocates.

Utilizing *storytelling techniques* - while getting away from the transactional relationship – is a very powerful technique and will help to create a strong emotional bond with your customer. Storytelling, although one of the main business buzzwords in 2013, is nothing new and is very much at the core of every great brand's DNA. Videos, pictures, and songs will become more dominant in the future. Working best, they will be blended into one consistent story (e.g. P&G's Proud Sponsor of Moms). Some weeks ago Instagram announced that it would join the visual playing field, alongside other messaging apps like Snapchat and WhatsApp, to enable consumers to share personable moments. On top of being compelling, your content needs to do two things. One, create an emotional connection with your brand, and two, drive customers to action.

Speed and Spontaneousness will be crucial, too. Real-time communication and feedback means to interact and respond quickly to any relevant occurrence, question, etc. Brands can use Twitter feeds during certain TV shows, sports events, etc., to communicate live and instantly with existing and potential new customers. It will take planning, flexibility, humor, creativity, and courage.

Being Best in using Customer-Focused Technology

Mobile technology and communication will become even more important. Already now, half of all social interaction happens on mobile platforms. In consequence, all brand communication must be designed based on a mobile-first perspective. Responsive design has almost become a basic requirement, and it's important to tailor each piece of content to the device or channel where it will most likely be viewed by the consumer. Mobile technology will soon replace all other communication devices as the predominant means. No doubt, in 2014 we are going to see a huge increase in location-based marketing.

Other key technologies are *Streaming* and *On-Demand* media. They are rewiring the way consumers think and process information. People are getting used to having everything customized and delivered instantly, when and where they want it.

Also, *Cognitive Computing* will further evolve, i.e. systems learning and interacting naturally with people. Rather than being programmed to anticipate every possible answer or action, cognitive systems are trained using artificial intelligence and machine learning algorithms to understand and to predict. Applying this to marketing will help managers to better understand and communicate with customers.

Being Best in Data-Driven Customer Experience and Customer Services

Big Data was one of another major buzzword in 2013 in many organizations around the globe. It's a fact that with today's technology we can collect, analyze, and process tons of (consumer) data to better understand consumption patterns, to evaluate commonalities and differences, to anticipate trends, and to identify new business and product opportunities. The real task, however, is to use all of these information – and by respecting possible and legitimate privacy concerns – in a way as to match them with real consumer wants and needs in order to improve the experience of your customers: e.g. new wearable devices like Samsung's Galaxy Smart Watch to improve personal health.

The key is not merely measuring what happened, but trying to predict future outcomes, i.e. to understand why and how it will play out in the future. Analytics have to go from passive to active.

Moreover, collected and stored data needs to be used to establish personal, trustworthy, and – most importantly – respectful relationships with existing and new customers. Big data needs to be seen as a vehicle to dramatically boost an organization's customer obsession and not its capability to spy on consumers and customers. Companies must implement whichever needed security measures to avoid discussions like those currently happening at Target.

Being Best in Corporate Social Responsibility

Companies clearly should make some 2014 resolutions to ensure their CSR and sustainability efforts start off on the right foot in the new year. While it's more or less standard practice for companies to address the environmental and carbon impacts (e.g. resulting from their operations and products), the time has come to take a closer look at how climate change (e.g. storms, floods, resources scarcity) could impact the company from the outside in and across their entire supply chain.

With the gradual depletion of many resources, some organizations are intensively searching for novel alternatives to the materials currently used in their products - an evolution and necessity which will need to be more widely applied. One example is Nike, which has already started to research for more sustainable textiles by partnering with the U.S. State Department, NASA, etc. Other good examples are Coca-Cola and Nestlé.

Leading brands will further stimulate employee engagement around CSR by having already started turning to gamification or micro-volunteerism to make engagement easy, fun and personalized. German airline Lufthansa has been running for some years a company-wide initiative called HelpAlliance, which supports nearly 40 projects in 19 countries. Responsibility for a project of this kind is always assigned to an employee of Lufthansa.

These employees donate their free time to helping people in developing economies. In return they receive some support from the company for THEIR project.

Finally: The Need of Having the Right Organization, Processes, and People in Place

Misaligned organizational structures and processes often hinder the flow of information and know-how across brand, marketing, and business goals. There needs to be a close integration between traditional marketing programs and digital initiatives on the one hand and between marketing and other departments on the other hand. As brand managers for the most part are responsible for the overall performance of a brand, and most recently also for an increasing volume of content and messaging, moving forward they should also have the digital marketing managers within their teams and have them report into brand management. Brands need active senior leadership support and focus more than ever. Chief Marketing Officers (CMOs) are in an ideal position to help facilitate and advance these efforts.

There is also a strong need for an improved alignment and reorganization around agency selection and management. It is known that more traditional agencies often still lack digital expertise (which normally they would not admit). As a consequence, brand marketers are managing various agencies at the same time. In the future this would need to be simplified and streamlined to improve efficiency and effectiveness of the marketing teams.

Last, but not least, when hiring for marketing and branding expertise, it is advised to look for a top technical skill set (e.g. candidates having a very solid marketing basis, first comprehensive digital branding and media experience) and core characteristics such as the ability to cross-communicate, to connect to business goals, to show strong backbone, to be willing to convince senior management to implement new methods, and to be willing to permanently learn and constantly educate the business.

Marketing and branding in 2014 will require more than ever the integration of marketing into all business efforts and departments, including customer experience, design, sales, and product development.

6. HOW ZAPPOS WOWS ITS EMPLOYEES

In a previous blog article I wrote about the key elements of how to build A Culture of Employee Engagement.

I argued that any organization can raise the bar on team and employee engagement to achieve significantly better business results by applying the following straight-forward, yet very powerful principles:

- Understand What Your Employees Think And Want
- Build A Trust Culture
- Practice Open Communication
- Provide Clear Career Paths
- Demonstrate Appreciation For Contributions
- Inspire Employees Beyond Turnover
- Communicate Your Employee Focus

There are various top companies which successfully follow these principles. One of them being online retailer Zappos. I'd like to present you today the Zappos employee engagement approach by sharing its 6 ways of how to build relationships and engage employees.

Coworker Bonus Program

At Zappos they offer a coworker bonus program that allows employees to award an extra $50 to a coworker each month for really WOWing their socks off (e.g. if one coworker helped another one getting her work done, etc.).

Grant-a-Wish Program

Zappos Grant-a-Wish program allows its employees to submit and grant wishes and is a great way to build a team and family spirit in the company (e.g. learning how to play guitar, ride a motorcycle, etc.). In addition to employees granting wishes, Zappos as a company grants wishes. One of the most inspiring wishes granted was for an employee who wanted to become an American citizen, but was unable to afford the citizenship program. Zappos granted his wish and he went on to become a US citizen.

Zappos $$$

The currency of Zappos employees is called "Zollars". You have to earn your Zollars and they are used as a way to recognize employees for times when a co-worker or manager feels they've gone above and beyond. Employees can spend their Zollars on Zappos branded swag such as sweatshirts, glasses, and sun shades or they can buy movie tickets, donate them for a charitable donation, or enter them into a raffle for bigger prizes.

Shadow Sessions

As a great way to build relationships across the company Zappos allows employees to "shadow" an employee for a few hours to gain an understanding of what they do on a day-to-day basis. Not only does this allow employees to learn the ins and outs of the company, but it also builds working relationships with people in other departments.

New Hire Scavenger Hunt

All employees at Zappos are required to go through a month-long new hire training. At the end of the training they are assigned challenges to locate employees around the company. For example, find someone with a Zappos shirt on and find out how long they have been at the company, or find who schedules training classes and take a picture with them, and find the longest tenured employee in the finance department.

Apprenticeships

Zappos prides itself in promoting and hiring within the company. One way the company encourages growth and learning is through its apprenticeship program. Employees can apply to become a Z'apprentice even in an area where they may not have previous experience/skills. It allows the employee to check out a new career path and a hiring manager to see if the employee has the right potential to fit the role and team. When a person is selected for a Z'apprenticeship, they have a 90-day tenure in the role. After the 90 days, a mutual decision is made regarding whether or not the person is right for the position. If they are, they become a full-time member of the team. If they are not the right fit for the position, they are able to return to their previous position and department.

7. 25 HOT STARTUPS TO WATCH IN 2015

Predicting the future? Pretty tough and not the objective of this article. Instead, like at the beginning of last year, I want to present you a list of 25 hot startups you should closely follow in 2015.

Interestingly, now more than ever, innovations happen anywhere, i.e. there are some great startups outside of Silicon Valley and the US. In the past 12 months I've surveyed the landscape of many promising startups.

I think I have found some very exciting ones to keep an eye on — pretty hot startups which have the potential to take really off and make it into the mainstream in 2015.

Please note that it's my own personal compilation and that it does not claim to be complete. Saying that, I believe that it gives a good overview for experts and anyone interested in startups:

Ginger.io

Ginger.io is comprised of experts in data science, software engineering, interaction design, clinical research, and medicine to empower researchers, physicians and healthcare providers to improve patient care. The company sits at the interface of big data, healthcare, and mobile. Based on information from a patient's smartphone app, Ginger.io helps hospitals and caregivers manage patients and detect changes in behavior and health.

Spire

These days digital health is very popular among investors, although most startups still have to prove the effectiveness of their devices and apps. One promising startup is Spire, which even considers getting FDA approval as a true medical device. Spire is a sophisticated activity tracker that senses physical movement, position, and breathing patterns. It uses this information to provide you with insights about your daily activity and state of mind through the mobile app. The app, although still missing an Android version, is supposed to contain the ability to help boost your activity, relaxation, and focus.

Headspace

Already over a million users are getting some Headspace to experience meditation and relaxation in a new way. And I'm one of them. This is a great app to map your journey, track your progress, and get rewards as you go. You can even buddy up with friends and motivate each other along the way. Find some extra calm and clarity with their free "Take 10 programme" - just 10 minutes a day.

Canva

Aussie startup Canva is a site that lets non-designers create graphics using drag-and-drop tools. Over the past 16 months, Canva's one million users have created more than seven million designs. They've just launched a new feature to share and discover design, enabling people to post their designs publicly, follow their friends, and interact with others. The Canva Design School, a new platform, offers workshop series' and a teacher resource hub.

Electric Objects

The New York-based startup founded by Jake Levine developed a computer – called E01 - designed specifically to display the art of the Internet in your home. The company is one of the first to offer the complete package of a digital display, distribution system, and artwork itself. You can explore and display thousands of objects, including original artwork, or upload your own. The E01 can easily be wall-mounted or used with a stand. It is controlled completely with your phone and executed in real time. A limited number of E01s will be shipped in May 2015. Hurry up and reserve yours today! Jake, I'm also looking forward to receiving mine!

Simpolfy

Seattle-based political startup Simpolfy, currently in beta, is a new non-partisan political startup which aims to tell its members what representatives and bills they support, and allows them to easily contact their representatives through the website. Simpolfy aims for the voters using their site to rely on hard data in the format of a "report card" to have more empowered citizens who will improve democracy.

Blinkist

You love to read great professional books, but lack time (who doesn't...)? Berlin-based Blinkist developed an app that distills key insights from popular nonfiction books into fifteen-minute, made-for-mobile reads. These so-called "blinks" are original, thoughtful, and engaging. They can be read on iOS, Android and any web browser. Currently they feature over 500 books; it's adding more than 40 new ones every month. There's a free version where you can read one pre-selected book per day. In the premium version ($99/year) you can read all books and listen to some new ones with Audio. Check out the 3-day-free-trial.

Kytabu

Kytabu (from the word "Kitabu", Swahili for "book") is a Kenyan startup which digitizes textbooks and allows users to buy portions of a textbook or an entire textbook on their mobile platform of choice. As such, it's making education increasingly more affordable and accessible. With 7.5 million children in formal schools and another 7.2 million in informal learning environments in Kenya, there is a lot Kytabu can achieve. Certainly, it's also a blueprint for other African countries.

Crypho

Crypho is a Norwegian startup building encrypted real-time communications solutions for the web. It enables you to set up a secure, end-to-end encrypted, communications channel for your business in a matter of minutes, with no need to install software. Crypho runs in the cloud. Participants can be from different organizations and networks. There are different plans available, from a free personal account to an account for large organizations.

Fuel3D

Just as 3D printing is set to bring micro-manufacturing to the masses, so too is 3D scanning. Fuel 3D is an Oxford-based university spin-out that develops handheld 3D scanners for use in 3D modelling applications and 3D printing. For example, their Fuel3D handheld scanner, a point-and-shoot 3D imaging system that captures high resolution (~350 microns) shape and color information of objects, costs just less than one tenth of the cost of comparable handheld 3D scanning systems.

Metamind

MetaMind delivers pretty impressive Artificial Intelligence solutions for enterprises, powered by deep learning (DL). DL comprises a set of techniques that don't require domain experts to program knowledge into algorithms. Instead, these techniques - by learning to observe data - provide solutions for natural language processing, computer vision and database predictions: e.g. automated medical image diagnostics, sentiment modules to be used in finance, marketing and social media analysis, etc.

Wearable Experiments

Wearable Experiments (We:eX) is a socially driven wearable technology company. Their mission is to bring together fashion and technology with a functional design aesthetic. For example the newly launched Alert Shirt, for which the company weaves hardware, software, and stylish design together with real-time sports data, which is transmitted via a smartphone app to the electronics within the jersey. The Alert Shirt then converts the data into powerful sensations that simulate live sports action.

Ello

Ello only launched in late August 2014 with just 90 friends on the new social network back then. A little more than four months later, millions of people have joined Ello worldwide. It's a global community that believes that a social network should be a place to empower, inspire, and connect — not to deceive, coerce, and manipulate. As such, Ello refuses to support itself through advertising and selling user data.

Cratejoy

Yep, we're in the middle of the "sharing economy." And one key part of it are subscription models. Cratejoy is an all-in-one platform, built from the ground up just for subscription businesses. It assists you to save time and focus on what really matters: growing your business. It contains a website builder, a subscription builder, and some pretty cool reporting tools specifically designed for any subscription business. Additional helpful features are the subscription school and the discussion forum to exchange with like-minded people.

Alfred

For $99 a month, your personal butler Alfred, i.e. a friendly helper, will drop by your house once a week to take care of your weekly errands: Groceries, fridge stock, laundry, dry cleaning, tailoring, and sending packages. Alfred – which launched in New York and Boston at the end of 2014 - pairs busy individuals with organized, knowledgeable, intuitive people. It hums along quietly in the background of your life – so you can be free to live yours. If Alfred were able to maintain a high service level whilst catering to millions of customers, then the service will be a blockbuster. No doubt.

Spring

Spring, featured as one of Apple's best 2014 apps, is a great mobile marketplace that gives brands a simple opportunity to let consumers shop with them by directly using the brands' existing e-commerce infrastructure. Any purchased products are shipped from the brand (incl. handling of returns). Spring - like Seamless or Grubhub – only acts as a referral engine. With its lifestyle photos it looks more like Instagram or Pinterest than a traditional shopping app. However, and this is the amazing part, via their one-swipe solution you can buy a product in a second in Spring.

Fits.me

In a physical store, the single most significant engagement milestone is reached when shoppers move into the fitting room: Customers who try on clothes convert much higher than without one. Fits.me's virtual fitting room enables retailers to provide this shopper engagement mechanisms online and helps shoppers to choose the right size for them, reduces their fit-related returns, and increases their average order value.

Bringg

This Israeli startup offers businesses - via their SaaS and mobile-based platform - the ability to show their customers where their order currently is in real-time. For example, customers can see the pizza driver's or cable guys' location on the map, get his contact details and a picture of him. Customers receive proactive smart alerts (e.g. idle, out of route, late), any other updates and special offers, and can rate the service.

Carwow

Based in Holborn, London this small startup gives customers an excellent experience throughout the entire car buying process, guiding you seamlessly and painlessly from research to purchase. Users can configure their ideal car with the online program and then optionally buy what they've created directly from handpicked dealers listed on the site.

Satellogic

If the new space revolution were to come from small startups, then Argentinian Satellogic might play a key part in it. The company, which launched three satellites in 2014, aims to build a constellation of nano-satellites to image any spot on earth every few minutes. This would provide real-time coverage of the living earth: From global commercial activity, to the health of the planet, social conflict and natural events.

Affectiva

This startup possesses the world's largest database of emotion analytics (2.3 million faces analyzed to date) and owns a highly sophisticated patented advanced face and emotion recognition software. Allowing to derive unique insights with high accuracy, Affectiva's technology and data are very interesting for market research, advertising, education, and many more industries.

Exotel

Bangalore-based Exotel offers intelligent cloud telephony that tracks, records and routes every call. It has smart analytics and can be easily integrated in your existing CRM system using their APIs. Exotel – currently having more than 500 business clients - found an affordable way to replace expensive call centers.

We Are Pop Up

We Are Pop Up helps tenants to find and rent their ideal pop up space quickly and easily. From shops and restaurants to quirky spaces, tenants search through hundreds of landlord-listed spaces and contact the ones they like directly via the platform. If you were tight on budget, you can use their Shop Sharing which allows you to pop up within an existing shop. You can even rent a rail, a table, a shelf or a concession and collaborate with an established destination.

Gimlet Media

Gimlet Media is a network of narrative podcasts (you might remember that I considered both videos and podcasts as a major focus for marketers this year). In 2014 they launched "StartUp" and "Reply All," with more shows on the way. For the full story of Gimlet's creation, go to their site and listen to StartUp, a documentary mini-series hosted by its CEO Alex Blumberg.

Nuzzel

This startup is a straightforward and well-designed social news aggregator. It helps you to find and read news articles that have been shared most often by people you follow on Twitter, Facebook, etc. without being overwhelmed or having the feeling to miss anything.

In case I missed a great startup, please let me know in the comments below. By the way, I did a 2014 list of exciting startups to watch for at the beginning of last year. Have a look at my last year's picks and decide for yourself how they went (see article below).

8. 25 HOT TECH STARTUPS TO WATCH FOR IN 2014

There are a lot of hot tech startups around these days. Many of them are relatively new; others which have been operating for some years are getting significant momentum most recently. I have tried identifying 25 very promising ones - those I think you should keep an eye on.

Please note that it's my own personal compilation and that it does not claim to be complete. Saying that, I believe that it gives a good overview for both experts and anyone interested in tech startups:

www.distractify.com

Launched in October 2013, Distractify is one of those viral story sites like BuzzFeed, Viral Nova and Upworthy. It aims for a mix of original content and repackaged content meant to go viral. Its founder and CEO Quinn Hu is not only just 20 years old, but also the boss of one of the fastest growing new Internet sites.

www.storenvy.com

Storenvy is a fascinating site and home to emerging brands and inspired goods. It's a place where you can launch your own custom store in minutes, and a site where you'll discover amazing, one-of-a-kind things you can't find anywhere else.

www.eyeka.net

eYeka, founded in France in 2006, enables marketers and their agencies to leverage a wealth of creative ideas developed by a community of 250,000 creative individuals in 154 countries. 40 leading brands such as P&G, Kraft, Coca-Cola, Unilever, Nestle, Danone, Hyundai, Citroen and Microsoft are already tapping into eYeka's community.

www.hukkster.com

Expected to have more than 1 million registered users in 2014, Hukkster is a free shopping tool which tracks products online for users and notifies them via text, email or push notification when products they want go on sale. You only need to "hukk" a product from more than 1,000 retailers, and Hukkster informs you whenever their prices drop.

www.clarity.fm

Clarity is a marketplace that connects entrepreneurs with top advisers and industry experts to learn new skills, conduct market research, or get strategic advice on how to grow their business. Clarity has over 30,000+ verified experts; many of whom are very successful entrepreneurs (i.e. Mark Cuban, Eric Ries, etc.).

www.lyft.me

Lyft, founded in 2012, facilitates peer-to-peer ridesharing by enabling passengers who need a ride to request one from drivers who have a car. Unlike traditional taxis, Lyft drivers do not charge "fares" but receive "donations" from their passengers.

www.nimble.com

Nimble is an innovative web-based CRM solution that brings together all contacts, calendar, communications and collaborations in one simple, free platform. Nimble's core benefit lies in its ability to unify email, calendar activities and the most popular social channels (LinkedIn, Facebook, Google+, and Twitter) and automatically link this functionality to business contacts. No more jumping from application to application.

www.thumb.it

Launched in 2010, people use Thumb to get and give feedback in virtually every area of life (music, artwork, shopping, hairstyles, relationships, movies, food, etc.). Thumb is a vibrant community where you'll discover interesting things and people via an insanely engaging and instantaneous experience. Thumb it!

www.coinbase.com

Launched in 2012, San Francisco-based Coinbase has become the most widely-used way to buy and transfer the online currency Bitcoin in the U.S. It's growing into an international digital wallet that allows to securely buy, use, and accept Bitcoins.

www.oysterbooks.com

Experts are betting that e-book subscription start-up Oyster can do for books what Spotify has done for music and Netflix for movies. Its library has over 100,000 titles with HarperCollins being the largest partner publisher.

www.rolepoint.com

The London-based social recruiting software startup matches relevant roles with potential candidates in the social networks. It is a smart, well-designed business software that is easy to use.

www.memrise.com

Memrise is a learning platform and community to learn vocabulary, languages, history, science, trivia and just about anything else. There are thousands of courses on Memrise, all free and all created by members of the community. Courses are available in many languages. If they don't have what you want, you can join and create your own course.

www.gotinder.com

Tinder is an edgy mobile dating app that lets users browse for potential suitors. The free app, which has quickly grown into a global phenomenon, is currently spreading like wildfire.

www.duckduckgo.com

Founded in 2008 by Gabriel Weinberg, DuckDuckGo is a search engine that experts describe as the biggest long-term threat to Google. It protects searchers' privacy by avoiding the "filter bubble" of personalized search results. DuckDuckGo also emphasizes getting information from the best sources rather than the most sources.

www.adyapper.com

Chicago-based AdYapper tracks display and mobile ads, generating detailed verification data, consumer sentiment, real-time analytics across the entire ad buying ecosystem and centralizes the data into one platform. AdYapper makes advertising performance data actionable so advertisers can optimize and increase the efficacy of their ad buys.

www.plated.com

The "curated food" startup Plated assembles and delivers meal "boxes" to its customers that contain all the ingredients and instructions they need to cook a tasty, healthy meal at home from locally sourced ingredients.

www.cir.ca

The San Francisco-based company has a great app to read news in a well-structured manner on the go. It provides the most critical pieces of information first, followed by expanded explanations, photos, related suggestions, etc.

www.doublerobotics.com

Double takes everything you love about video calls on an iPad and puts that on a mobile base that puts the remote worker in control. Having your own Double in the office means you can be free to roam around anywhere without having to schedule a meeting.

www.smartthings.com

Smartthings is a startup that provides tools to help users connect their homes to their smartphones. It's about turning your home into a smart home.

www.whisper.sh

Whisper, a hit since day one, allows users to send messages anonymously and receive replies. Users post messages that are displayed as text superimposed over an image, similar to greeting cards.

www.opencare.com

A network and exchange forum of more than 7,000 health providers and almost 4 million patients, Opencare's mission is to create a healthier world by connecting patients with health providers and health data.

www.estimize.com

This New York online startup is the first open financial estimates platform. They allow buy-side, sell-side, and independent analysts to publish their forecasts for the fundamental metrics of public companies.

www.nationbuilder.com

NationBuilder is the world's first Community Organizing System: an accessible, affordable, complete software platform that helps creators grow and organize communities to achieve great things. A nation is a group of people united behind a common purpose. Everyone who cares about what you are doing – your fans, followers, constituents, members, donors, volunteers, customers.

www.spacemonkey.com

Founded in 2011 in Salt Lake City, USA it's been described as "The cloud on your desk." Space Monkey is taking the cloud out of the datacenter by providing an affordable, subscription-based data storage solution, creating a faster and more durable way to store data from any device. It provides a device that stores one terabyte of online storage for $49 per year.

www.flipboard.com

Although Flipboard has been around for some years, with users now having the option to create their own magazines, it's more attractive than ever. A great way to have one's favorite social networks, publications and blogs combined.

9. INSPIRATION - THE HEART AND SOUL OF LASTING SUCCESS

Over the years I've observed with a constantly increasing level of admiration the impact "inspiration" can have on both people and organizations. How inspiration can set off the creation of a powerful vision and how vision itself can cause lasting success. The words – Inspiration – Vision – Lasting Success - seem to form a magical flow.

Innovation as the Starting Point

Originally, "inspiration" derives from the middle English word "divine guidance". It is defined as «the process of being mentally stimulated to do or feel something, especially to do something creative."

There exist different sources of inspiration for every one of us: a stimulating piece of music, an engaging and thought-provoking book, a beautifully built ancient temple somewhere in the nowhere of a tropical jungle, a deliciously tasting chocolate bar when you feel it melting on the tip of your tongue, the roaring sound of a sports car screaming its power into the world, the first warming heat of the spring sun when it touches your skin, the infectious laughter of children when they're fooling around...

Each of those feelings and impressions can inspire us and trigger thoughts, and sometimes eventually actions, which make us create something unique, something visionary, something lasting. To get yourself into an inspirational state of mind right now, may I suggest that – whilst you continue reading this article – you listen to and become enchanted by Anna Netrebko & Elina Garanca singing Offenbach's Barcarola.

To further grasp the holistic concept of inspiration, and after having digested this article, you might want to read the stimulating book "Igniting Inspiration - A Persuasion Manual for Visionaries" by communication expert John M. Roberts. In his book, Roberts presents Inspiration in the context of systems theory, developmental psychology, and common sense. He also believes and explains that inspiration stimulates the creation of a Vision, i.e. it enables us to think about or plan the future with imagination or wisdom.

The Relevance of Vision and Action

Only once this vision – which as we've just learned before stems from the concept of inspiration – results into concrete actions, there is the chance to build something successful and lasting. When talking with friends about the expression "Built to last," some would probably refer with awe to the last studio album of the band Grateful Dead and its uniquely eclectic style which fused elements of various music styles. Influenced by an unbelievable degree of artistic inspiration.

When business professionals and academics hear the expression "Built to Last", their eyes might shine and they speak passionately and with loud voices of one of the most influential and groundbreaking business books: "Built to last – Successful habits of visionary companies," written by Jim Collins and Jerry Porras. It studies some of the most successful businesses, called leading companies, and the following companies, the non-leaders in an industry.

The most inspiring Companies

Business has never had more of an opportunity than today to do something inspiring. This is also, and especially, true for consumer goods and retail companies.

A new consumer survey conducted by the US consulting and training firm Performance Inspired aimed at finding a correlation between successful companies and those that inspire their consumers. After they had surveyed 2,175 consumers, they identified America's 25 most inspiring companies: Apple – what a surprise – topped the list for the second straight year, followed by Wal-Mart (which is a kind of surprise), Target, Google, Microsoft, and Amazon. Only on rank 16 is Ford, the first company which is not from the consumer goods and retailing sector:

"According to our latest research, consumers are not only feeling inspired by certain businesses, but are acting inspired by spending more with these companies while evangelizing to others about their inspiring experience," says Terry Barber, chief inspiration officer for Performance Inspired. *"We now see there is a validated set of drivers to inspiration and when these drivers are activated, it elevates employee engagement that shows up in the customer experience."*

Reasons for being inspiring - A Consumer's Perspective

The key drivers of an inspiring and therefore successful company and/or brand as identified per the study are as follows:

- Its ability to build a sense of community; the brand has become part of the consumer's personal identity
- It makes consumers feel more creative, more entrepreneurial
- People were also inspired by certain companies' ability to permanently innovate
- Winning and inspiring companies were seen as keeping their promises, following clear values and staying authentic

- Others were top ranked because of their global and/or community improvement projects, e.g. by donating a certain amount of profits, etc. to social community projects

However, the successful application of inspiring products and services does not only excite consumers. It also increases the engagement and performance of employees, keeps companies on the tips of their toes by staying agile and customer-focused, and causes ongoing organizational transformation processes resulting in permanent improvement and invention plans.

In summary: Inspiration, followed by vision and action, guarantees a company's long-term growth and its lasting success!

10. 12 MINUTES TO CREATE A MIND-CHANGING PRESENTATION

Reading this article will take you only 12 minutes — 12 minutes to find out how to draft great presentations and to become a more effective and convincing presenter. Twelve minutes which can change your professional and – most likely –your personal life.

So, what's the reason for this article? Last week I attended (another) of those meetings where most of the speakers stared 80% of the time at the screen just to read every single bullet point on each of their cluttered slides. I believe that after three minutes tops the audience fell into a deep trance and was neither able nor willing to follow many of the presentations any longer.

I am not the most talented speaker nor presenter. Over the years, however, I have continuously worked on improving both the quality of my slides and my presentation skills. With focus and vigour I thoroughly prepare and rehearse each presentation. After each meeting I ask colleagues and team members for their honest feedback to improve again for the next one.

Besides that, there are two experts who have strongly influenced my way of delivering speeches and presentations. I have not visited any of their — nor any other related — seminars. Instead I read their books, and practiced, practiced, practiced.

One of them is communication expert *Nancy Duarte* who wrote two excellent books on the subject: «Slide:ology" and "Resonate." I strongly suggest you read at least "Slide:ology." To get a taste of her approach watch the following short video clip.

The second person who strongly encouraged me to think differently and more creatively about the preparation, design, and delivery of presentations is designer and communication expert *Garr Reynolds*. His beautiful book "Presentation Zen" combines solid principles of design with the tenets of Zen simplicity. It is very clear, direct, takes just a few hours to read and can help you to save days of work by developing straightforward and very effective presentations.

Some of Garr's Key Points

Use multimedia wisely. Presentations must be both verbal and visual. Don't overwhelm your audience with too much information, animations and pictures. Question: Can your visual be understood in 3 seconds? If not, don›t use it!

Include short stories to explain your main points. The best presenters illustrate their points with the use of stories, especially personal ones. Stories are easy to remember for your audience.

Respect your audience. There are three components involved in a presentation: the audience, you, and the medium (e.g. PowerPoint). The goal is to create a kind of harmony among the three. But above all, the most important thing is that you get your audience involved and engaged.

Limit your ideas to one main idea per slide. If you have a complicated slide with lots of different data, it may be better to break it up into 2-3 different slides.

Move away from the podium. Connect with your audience. If at all possible get closer to your audience by moving away from or in front of the podium.

Take it slowly. When we are nervous we tend to talk too fast. Get a videotape of one of your presentations to see how you did — you may be surprised at the pace of your talk.

Keep the lights on. If you are speaking in a meeting room, etc. the temptation is to turn the lights off so that the slides look better. Turning the lights off — besides inducing sleep — puts all the focus on the screen. The audience should be looking at you more than the screen.

Two final Pieces of Advice

Keep it simple. Avoid cluttered slides. Be brave and use lots of «white space» or what the pros call «negative space.» The less «chunk» you have on your slide, the more powerful your message will become. Already *Leonardo da Vinci* knew: «Simplicity is the ultimate sophistication.»

Talk "to" the audience. Never turn your back towards the audience. You do not want to conduct a monologue with the screen. Look at your audience instead and make good eye contact. Try looking at individuals rather than scanning the group.

Well, how have you experienced the last 12 minutes? Have you enjoyed it? Are you now ready to embark on the exciting journey to draft and deliver really mind-changing presentations?

I bet that you are! I bet that you can do it! And I bet that you will do it!

11. IF YOU WERE ABLE TO LIVE YOUR LIFE ANEW, WHAT WOULD YOU DO?

Today is a new day. Why not also decide to be at the beginning of a new life from today on, before it might be too late?! Why possibly regret later in life that which we have not really done what we've always aspired to do? Why waste time?

We are always on the go; there is not enough time to rest and no time to contemplate. Yes, we might be successful on the job, but what's the prize we're paying for it? Do we, do you, invest enough time for a fulfilling private life?

Invest 5 minutes in yourself by reading the following, beautiful poem - called "Instants" - by Jorge Luis Borges. Afterwards, please close your eyes for a couple of minutes and enjoy the words, sentences, and related thoughts:

"If I were able to live my life anew,
In the next I would try to commit more errors.
I would not try to be so perfect,
I would relax more.

I would be more foolish than I've been,
In fact, I would take few things seriously.
I would be less hygienic.
I would run more risks.

I would take more vacations,
Contemplate more sunsets,
Climb more mountains, swim more rivers.

I would go to more places where I've never been,
I would eat more ice cream and fewer beans,
I would have more real problems and less imaginary ones.

I was one of those people that lived sensibly
And prolifically each minute of this life;
Of course I had moments of happiness.

If I could go back I would try
To have only good moments.

Because if you didn't know, of that is life made:
Only of moments; Don't lose the now.

I was one of those that never
Went anywhere without a thermometer,
A hot-water bottle,
An umbrella, and a parachute;
If I could live again, I would travel lighter.

If I could live again,
I would begin to walk barefoot from the beginning of spring
And I would continue barefoot until autumn ends.
I would take more cart rides,
Contemplate more dawns,
And play with more children,
If I had another life ahead of me.

But already you see, I am 85,
And I know that I am dying."

If you were able to live your life anew, what would you do differently? Will you be brave enough to do it? To change it? At least some parts of it?

12. A DISGUISED AND INSPIRATIONAL LEADERSHIP SPEECH

Without doubt there exist many great leadership speeches about vision, charisma, teams, communication, delegation, commitment, clarity, honesty, etc. given by respected and famous business leaders and managers.

There is one, however, that I believe to be a rather unique and inspirational one. At the same time, it's a very unusual one. One that talks about exceptional leadership only at a second glance. Why?

It's a speech about a simple word: Love! What love means and what it stimulates in you and your environment. The answer: Nothing less than authenticity, respect, maturity, self-confidence, simplicity, modesty, fulfillment, and even a special sense of wisdom. Key leadership characteristics in order to love – and as a consequence – to grow yourself, your team, and your customer base. Without these attributes you will not be able to manage and lead a successful business.

The speech is called *As I Began to Love Myself*

As I began to love myself I found that anguish and emotional suffering are only warning signs that I was living against my own truth. Today, I know, this is AUTHENTICITY.

As I began to love myself I understood how much it can offend somebody as I try to force my desires on this person, even though I knew the time was not right and the person was not ready for it, and even though this person was me. Today I call it RESPECT.

As I began to love myself I stopped craving for a different life, and I could see that everything that surrounded me was inviting me to grow. Today I call it MATURITY.

As I began to love myself I understood that at any circumstance, I am in the right place at the right time, and everything happens at exactly the right moment, so I could be calm. Today I call it SELF-CONFIDENCE.

As I began to love myself I quit steeling my own time, and I stopped designing huge projects for the future. Today, I only do what brings me joy and happiness, things I love to do and that make my heart cheer, and I do them in my own way and in my own rhythm. Today I call it SIMPLICITY.

As I began to love myself I freed myself of anything that is no good for my health – food, people, things, situations, and everything that drew me down and away from myself. At first I called this attitude a healthy egoism. Today I know it is LOVE OF ONESELF.

As I began to love myself I quit trying to always be right, and ever since I was wrong less of the time. Today I discovered that is MODESTY.

As I began to love myself I refused to go on living in the past and worry about the future. Now, I only live for the moment, where everything is happening. Today I live each day, day by day, and I call it FULFILLMENT.

As I began to love myself I recognized that my mind can disturb me and it can make me sick. But as I connected it to my heart, my mind became a valuable ally. Today I call this connection WISDOM OF THE HEART.

We no longer need to fear arguments, confrontations or any kind of problems with ourselves or others. Even stars collide, and out of their crashing new worlds are born. Today I know THAT IS LIFE!

13. NELSON MANDELA'S MOST INSPIRING SPEECHES

After a long illness, South Africa's first black president and anti-apartheid legend Nelson Mandela died on December 5, 2013 at the age of 95. One of the giants of the 20th century who will be missed by many. Personally, I have admired Mr. Mandela a lot for having evolved from a freedom fighter, to a political leader, a unifier, and later to an elderly statesman and father figure of almost unmatched stature and greatness.

Mandela has become a yardstick for many leaders with his warm, humble, charismatic, humorous, down-to-earth style. Never afraid of admitting his own shortfalls and areas of weaknesses, he would be able to do it even with a flashy, honest, and respectful smile. Something most leaders usually would not dare to do.

Many were strongly influenced and inspired by his visionary, authentic, and thoughtful speeches. Speeches about freedom, respect, human dignity, equality, the right to live your own life and to become the person you'd like to be.

The Nelson Mandela Centre of Memory has archived almost every speech ever given by Nelson Mandela. In the following I'd like to share with you some beautiful excerpts of three of his most memorable speeches which I have screened and selected during the past day (I'd like to encourage you to browse through the database yourself to find the speech which might inspire you the most).

An Ideal I Am Prepared to Die For, 1964

This is one of Nelson Mandela's most famous speeches. It was delivered from the dock of the Pretoria courtroom in 1964 at the opening of the defense case in the Rivonia Trial. He was imprisoned for two years already by then. The original speech is approximately 176 minutes long.

"I have been influenced in my thinking by both West and East. All this has led me to feel that in my search for a political formula, I should be absolutely impartial and objective. I should tie myself to no particular system of society other than that of socialism. I must leave myself free to borrow the best from West and from the East.

South Africa is the richest country in Africa, and could be one of the richest countries in the world. But it is a land of extremes and remarkable contrasts. The whites enjoy what may well be the highest standard of living in the world, whilst Africans live in poverty and misery.

The complaint of Africans, however, is not only that they are poor and whites are rich, but that the laws which are made by the whites are designed to preserve this situation. There are two ways to break out of poverty. The first is by formal education, and the second is by the worker acquiring a greater skill at his work and thus higher wages. As far as Africans are concerned, both these avenues of advancement are deliberately curtailed by legislation.

The lack of human dignity experienced by Africans is the direct result of the policy of white supremacy. White supremacy implies black inferiority. Legislation designed to preserve white supremacy entrenches this notion. Menial tasks in South Africa are invariably performed by Africans.

The only cure is to alter the conditions under which Africans are forced to live and to meet their legitimate grievances. Africans want to be paid a living wage. Africans want to perform work which they are capable of doing, and not work which the Government declares them to be capable of.

Above all, My Lord, we want equal political rights, because without them our disabilities will be permanent. I know this sounds revolutionary to the whites in this country, because the majority of voters will be Africans. This makes the white man fear democracy.

During my lifetime I have dedicated my life to this struggle of the African people. I have fought against white domination, and I have fought against black domination. I have cherished the ideal of a democratic and free society in which all persons will live together in harmony and with equal opportunities. It is an ideal for which I hope to live for and to see realized. But, My Lord, if it needs be, it is an ideal for which I am prepared to die."

Nelson Mandela's Address to a Rally in Cape Town on his Release from Prison, 1990

The first public speech by Nelson Mandela in 27 years, after his release from prison. Mandela ends this address with a quote from the words of his trial in 1964.

"Friends, Comrades and Fellow South Africans, I greet you all in the name of peace, democracy and freedom for all. I stand here before you not as a prophet, but as a humble servant of you, the people. Your tireless and heroic sacrifices have made it possible for me to be here today. I therefore place the remaining years of my life in your hands. On this day of my release I extend my sincere and warmest gratitude to the millions of my compatriots and those in every corner of the globe who have campaigned tirelessly for my release.

Today the majority of South Africans, black and white, recognize that apartheid has no future. It has to be ended by our own decisive mass action in order to build peace and security. The mass campaigns of defiance and other actions of our organisation and people can only culminate in the establishment of democracy. The apartheid destruction on our sub-continent is incalculable. The fabric of family life of millions of my people has been shattered. Millions are homeless and unemployed, our economy lies in ruins and our people are embroiled in political strife.

The need to unite the people of our country is as important a task now as it always has been. No individual leader is able to take on this enormous task on his own. It is our task as leaders to place our views before our organisation and to allow the democratic structures to decide on the way forward. On the question of democratic practice, I feel duty bound to make the point that a leader of the movement is a person who has been democratically elected at a national conference. This is a principle which must be upheld without any exceptions.

The people need to be consulted on who will negotiate and on the content of such negotiations. Negotiations cannot take a place above the heads or behind the backs of our people. It is our belief that the future of our country can only be determined by a body which is democratically elected on a non-racial basis.

We have waited too long for our freedom. We can no longer wait. Now is the time to intensify the struggle on all fronts. To relax our efforts now would be a mistake which generations to come will not be able to forgive. The sight of freedom looming on the horizon should encourage us to redouble our efforts. It is only through disciplined mass action that our victory can be assured. We call on our white compatriots to join us in the shaping of a new South Africa. The freedom movement is a political home for you too. We call on the international community to continue the campaign to isolate the apartheid regime.

In conclusion, I wish to quote my own words during my trial in 1964. They are as true today as they were then. I quote: 'I have fought against white domination and I have fought against black domination. I have carried the ideal of a democratic and free society in which all persons live together in harmony and with equal opportunities. It is an ideal which I hope to live for and to achieve. But, if needs be, it is an ideal for which I am prepared to die.'"

His Retirement Anouncement, 2004

"Thank you very much to all of you for taking time out of your very busy schedules to come and listen to me this morning. I have always said that many people come to such gatherings where we are present merely out of curiosity to see what an old man looks like. Having observed the media speculation in recent weeks about my retirement and pending demise, I am even more certain you are present today for exactly that reason. But that does not in any way lessen my appreciation for your presence; on the contrary, we are very happy that old age can still inspire such undeserved attention.

One of the things that made me long to be back in prison was that I had so little opportunity for reading, thinking and quiet reflection after my release. I intend, amongst other things, to give myself much more opportunity for such reading and reflection. And of course, there are those memoirs about the presidential years that now really need my urgent attention. When I told one of my advisors a few months ago that I wanted to retire he growled at me: "you are retired." If that is really the case then I should say I now announce that I am retiring from retirement.

I do not intend to hide away totally from the public, but hence forth I want to be in the position of calling you to ask whether I would be welcome, rather than being called upon to do things and participate in events. The appeal therefore is: don't call me, I'll call you.

That is also for our generous business community not to feel too disappointed: I shall not totally forget you. When I notice a worthy cause that needs your support, I shall certainly call you. Seriously therefore: my diary and my public activities will, as from today, be severely and significantly reduced. We trust that people will understand our considerations and will grant us the opportunity for a much quieter life. And I thank all of you in anticipation for your consideration. This does, however, not mean that the work that we have been involved in, supported and promoted comes to an end. It has been our practice to establish organizations to do certain work and then to leave it to those organization to get on with the job."

Chapter 2

LEAD & EXECUTE!

Tomorrow's top leaders avoid what quite often causes today's experienced and successful business leaders to arrive at utterly wrong conclusions, since the latter lack comprehension of how to live by two of today's most relevant business and leadership principles. First, they are not VUCA leaders. Second, they have not been able to grasp the concept of DyBoPe leadership. These are two crucial concepts for future leaders which I'll explain in this chapter.

Tomorrow's top leaders follow a poet and peasant approach, i.e. they have a strategic mindset and simultaneously roll up their sleeves and get their hands dirty whenever needed. They are more human, more approachable, and less arrogant than many of today's leaders. They are both effective and efficient by aiming at doing the right things in the right way. They are not driven by short-term results, instead they are completely customer-centric following a long-term perspective. They strongly believe in the art of execution and know how hard and painful it can be to have things seamlessly implemented.

The outstanding leaders of the future master one of the ultimate balancing acts of superior leadership – they know how to lead with head and heart. Meaning they are respected for having both a strong results focus and social skills. Or, as Eleanor Roosevelt stated:

"To handle yourself, use your head. To handle others, use your heart."

They follow a strong set of both company leadership principles and personal principles, and look for a strong congruency and link between the two of them. They feel and act in an accountable manner; they commit, love making decisions, and constantly need to earn the right to lead.

14. LEADERSHIP TODAY – THE HORSE IS NOT HERE TO STAY

In 1903, an educated and well-known businessman proclaimed:

"The horse is here to stay but the automobile is only a novelty – a fad."

The gentleman was the distinguished president of the Michigan Savings Bank advising Henry Ford's lawyer not to invest in the Ford Motor Company.

More than a hundred years later another, much more famous businessman vocalized:

"There's no chance that the iPhone is going to get any significant market share. No chance."

It was Microsoft's then CEO Steve Ballmer laughing off the iPhone when being asked in an interview in 2007 what he thought of the coming iPhone launch.

Certainly you've heard of similar anecdotes and related misjudgments. Many companies are still having to bear the consequences until present time. At least those which have survived.

So, what is it that quite frequently causes experienced and successful business leaders to arrive at utterly wrong conclusions? Ignorance? Arrogance? Lack of vision and imagination? All of the above?

In my opinion they lack comprehension of how to live by two of today's most relevant business and leadership principles: First, they are not VUCA leaders. Second, they have not been able (yet) to grasp the concept of DyBoPe leadership.

The VUCA Leader

VUCA is a term, or more precisely, an acronym which was coined by the military and describes volatility, uncertainty, complexity and ambiguity of general conditions and situations. Also, in the business world it relates to how people view the conditions under which they make decisions, manage risks, plan ahead, drive change and solve problems.

VUCA leaders are trained to anticipate future issues, are aware of consequences of possible actions, understand how multiple variables interact, develop alternative plans, are well prepared for crisis management, and are clear about how to detect and quickly seize new opportunities. VUCA leaders have figured out that the horse is a horse. Not a car. And not a plane.

The DyBoPe Leader

VUCA, with its more practical code for awareness and readiness, assists leaders in spotting the coming wave and helps bypass or avoid it. However, to ride the wave, i.e. to be disruptive, to be innovative, and to actively define the rules of the game, it takes leaders who are extremely agile, courageous, and who love building top performing teams.

Dynamic (Dy), bold (Bo), and people-focused (Pe) leaders possess the following distinct characteristics:

Willingness to learn by doing and by experimentation; after having conducted some solid analyses first.

Use of greatly flexible decision making models; e.g. algorithm-based probabilistic modeling.

Cultivation of just-in-time decision making.

Upbringing of emerging issues at a very early point of time, i.e. before they get (too) big and nasty.

Obsession by fewer, bigger, better. They pursue no more than 3 major initiatives and projects at the same time. In parallel their teams are empowered and have the right to stop non-priority tasks.

Honest joy in supporting their peers and teams.

Pace-setting if multiple tasks need to be accomplished in tight time frames. Best done with experienced teams.

Coaching and building on team members' individual strengths. Works very well when the team is self-proficient, self-disciplined, and willing to think outside of the box with almost no direction from the top needed.

Building of long-term relationships which are founded on trust, values, ethics, and fundamental principles. They love "to give without any strings attached."

Installing VUCA and DyBoPe Structures and Processes.

To make the two concepts become a reality, existing structures, processes, and procedures need to be radically redesigned. They need to become simpler, leaner, and geared towards quick and smart decision making.

In today's fast-paced world, a successful leader should be able to draw from a variety of resources and skills to build a holistic leadership style that is anticipative, dynamic, innovative and bold. No leader can predict the future. However, she can build dynamic organizations that will flourish in whatever possible future scenario.

Final Thoughts

To summarize, let me quote Peter Lake, the main character in Mark Helprin's book *Winter's Tale*:

"Who is worse? The horse who won't listen to his master or the master who listens to his horse?"

Or, in my own words: Start immediately to VUCA-nize and to DyBoPe-nize yourself, your life, and your business!

15. THE 17 QUALITIES AND VIEWS OF GREAT LEADERS

Countless books, studies and articles have been published about which characteristics great leaders possess. Some authors argue that it takes certain personality traits such as charisma, authenticity, etc. Others maintain the view that it's all about skills and abilities. Another group of experts blends the two previous options and even adds behavior as a third key ingredient. In addition, to make things more complicated, there exist further schools of thought.

Over the last 20 years of having worked with many exceptional managers and leaders of some of the finest companies in the world, I have tried summarizing key leadership traits which I have observed and experienced. In my opinion it boils down to the following 17 qualities and views which successful leaders have in common:

Fail young, often, and hard – Learn from mistakes, admit them, and stay humble.

Think the impossible to realize the possible – Be bold and brave.

Exercise tough empathy towards your team – Give them what they need in your opinion, and not necessarily what they want.

Be effective and efficient at the same time – Do the right things in the right way.

Practice execution as an art – Be focused on making decisions and implement them until the very end in the best possible manner.

Embrace a *Poet and Peasant* approach – Have a strategic mindset and simultaneously don't mind diving into details and rolling up your sleeves.

Stay human, approachable, and show respect – Choose being people-focused over task-focused, even and especially when push comes to shove.

Be resilient and display a can-do-attitude – If something does not work, try something else. Be positive and radiate confidence and strength.

Over-communicate and you'll over-perform – Teams, peers, business partners, etc. need clarity and transparency.

Recruit, develop and empower the best fitting ones – Make sure that there is a "cultural" and mental fit between company and employees built on a "psychological contract."

Work hard, smart and have fun – No output without input. At the same time you should love and enjoy what you do. Only then you can be highly passionate and committed.

Under-promise and over-deliver – Walk your talk.

Inspire – Think, behave and communicate beyond pure targets and figures. Stimulate people around you to play and to experiment.

Stay true to yourself and your core values – Adapt yourself, if necessary. Never bend yourself. If not, you might break and might lose your heart and soul.

Believe in the good – Always stay open-minded and curious without being naive.

It's all about the long-term – If needed, forgo and sacrifice short-term profit and benefits for the sake of long-term growth and sustainability.

Lead a holistically fulfilled life – Life is much more than work and making a career. Spend enough time with family, friends, and loved ones. Relish your hobbies and passions without bad feelings.

16. HAVE YOU EARNED THE RIGHT TO BE A LEADER?

Steering change initiatives and helping organizations find the good way through these turbulent times might become the ultimate test for many of us in the next months and years to come, especially for those who call themselves "Leaders." Are you prepared? Are we prepared? Have we prepared our teams and will they follow us?

There are many excellent books and articles published on leadership and change management. There is Abraham Zaleznik's inspiring article "Managers and Leaders – Are they different?" (Harvard Business Review, 1977). Managerial development at the time focused exclusively on building competence, control, and the appropriate balance of power. Managers, Zaleznik argued, are concerned about the status quo and about solving problems in a rational, systematic and more analytical way. In his opinion, that view omitted the essential leadership elements of inspiration, vision, and human passion which drive corporate success in modern times. For Zaleznik, business leaders have much more in common with artists than they do with managers.

John P. Kotter deepened end extended Zaleznik's ground-breaking work. In his major books "The Leadership Factor" (Free Press, 1988) and "A Force for Change" (Free Press, 1990), he proposed that management and leadership are different but complementary, and that in a changing world, one cannot function without the other.

And then there is one of my favorite pieces of research on leadership: "Why should anyone be led by you?" A superb article published by Robert Goffee and Gareth Jones (Harvard Business Review, 2000). In this article they substantiated previous findings about management and leadership. They claimed, however, that a true and inspirational leader would possess four additional characteristics:

Reveal weaknesses: It helps in establishing trust and getting people on board. Do it in a careful, considerate and genuine way.

Become a sensor: Rely often upon intuition and not only on facts and data. Try to read silence and pick up non-verbal clues. Be careful with projections you might make and always make a reality check.

Practice tough empathy: It means giving people what they need, and not necessarily what they want. At its best, it balances respect for the individual and for the task at hand.

Dare to be different and be authentic: Capitalize on what is unique about you and be truthful to yourself. By doing so, don't lose contact with your followers and your team.

Are we possessing those four characteristics? Should our people and teams be led by us?

17. HOW TO LEAD WITH HEAD AND HEART – THE ULTIMATE BALANCING ACT

Whether your leadership style is more focused on business objectives and getting things done (leading with your head), or more on people engagement, motivation, and relationships (leading with your heart), your approach likely has several benefits and pitfalls.

People tend to be stronger in one or two of those areas and weaker in the others. I argue that in today's business environment – which is characterized by constant change and multiple and highly complex challenges - neither approach is sufficient in itself. Rather, both are needed to make real headway in increasing employee engagement.

Various studies like the ones of Jack Zenger and Joseph Folkman revealed that great bosses are often seen as those who have both a strong results focus and social skills.

Let's have a look at these two main styles, how to develop them, and how to possibly balance them to become a holistic leader.

Head Leadership

Head leaders are great at creating a strategy and a plan, setting goals, following a budget, and holding their team accountable to the plan's actions and processes. They know how to create systems and plans. Leading with your head is about competence, skills, and knowledge.

Head leaders are usually task-oriented which ensures that things get done in a manner that is both effective and efficient. They usually set up concrete, logical, and deadline-driven schedules with specific requirements. Those leaders try to maintain high standards with optimal allocation of resources. Employees who need structure and who struggle with managing their time work best under this kind of leadership.

There are a great number of tough questions to be addressed in any organization. Whilst heart leaders can seem overly emotional - with the leader basing their decisions on whether or not someone's feelings may get hurt - head leaders usually are not afraid of tackling difficult issues directly. They face them with structured sessions and discussions to resolve them quickly.

Strength or competence can be established by virtue of your reputation, your position, and your actual performance. But your behavior and presence always count, too. Therefore, the nip is to groom a demeanor of strength without being considered as threatening.

Recommended Techniques

Stand Up Straight. Realize the importance of good posture in projecting authority and an intention to be taken seriously. Be aware of who you are and that you can master your circumstances. Reach your full body height, use your muscles to straighten your spine, and speak with clarity and conviction.

Get Hold Of Yourself. When you move, move precisely and with drive to a specific spot rather than casting your limbs about loose-jointedly. And when you are finished, stand still. Stillness demonstrates calm.

Prepare Yourself. One important key to strength is self-confidence. An important key to self-confidence is preparation. Be prepared about your next steps. Then you will not get lost in vague, foggy imprecision and possibly even fear. Instead, develop precise plans and construct positive scenarios in your mind of what may happen if you give it a try.

Go Exploring. Another technique to build and find more confidence in yourself is to get to know yourself better. How to do it? Go exploring! Face some of your fears. Fail over and over and understand that it isn't really that big of a deal. Grow stronger through such experiences. Figure out what really happened and how to possibly handle it better moving forward.

Admit Mistakes And Weaknesses. Don't put too much pressure on yourself. So, when you don't do the right thing, admit it. Be transparent, authentic and willing to talk about your mistakes and faults in a constructive manner. When you are vulnerable and have nothing to hide you radiate trust. That's what people love.

Feel In Command And Be Present. If you see yourself as an impostor, others will, too. Feeling in command and confident is about connecting with yourself. And when we are connected with ourselves, it is much easier to connect and to be with others.

Heart Leadership

The idea of bringing the heart into workplace leadership traditionally has been seen as a soft and weak approach that inherently undermines business focus and profit.

However, given that emotion is a much more powerful driver of behavior than logic and reason alone, it explains why so many intellectually brilliant and brainy leaders struggle with people-centered leadership. Their speeches and argumentations may hit the head, but often miss the heart; as such they do not really engage employees.

Heart leaders are great at making their people feel special, giving them a sense of purpose and making them feel appreciated for the work they do. They strongly focus on employee relationships and undertake many efforts to make team members feel that they're a part of an organization's success. Heart leaders care about the teams' happiness and about their ambitions and welfare.

Heart leaders have a strong desire to speak from the heart, rather than deliver highly academic and watertight lectures from the head. They've understood that what comes from the heart, lands on the heart.

Recommended Techniques

Efforts to appear people-focused, warm, and trustworthy all too often come across as inauthentic and wooden. Some proposed ways to avoid that trap:

Show People That You Care About Them. Be out for others and not primarily for yourself. Appreciate all people you're dealing with. Show sensitivity to their interests, wishes, and needs. Value them and thank them. Express sincere gratitude rather two times too often than missing it just once. Do it from the heart.

Be Aware Of What You Do Not Verbally Say. We always communicate. Even – and especially – when we're not speaking explicitly. Even a few small nonverbal signals like a nod, a smile, an open gesture, etc. can show people that you're pleased to be in their company and attentive to their concerns. It demonstrates that you hear them, understand them, and can be trusted by them.

Focus On The Positives. Don't punish mistakes. As they can happen think and speak about them in a results-oriented and forward-looking way. Jointly look with others for solutions and implement actions to avoid them happening again.

Walk Your Talk. Mean what you say and keep your word. Deliver your committed tasks and duties on time and in full. Lead by example and permanently demonstrate that you deliver on your promises and that others can count on you.

Empower Others. Show people that you trust them. Grant flexibility, stimulate initiative-taking, and ask for regular feedback. Have faith in others' skills and capabilities. Be willing to let go and to share power.

Establish Long-Term Relationships. Displaying warmth is stemming from deeper values, ethics, and fundamental principles. Take your time and don't rush. The best trust fertilizer is to "give without any strings attached." Don't always expect something in return.

Balancing Head and Heart

Leaders with highly engaged employees know how to demand a great deal from employees (head), but are also seen as transparent, collaborative, and great developers of people (heart). Our goal as leaders should be to have a healthy combination of the head and the heart when we lead. As we grow our leadership skills we will become better at understanding when to use each.

Or as Eleanor Roosevelt stated: *"To handle yourself, use your head. To handle others, use your heart."*

The key is to take the best parts of each management style and combine them to create your own approach - one that suits your personality and that gets the tasks done while also cultivating positive working relationships. Be flexible and aware of the fact that different approaches work better in specific situations.

18. OH CAPTAIN, MY CAPTAIN! LESSONS FOR LIFE

Robin Williams, who on August 11, 2014 was found dead at his home in Northern California, was a remarkable actor, genius, and man whose movies have inspired my whole life (and I think I saw most of them). For this privilege I'm deeply grateful.

The one film of Robin Williams' which went under my skin like none before is Dead Poets Society. It is one of those films that has the power to change your life due to their plot, their messages, their emotions, and their actors.

When I was a young man at the age of 20, I saw Dead Poets Society in autumn 1989. In the film I heard for the first time the words "Carpe diem" (seize the day). Immediately in this very moment I realized that this film was special, very special to me, and that it would have a great influence on my whole life.

There was a unique energy, power, and inspiration in those dialogues and words which gave me the courage to stand up for what I wanted. To be bold. To decide to lead my own life. Some months later I left Germany and went to the States to work for Disney. And ever since, I've been writing the script of my own life. Trying to lead it in a meaningful, passionate, and responsible way.

The Plot

Set in 1959, Dead Poets Society tells the story of the English professor John Keating (Robin Williams) who inspires his students with his love of poetry and encourages them to seize the day. He is employed at the very traditional Welton School, which is based on the four principles "Tradition, Honor, Discipline, and Excellence." His teaching methods are unorthodox, including taking them out of the classroom to focus on the idea of carpe diem.

He tells the students that they may call him "O Captain! My Captain!" in reference to a Walt Whitman poem, if they feel daring enough. In another class, Keating instructs his pupils to rip the introduction out of their books, to the amazement of one of his colleagues. Later, he has the students stand on his desk in order to look at the world in a different way.

The Poem

"O Captain! My Captain!" is a poem written in 1865 by Walt Whitman, about the death of American president Abraham Lincoln.

The following lines are from the first of three stanzas. The captain in the poem refers to Abraham Lincoln who is the captain of the ship, representing the United States of America:

"O Captain! My Captain! our fearful trip is done;
The ship has weather'd every rack, the prize we sought is won;
The port is near, the bells I hear, the people all exulting,
While follow eyes the steady keel, the vessel grim and daring:
But O heart! heart! heart!
O the bleeding drops of red,
Where on the deck my Captain lies,
Fallen cold and dead."

Learning

There are many lessons one can learn from this beautiful film. Lessons for all areas of life:

Be Unorthodox – Dare to be different. Experience. Try out new things. Don't care too much about opinions of others. Trust in yourself and your judgement. Only cowards do not question and change.

Carpe Diem – Seize the day. Enjoy life. Make your life extraordinary. It's your personal obligation. Take over responsibility for your life. The script is yours to write.

Apply Different Perspectives – Look at the world and various situations from different angles. Yes, you might even think about standing on your desk. Ever tried it?

Inspire – Yourself and your team. Dream. Think big. Be aspirational. Be positive. Spell out your visions.

Stand Up – Have courage. Raise your voice to make yourself heard. Challenge others and the system if you truly believe in something. Don't give up easily.

Be Wise, Not Stupid – Wait and look for the right moment. Then go for it.

Be Curious – Be hungry to learn and to discover new things. Even completely unknown and "silly" things. Risk and enjoy to fail. That stimulates your growth and transformation.

Be Humble – Earthen yourself. Don't lose contact with others and your inner soul. Treat people and yourself with respect. Show feelings and be human.

Tribute To Robin Williams

Who could do that better than Chris Columbus, director of Williams' splendid movie Mrs Doubtfire:

"We have lost one of our most inspired and gifted comic minds, as well as one of this generation's greatest actors. To watch Robin work was a magical and special privilege... He truly was one of the few people who deserved the title of 'genius'."

19. SUCCESSFUL LEADERS LIVE BY LIGHTING PRINCIPLES

What is in your opinion more important in order to become and stay a successful leader?

To acquire and to possess the "right" leadership characteristics, or to follow and to live by clear leadership principles?

From my perspective, and although the two aspects are certainly interlinked, they are two separate issues which are equally important. Unfortunately, it is a neglected facet in today's debate on effective and sustainable leadership.

Let me start with a short anecdote: Some weekends ago I privately attended a seminar about leadership and team development. Sunday over lunch I had the pleasure being seated together with some C-level executives of multinational organizations as well as owners of small and mid-sized companies.

We talked a lot about generic business challenges, current and anticipated management trends, complex leadership situations which we've been in over the years, and possible training and development ideas for future leaders. The discussion gained significant momentum when we started talking about which traits great leaders possess. Some put forward the idea that it requires specific personality traits like authenticity, charisma, etc. Others argued that it's all about skills and abilities. A third group mixed the two previous opinions. As you rightly imagine it was a very diverse exchange of statements and comments which never stood a chance arriving at a mutual consent.

The conversation got really stimulating when one executive – she's the COO of a large financial firm – expressed that, based on her experience, the crucial influencing factor of true and lasting success of any leader is not only to possess the (presumably) right leadership characteristics, but also and foremost to follow and to live in an honest and authentic way with clear leadership principles.

The Importance of Leadership Principles

I wholeheartedly agree with her in the sense of defining the term principle as *a fundamental truth or proposition that serves as the foundation for a system of belief or behavior or for a chain of reasoning.*
Saying that, there's no doubt in my mind that you can only become a good leader if you exhibit and display certain leadership qualities and characteristics (read more about them here). In addition, however, to evolve into an outstanding leader, you need to be clear about your and your organization's leadership

principles which you should constantly and rigorously communicate, apply, and live by.

Solid leadership principles allow you, your teams, peers, and business partners to obtain and to give guidance. They transmit purpose to your work and life. Like a torch or a compass they assist in directing behavior towards objectives and activities. Moreover, when principles are sincerely practiced based on authenticity, honesty, generosity, courage, respect, and flexibility, then you can build valuable and lasting relationships.

In this respect, the following three dimensions should be addressed and evaluated:

Company Leadership Principles: Do they exist in your company? Are they aligned with the company's mission statement, values, and its overall objectives? Are they precise enough and clear to everyone? Are they stimulating and aspirational? Are they communicated to everyone on a regular basis? Are they implemented and being respected? Are they being reviewed and, if needed, being adjusted every 5-8 years?

Personal Leadership Principles: Have you formulated your own principles based on your values and long-term ambitions? Do you feel comfortable with them? Do you follow them and do you live them in a transparent and authentic manner?

Congruency: Is there a strong overlap and fit between your organization's and your own principles? Do they match, stimulate, and strengthen each other? Is it feeling right?

You should be able to answer all questions with "Yes," if your aspiration were to become a truly successful leader in your current organization.

Examples of selected Leadership Principles

In order to acquire a sound understanding about how to adequately phrase your and/ or your company's leadership principles, let's have a look at various leadership principles of some of the World's Most Admired companies:

It's best to do one thing really, really well
Invent and simplify
Fast is better than slow
Insist on the highest standards
You don't need to be at your desk to need an answer

Bias for action
If something does not work, try something else
There's always more information out there
If you can dream it, you can do it
Vocally self-critical
Deliver results
You can be serious without a suit
Think big
Have backbone, disagree and commit
Great just isn't good enough
Execute in excellence
Earn trust

20. DO WE NEED BLUE OCEAN LEADERS?

In the May 2014 edition of the Harvard Business Review, W. Chan Kim and Renée Mauborgne, the authors and inventors of the famous Blue Ocean Strategy (which I like a lot), write about a concept they've coined Blue Ocean Leadership.

When I read the title of the article for the first time momentarily two thoughts popped up: First, in the spirit of a classic line expansion approach it seems comprehensible trying to stretch a very successful idea and name via a new product into the popular and profitable leadership and training segment. Second, I wondered if Blue Ocean Leadership is old wine in new skins. Or a true, new value-adding leadership concept which would help developing better leaders.

So, before making our call, let's have a look at their main ideas and recommendations which are based on hundreds of interviews over the last 10 years:

Underlying Insight

According to Chan and Mauborgne, leadership can be thought of as a service that people in an organization "buy" or "don't buy." Every leader in that sense has customers: the bosses to whom the leader must deliver performance, and the followers who need the leader's guidance and support to achieve. When people value your leadership practices, they in effect buy your leadership. They're inspired to excel and act with commitment. But when employees don't buy your leadership, they disengage, becoming non-customers of your leadership.

Key Differences from other Leadership Approaches

Blue Ocean Leadership is supposed to be distinct in at least three ways from traditional leadership approaches:

Focus On Acts And Activities

Blue Ocean Leadership focuses on what acts and activities leaders need to undertake to boost their teams' motivation and business results, not on who leaders need to be. Meaning, that Blue Ocean Leadership does not put an emphasis on values, qualities, and behavioral styles. Of course, altering a leader's activities is not a complete solution, and having the right values, qualities, and behavioral traits matters. But activities are something that any individual can change, given the right feedback and guidance.

Connect Closely to Market Realities

Blue Ocean Leadership claims that the people who face market realities are asked for their direct input on how their leaders hold them back and what those leaders could do to help them best serve customers and other key stakeholders. And when people are engaged in defining the leadership practices that will enable them to thrive, and those practices are connected to the market realities against which they need to perform.

Distribute Leadership Across All Management Levels

For Blue Ocean Leadership the key to a successful organization is having empowered leaders at every level, because outstanding organizational performance often comes down to the motivation and actions of middle and frontline leaders, who are in closer contact with the market. It calls for profiles for leaders that are tailored to the very different tasks, degrees of power, and environments you find at each level.

The four Steps of Blue Ocean Leadership

To overcome the "Here comes another change initiative" syndrome, Blue Ocean Leadership has incorporated good execution into its process. The four steps to implement it are founded on the principles of engagement, explanation, and expectation clarity:

1. See Your Leadership Reality

A common mistake organizations make is to discuss changes in leadership before resolving differences of opinion over what leaders are actually doing. Without a common understanding of where leadership stands and is falling short, a forceful case for change cannot be made. The aim is to uncover how people experience current leadership and to start a company-wide conversation about what leaders do and should do at each level. The customers of leaders are asked which acts and activities—good and bad—their leaders spend most of their time on, and which are key to motivation and performance but are neglected by their leaders. It takes the form of what they call as-is Leadership Canvases, analytic visuals that show just how managers at each level invest their time and effort, as perceived by the customers of their leadership. An organization begins the process by creating a canvas for each of its three management levels.

2. Develop Alternative Leadership Profiles

At this point the sub-teams are usually eager to explore what effective Leadership Profiles would look like at each level. To achieve this, they go back to their interviewees with two sets of questions. The first set is aimed at pinpointing the extent to which each act and activity on the canvas is either a cold spot (absorbing leaders' time but adding little or no value) or a hot spot (energizing employees and inspiring them to apply their talents, but currently underinvested in by leaders or not addressed at all).

The second set prompts interviewees to think beyond the bounds of the company and focus on effective leadership acts they've observed outside the organization, in particular those that could have a strong impact if adopted by internal leaders at their level. Here fresh ideas emerge about what leaders could be doing but aren't. The key tool used in this step is the Blue Ocean Leadership Grid; an analytic tool that challenges people to think about which acts and activities leaders should do less of because they hold people back, and which leaders should do more of because they inspire people to give their all.

3. Select To-Be Leadership Profiles

After two to three weeks of drawing and redrawing their Leadership Canvases, the sub-teams present them at what they call a "leadership fair." Fair attendees include board members and top, middle, and frontline managers. The event starts with members of the original senior team behind the effort describing the process and presenting the three as-is canvases.

With those three visuals, the team establishes why change is necessary, confirms that comments from interviewees at all levels were taken into account, and sets the context against which the to-be Leadership Profiles can be understood and appreciated.

All levels are being presented and discussed. Armed with this information and the votes and comments of attendees, the top managers convene outside the fair room and decide which to-be Leadership Profile to move forward on at each level. Then they return and explain their decisions to the fair's participants.

4. Institutionalize New Leadership Practices

After the fair is over, the original sub-team members communicate the results to the people they interviewed who were not at the fair. Organizations then distribute the agreed-on to-be profiles to the leaders at each level. The sub-team members hold meetings with leaders to walk them through their canvases, explaining what should be eliminated, reduced, raised, and created. This step reinforces the buy-in that the initiative has been building by briefing leaders throughout the organization on key findings at each step of the process and tapping many of them for input.

The leaders are then charged with passing the message along to their direct reports and explaining to them how the new Leadership Profiles will allow them to be more effective. Leaders are tasked with holding regular monthly meetings at which they gather their direct reports' feedback on how well they're making the transition to the new profiles. All comments must be illustrated with specific examples.

Final Assessment

Clearly, I like the pragmatism and fairness of Blue Ocean Leadership as it aims at all levels. The rather straight-forward process makes the implementation and monitoring of changes easier acceptable than the application of top-down approaches. The notion that every leader is serving internal customers, i.e. her team, her line managers, and her colleagues is beautiful. Also, its four-step-implementation process is very solid by using a comprehensive grid and putting a strong emphasis on execution.

If companies were able to really change the tasks and habits of their managers by only addressing acts and activities of its leaders – and not their values and behavioral styles – then indeed Blue Ocean Leadership initiatives would take less time and effort than many other ones. Real case studies will have to prove its sustainability and mid-term impact.

Saying that, Blue Ocean Leadership contains some potent and effective ideas and measures which could complement and/or challenge existing leadership concepts.

21. THE MOST UNDERESTIMATED SKILL OF A GREAT LEADER

Highly respected management guru Warren Bennis once stated that as a successful leader you need to be *effective* and *efficient* at the same time. Effective being defined as «Doing the right things.» Efficient meaning «Doing things the right way.» In summary, a successful leader would do the right things in the right way. It›s so simple, at least in theory. But, why not in reality?

The answer in a nutshell: Most organizations do not spend enough time on "detailing how to implement" nor do they put the required high level of attention, commitment, and passion into *getting things done in an excellent manner until the very, very end.* They do not have leaders who are capable of and willing to focus with firmness and love on *Executing in Excellence.*

Many corporations severely underestimate the immense importance of a rigorous *Obsession of Execution Mentality,* which needs to run throughout the entire organization. Every single employee would need to embrace and to love getting things done in a complete manner. Let's apply some common sense by addressing the following question: How valuable are your objectives and your strategy – even if they were developed by the brightest people in the most sophisticated way – if you just can't realize them, or if you do not have a leader who can make people achieve the defined goals and plans?

Execution is the Great Unaddressed Issue in Today's Business World

What I've observed over the years is that many corporations spend an awful lot of time trying to figure out what they should do. For example, pondering in which market segments to invest, which products to launch, which services to offer, should they focus on growth, on cutting cost and so on. Afterwards, in a second step, they again invest a significant amount of time to discuss the "how," thinking about the strategy they would like to follow. Should they improve the quality of their offering, or should they instead increase volumes to benefit from economies of scale, should they focus on their home market or should they go international, etc.

In a third step, and following good management practice as it's being taught at every business school, they would focus on the tactics, i.e. drafting action plans in order to implement their strategy and to aim to achieve the predefined goals.

Lacking a Culture of Executing in Excellence

Many companies naively believe that once they have drafted the action plans, and listed what has to be done by whom by when by using which resources, the work is done. Almost in a Harry Potteresque manner. Or they think things get taken care of by anonymous subordinates somewhere in their organizations.

I met executives who regarded detail work as something which is beneath the dignity of a business leader. You might assume that they have most likely spent too much time either in the sun without wearing a hat or with overpaid consultants. Or, possibly even worse, they might have done both things simultaneously.

I would argue, however, that they are completely wrong. Execution is an art; an art that separates successful organizations from less successful ones.

As such, *Execution* is one of a leader›s most important job. Full stop.

The fundamental problem is that an army of business leaders still think of Execution as the tactical side of business – something which they delegate while they indulge themselves in the perceived "bigger" topics. Consequently, they do not comprehend that Execution is not just tactics – it is a discipline and a system of its own. It has to be ingrained into an organization's objectives, culture, structure, and processes. The leader himself must be the grandmaster of Execution both in big and in small companies.

How to become a Master of Execution

In their excellent book *Execution – The Discipline of Getting Things done*, Larry Bossidy and Ram Charan list the following three building blocks that need to be in place in order to make Execution happen in your organization.

Building Block One: The Leader›s Seven Essential Behaviors

To install and to keep up the real spirit, concept, and processes of Execution – and to avoid becoming a micromanager – there are seven essential behaviors which characterize a leader of execution:

Know your people and your business: Be engaged with your business, live your business, and be where the action is.

Insit on realism: It›s the heart of execution. Start by being realistic yourself. Then you make sure realism is the goal of all dialogues in the organization.

Set clear goals and priorities: Focus on 3-4 clear priorities that everyone can grasp. Speak and act simply and directly.

Follow through: Lack of it is a major cause of poor execution. Implement detailed action plans and make specific people accountable for results.

Reward the doers: If you want people to produce specific results, you need to reward them accordingly. Either in base pay or in bonuses and stock options.

Expand people's capabilities through coaching: Pass on your knowledge, wisdom and experience to the next generation of leaders. Every encounter is an opportunity to coach.

Know yourself: It takes emotional fortitude to be open to whatever information you need, whether it›s what you like to hear or not.

Building Block Two: Creating The Framework For Cultural Change

Most efforts at cultural change fail because they are not linked to improving the business outcomes. The ideas and tools of cultural change are fuzzy and disconnected from strategic and operational realities. To change a business's culture, you need a set of processes – social operating mechanisms – that will change the beliefs and behavior of people in ways that are directly linked to bottom-line results.

The basic premise is simple: Cultural change gets real when your aim is execution. You don't need a lot of complex theory or employee surveys to use this framework. You need to change people's behavior so that they produce results. First you need to explain people what results you're looking for. Then you discuss how to get those results, as a key element of the coaching process.

Then you reward people for delivering the results. If they come up short, you provide additional training and coaching, possibly withdraw rewards, look for other tasks and/or jobs for them, or even let them go, if it were the best option for all main stakeholders. When you do these things correctly and sincerely, you create a culture of getting things done.

Building Block Three: The Job No Leader Should Delegate – Having the Right People in the Right Place

An organization's human beings are its most reliable resource for generating excellent results year after year. Their judgments, experiences, and capabilities make the difference between success and failure. Sounds familiar? Yet the same leaders who exclaim that "people are our most important asset" usually do not think very hard about choosing the right people for the right jobs. They either do not have precise ideas about what the jobs require (not only today, but tomorrow) or they're too busy thinking about how to make their companies bigger. What they're overlooking is that the quality of their people is the best competitive differentiator.

Often leaders may not know enough about the people they're appointing. They may also pick people with whom they're comfortable, rather than others who have better skills for the job. They may not have the courage to discriminate between strong and weak performers and take the necessary actions. All of these reflect one absolutely fundamental shortcoming: The leaders aren't personally committed to the people process and deeply engaged in it. However, it's a job you have to love doing as a leader.

Conclusion

Execution-oriented companies are closer to reality; they change faster, are more flexible, and as a result are more successful. They have comprehended that sometimes – and especially if they lack certain know-how, time or particular capabilities – they are better off choosing the second or third best option available (the What), and then executing it (the How) better than any of their competitors.

Contrariwise, if an organization is able and fortunate enough to select the best chance at hand, but at the same time is not capable of executing it in excellence, their realized targets might easily be far behind the ones of group one.

Leading for execution is a straightforward and very rewarding exercise. The main requirement is that you as a leader have to be deeply and passionately engaged in your organization and honest about realities with others and yourself. Putting an execution environment and mentality in place is hard, but it's one of a leader's most important job. This is true whether you're in charge of a multinational or your own smaller company.

22. LEAD LIKE THE NEW CHESS WORLD CHAMPION

Magnus Carlsen, a 22-year-old Norwegian, was crowned chess' newest world champion in 2013 by having beaten six-year title holder Viswanathan Anand of India.

In 2004, Carlsen became a grandmaster at the age of 13. On Jan. 1 2010, at the age of 19, he became the youngest chess player in history to be ranked world No. 1. Carlsen is said to have a grasp on the game that would usually take players between 20 to 30 years to acquire.

With a rating of 2872 (calculated according to a win-loss formula) he's the highest-rated chess player in history. Carlsen, known for a fast and aggressive style of play, is also the first player not to come from Eastern Europe or Asia to claim the chess world championship since American Bobby Fischer was dethroned in 1975.

Russian grandmaster Garry Kasparov has dubbed the young Norwegian as the Harry Potter of chess, while others have compared him to Mozart. I'd call him the new global pop star of chess. Carlsen is young. He›s good looking. He›s got humor. And although he misses out on being the youngest player to win the title (that honour goes to the Russian Garry Kasparov), he›s already now building himself into a marketing juggernaut.

Carlsen was profiled on "60 Minutes", has modelled along with Liv Tyler, appeared on the front cover of GQ magazine, has 222k Facebook likes, 52k Twitter followers (me being one of them), and was even offered a role as a chess player in the next "Star Trek" film. Carlsen certainly knows how to use social media and to apply it as a key marketing channel to connect with and build his fan bases. After his win on Friday his brand value will rapidly go further up.

The 10 Leadership Characteristics of Carlsen

Work hard and never stop learning and growing - Carlsen developed his early chess skills by playing alone for hours at a time, searching for combinations and replaying games and positions shown to him by his father. He participated in his first tournament at the age of 8 years.

Plan ahead and still stay flexible – Although being a strategist, Anand says of Carlsen that "he's very flexible, he knows all the structures and he can play almost any position. ... Magnus can literally do almost everything."

Stay calm and believe in yourself - Carlsen is incredibly controlled and disciplined for his age. He's quiet and relaxed before his matches. When playing he's highly focused, concentrated, and self-confident.

Keep up until the end – Never give up. Both Carlsen's positional mastery and endgame prowess are being compared with those of the very best world-class players. When needed, he plays fearless moves.

Make quick and smart moves – That builds up pressure on competitors. After the match Anand said: "I congratulate Carlsen. He poked me into making mistakes."

Apply thoughtfulness and variety – Over the years Carlsen's style has evolved. Once known for his attacking style as a teenager, Carlsen later developed into a more universal player. Today he plays a variety of different styles, making it harder for opponents to prepare against him.

Stay true to yourself – Have your own style. Kasparov once said that although Carlsen would have characteristics of chess legends Karpov and Fischer, he's very unique by getting his positions and then never lets go of that bulldog bite.

Have a good sense of humor – No doubt that Carlsen is a witty young man who has a life beyond chess. That helps him to remain balanced and to re-energize himself for all of those challenging matches.

Good physical health- Carlsen is in excellent physical shape which enables him to avoid "psychological lapses." As a consequence he can maintain a high standard of play over long games and at the end of tournaments when the energy levels of others have dropped.

Stay humble, respectful and approachable – Carlsen is someone respecting very much the chess etiquette. He's well educated with great manners. He's not arrogant, but instead open-minded and approachable (you might want to follow him on Twitter).

23. THE FALL OF A MEGA BILLIONAIRE –
3 LESSONS TO BE LEARNED

Eike Batista was a Brazilian business magnate who had made a fortune in mining, oil and gas. He is the CEO of Brazilian EBX Group. The group includes five public companies: MMX (mining), MPX (energy), OGX (oil and gas), LLX (logistics), and OSX (offshore services and equipment).

According to Forbes in early 2012, Batista had a net worth of more than $30 billion, making him the 8th richest person in the world and the wealthiest in South America. Back then he was listed by Bloomberg among the 50 most influential people in global finance. An elite group of people "whose comments move markets; whose deals set the value of companies or securities; whose ideas and policies shape corporations, governments and economies," Batista has been known to have claimed publicly several times that he would overtake Mexican baron Carlos Slim to become the world's richest man by 2015.

Instead, Batista's wealth decreased 99% between March 2012 and August 2013 to just €200 million, making him the world's fastest destroyer of wealth.

What happened?

Business-wise, the reasons seem to be rather clear: The losses can be attributed to the downturn in the metals mining industry, an economic slowdown in Brazil and mismanagement that resulted in a collapse of Batista's flagship oil company OGX Petroleo & Gas Participacoes SA. Missed targets at OGX spurred selling of his group's securities. Investors worried that Batista couldn't pay a $45 million short term debt due in October.

Over the next 10 years, the struggling oil company owes $3.6 billion. Things got more complicated in July, when Moody's lowered Batista's OGX bond rating from junk level Caa2 to super junk level Ca with a negative outlook. The situation became really dramatic when some weeks ago Mubadala Co., the Abu Dhabi fund, converted a €2 billion investment in Batista's companies into debt, further eroding the value of his assets.

While there were economic and financial reasons to Batista's epic fall, there were also leadership, management, and personal deficiencies that might be even more relevant, even for those among us whose net worth is not even close to a billion.

Set meaningful Objectives

That's the undisputed starting point. Both as an entrepreneur and as a salaried manager, one should have worthwhile professional and personal objectives to strive for and to get motivation from. In a perfect world the two dimensions would match and complement each other. For example, in a business context you could decide to build the most customer centric organization in the world. At the same time, in a personal sense, you might want to determine to develop your personal services skills to a never-reached level of excellence. From such aspirations your customers, employees, other stakeholders, and eventually you, would benefit.

Aiming to become the richest person on the planet, however, might be somehow trivial; especially if you are already worth more than €30 billion. Whom do you want to motivate with such an objective? Whom do you want to impress? How do you add value to your organization and to society by just becoming the wealthiest person on the planet? Why not try instead to become the world's number one charitable donator? Why not set up your own foundation to help others in need and to become an admired social leader? I bet you would inspire thousands and millions in assisting and following you. And, most importantly, you would have a much more fulfilled life.

Worship Humility

Stay humble during your whole career. Display meekness and modesty in your behavior, attitude, or spirit. Avoid becoming arrogant. There is nothing wrong with being proud of you and your achievements, but never forget that it was not only you who made you successful. There are many other contributors. Show them and others sincere respect.

Research suggests that humility is a quality of leaders who are successful in the long-term. For example, Jim Collins found that a certain type of leader, whom he terms "level 5," possesses humility and fierce resolve. Humility is being studied as a trait that enhances leadership effectiveness. Research suggests that humility includes self-understanding, awareness, empathy, openness, and perspective taking.

Be trustworthy and credible

In the case of Batista, most experts would agree that key stakeholders lost trust in him. Credibility had been one of his most important assets, since he built vast parts of his conglomerate on debt. But he couldn't deliver on the results he promised when he listed his companies.

Particularly in times when markets are highly sensitive and volatile, a loss of trust can easily be the beginning of the end. As a consequence, there was a vicious chain reaction: Once Batista has lost credibility in one area, very quickly he lost it in all of them.

As Batista fell from billionaire-dom, he expressed regret at having taken his companies' public, saying that in retrospect, a private equity model of financing his ventures would have been more suitable. It seems that he's still missing the point.

Batista might leave a legacy of having been the greatest Icarus of modern times. According to Greek mythology, Icarus attempted to escape from Crete with wings that his father constructed from feathers and wax. He ignored instructions not to fly too close to the sun, and the melting wax caused him to fall into the sea where he drowned. The myth is usually taken as a tragic example of hubris.

Regardless, I hope – with €200 million remaining in his bank account – that Batista will very soon and very deeply reflect on his personal shortfalls. I strongly admire sustainable and responsible entrepreneurial success, and although it is currently difficult to believe in his comeback, I hope Batista gains back his credibility, to become and remain "earthened," and to define meaningful objectives for himself and his future business endeavors.

24. AS CEO I'M ACCOUNTABLE –
RESPECT TO GROUPON'S ANDREW MASON

Groupon's founder Andrew Mason was dismissed as its CEO on March 1, 2013 after the company – once again – missed analysts' expectations in regards to sales and profits.

With Groupon, Mason has built an inspirational start-up and a multi-million dollar company. At its peak, Groupon was said to have rejected a $6 billion acquisition bid from Google.

Still, the last couple of years have been an edgy ride for the one-time shooting star Mason and his company. Attacked by many copycats and having suffered from various management mistakes of its own making, the company lost lots of its former appeal and growth momentum. In 2012, Mason was even named "Worst CEO of the Year" by Herb Greenberg of CNBC. Greenberg wrote, in part, "Mason's goofball antics, which can come off more like a big kid than a company leader, almost make a mockery of corporate leadership – especially for a company with a market value of more than $3 billion. It would be excusable, even endearing, if the company were doing well, but it's not. Sales growth is through the floor..."

After Groupon ousted Mason as CEO yesterday after the stock declined more than 80 percent from its November 2011 high, Mason left a great and mature note to his former employees and team members:

People of Groupon,

After four and a half intense and wonderful years as CEO of Groupon, I've decided that I'd like to spend more time with my family. Just kidding - I was fired today. If you're wondering why... you haven't been paying attention. From controversial metrics in our S1 to our material weakness to two quarters of missing our own expectations and a stock price that's hovering around one quarter of our listing price, the events of the last year and a half speak for themselves.

As CEO, I am accountable.

You are doing amazing things at Groupon, and you deserve the outside world to give you a second chance. I'm getting in the way of that. A fresh CEO earns you that chance. The board is aligned behind the strategy we've shared over the last few months, and I've never seen you working together more effectively as a global company - it's time to give Groupon a relief valve from the public noise.

For those who are concerned about me, please don't be - I love Groupon, and I'm terribly proud of what we've created. I'm OK with having failed at this part of the journey. If Groupon was Battletoads, it would be like I made it all the way to the Terra Tubes without dying on my first ever play through. I am so lucky to have had the opportunity to take the company this far with all of you. I'll now take some time to decompress (FYI I'm looking for a good fat camp to lose my Groupon 40, if anyone has a suggestion), and then maybe I'll figure out how to channel this experience into something productive.

If there's one piece of wisdom that this simple pilgrim would like to impart upon you: have the courage to start with the customer. My biggest regrets are the moments that I let a lack of data override my intuition on what's best for our customers. This leadership change gives you some breathing room to break bad habits and deliver sustainable customer happiness - don't waste the opportunity!

I will miss you terribly.

Love,
Andrew

This is a remarkably mature and honest message for someone who often was referred to as a kid entrepreneur. Mason is not hiding behind any other dubious reasons nor behind someone else's fault and mistakes. Something which is not normal any longer in today's often selfish and egoistic business world.

This deserves respect!

Also, respect to Mason for having invented a new business model and a company which has disrupted the industry and created lots of creative and stimulating momentum for many other companies, entrepreneurs, managers, and employees.

25. JUST RETHINK!

There are not many really unique and inspirational business books around anymore. I don't mean the ones which just give you the same old advice: draft a situation analysis, set up a business plan, ask investors for money. You know the ones, with all the typical strategy, action plans yadda yadda yadda…

Now, guess what? I was lucky enough to come across another outstanding piece of business literature - a book about how to succeed in business, not written in a superficial way. Instead, it was written with wit, pragmatism, clarity and – yes – "INSPIRATION."

It is for everyone who has been having the feeling that sometimes (or even often) we have to break the established rules and ways of thinking in order to make an impact and to be successful in the long-term, regardless if you run your own business, work in a huge company or if you are just interested in practical mental stimulation.

One more thing you might be interested in: This time I will not tell you the book's title. Or, at least not for the time being. It's up to you to find it out as we go along discussing some of its key statements and phrases. You think that's cruel? Yes, maybe… You could think, however, like me in the opposite way:

I want you to focus on its contents first before being distracted by names, etc.

I want you to think, imagine, dream and question. Question the way you work. Question the way you live; Question yourself!

I want you to present and discuss your thoughts and ideas with us around this series of upcoming articles

Of course, I'm also very curious to see who will first find out which book we're talking about. Are you ready to join? If so, then let's get started with the first key thoughts of the book.

That will never work in the real world!

Sound familiar? You hear it all the time when you tell people about a fresh idea. All these "real world" inhabitants are filled with pessimism and despair. They assume society is not ready for or capable of change. Don't believe them. That world may be real for them, but it doesn't mean you have to live in it.

In other words: The real world isn't a place, it's an excuse. It's a justification for not trying. It has nothing to do with you.

Misconception: Learning from failures equals being successful

"Fail early and fail often." Yes and no. Don't get fooled. At the end of the day, there is only so much you can learn from mistakes and failures. Failure is not a prerequisite for success. You just learn what you should not do. You still don't know what you should do. Contrast that with learning from your successes. That shouldn't be a surprise. It's exactly how nature works. Evolution doesn't linger on past failures, it's always building upon what worked. And so should you!

26. COMMIT TO THINGS THAT NEVER CHANGE!

Here we go with the much awaited next article of our very successful "Rethink for Success" series. You don't have to have read any of the previous articles. Each of them covers an independent and very relevant (management) topic. The series is based on a very stimulating business book.

The book's title is still not revealed for the time being in order to fully focus on its unique contents. Let's get started.

In a previous article I presented the following Ideas and Advices

Be a curator: What makes a museum great is the stuff that's NOT on the walls. In other words: It's the stuff you leave out that matters. Advice: Constantly look for things to remove and to simplify.

Throw less at a problem: More people, more time, more money just makes the problem bigger. Advice: Cut back! Do less! And make the tough calls!

Time to move on with Today's Thoughts and Tips

Forget flings, commit to things that never change

Many companies focus on the next big thing... without really knowing what it will be. Then they latch on to what's hot and new. They simply follow the latest trends. That's a fool's path, since you're focusing on fashion instead of substance. Instead, the core of your business should be built around things that last and won't change. Things that people are going to want today and in ten years' time: quality, good service, affordability, choice, simplicity, etc. Remember, fashion fades away. Core features will stay.

An expensive golf club does not transform you into Tiger

In business, and other areas of life, too many people are obsessed with the latest technology, tools and tricks. Wrong! What really matters is content – substance to get customers to make money. There are no shortcuts to that. The good way: Use whatever you've got already or can afford cheaply. Then go! It's not the gear that matters. It's your head, heart and passion!

27. MAKE DECISIONS, DECISIONS & MORE DECISIONS!

Sorry for being a bit late with this part of our thought-provoking and heavily discussed "Rethink for Success" series. A series which is based on an insightful and exciting business book which I have found, read and reviewed especially for you.

As you know, I have not revealed the book's title for the time being in order to fully focus on its unique contents. Fasten your seatbelts and get stimulated with today's part 8. No need to have read my previous articles on this subject, you'll get the articles' contents and messages without any problems. No worries!

In a previous article I presented the following Ideas and Advices

Less is More (1): Big organizations talk and meet a lot without doing too much at the end. Stripped Down Advice: Keep your mass low and you can quickly move and change anything.

Less is More (2): Too many of us complain that there is not enough time, people, money, etc., etc., etc. to do certain things. Stripped Down Advice: Stop whining and see instead how far you can get with what you have.

Time to move on with Today's Thoughts and Tips

Ignore the details early on

Focusing on details too early means not seeing the whole picture. So ignore the details for a while. Nail the basics first and worry about the specifics later. Besides, you often can't recognize the details that matter most until after you start building. And that's when you need to pay attention, no sooner.

Commit to making decisions

Don't wait for the perfect solution. It does not exist. Instead, decide and move forward. Get into the flow of making decision after decision. Then you build momentum and boost morale. Decisions are progress. Each one you make is a brick in building your business. Also note: It doesn't matter how much you plan, you'll still get some stuff wrong anyway. Don't make things worse by over-analyzing and delaying before you even get going.

28. HAVE A POINT OF VIEW AND LIVE IT!

Let's move on with another article of our "Rethink for Success" series. Let's continue discussing a stimulating business book that I have found for you. For the time being we will not reveal the book's title. It's not to annoy you. It's to focus on its words and messages without being distracted by its title and the names of its authors.

And the best thing is that you can join us and our discussion at any time, even without having read my previous articles. Not a prob at all!

In a previous article I presented the following Ideas and Advices

Start making something: Ideas are cheap and plentiful. Stripped Down Advice: The most important thing is to begin. And then how well you execute.

No time is no excuse: The most common excuse people give is "there's not enough time." Stripped Down Advice: Don't let yourself off the hook with excuses. It's entirely your responsibility to make your dreams come true.

Time to move on with Today's Thoughts and Tips

Draw a line in the sand

Great businesses have a point of view, not just a product or service. You have to believe in something. A strong stand is how you attract superfans. Everything is debatable. But when you stand for something, decisions are obvious.

Start a business, not a startup

They say that the startup is a magical place. Why? It's supposed to be a place where expenses are supposed to be someone else's problem. It's a place where you can spend other people's money. The problem with this magical place is it's a fairy tale. The truth is that every business is governed by the same rules: revenue in, expenses out. Turn a profit or wind up gone. So don't use the idea of a startup as a crutch. Instead, start an actual business.

29. NO EXCUSES. GET STARTED!

Here we go with another part of our series, "Rethink for Success." In this series I'm discussing with you some thoughts and quotes of a stimulating business book. Its title is not being revealed for the time being. We strip it down to its bare words and meaning without being distracted by its title and the names of its authors.

In a previous article I presented the following Ideas and Advices

Make a Difference: Don't imitate, since you want your customers to say, "This makes my life better." Stripped Down Advice: What you do is your legacy.

Make something you want to use: The easiest, most straightforward way to create a great product is to make something you want to use. Stripped Down Advice: Do what you need and what you like most.

Time to move on with Today's Thoughts and Tips

Start making something

Ideas are cheap and plentiful. The original pitch idea is such a small part of a business that it's almost negligible. What you do is what matters, not what you think or say or plan. The most important thing is to begin. And then how well you execute.

No time is no excuse

The most common excuse people give is "there's not enough time." When you want something bad enough, you make the time - regardless of your other obligations. The truth is most people just don't want it bad enough. Then they protect their ego with the excuse of time. Don't let yourself off the hook with excuses. It's entirely your responsibility to make your dreams come true.

30. MAKING A COLORFUL DIFFERENCE

This is another article of our series, "Rethink for Success." As you know, in this series I'm discussing with you some thoughts and quotes of a stimulating business book which title I'm not revealing for the time being. We strip it down to its bare words and meaning without being distracted by its title and the names of its authors.

In a previous Article I presented the following Ideas and Advices

Workaholism is not a Virtue

Not only is workaholism unnecessary, it's stupid. Stripped Down Advice: Don't work ridiculous hours. The real hero is home on-time, because she figured out a faster way to get things done.

Enough with Entrepreneurs

Let's retire the term "entrepreneur." It's outdated and loaded with baggage. Stripped Down Advice: Let's call them "starters" instead. It's more down-to-earth. Anyone who creates a new business is a "starter."

Time to move on with today's Thoughts and Tips

Make a Difference

Do you want to build just another me-too product, or do you want to shake things up? Don't you want to feel that you're making a difference? You want your customers to say, "This makes my life better." Don't forget: What you do is your legacy!

Make something you want to use

The easiest, most straightforward way to create a great product is to make something you want to use. Something that lets you develop and design what you know - and you'll figure out immediately whether or not what you're making is any good. When you solve your own problems, the light comes on. You know exactly what the right answer is.

31. THE POWER OF SLOWNESS

Everything is becoming faster, more hectic. People have less time to enjoy life, nature and the wonderful things around them. Fortunately for some, time this seems to have started to be reversed: Instead of doing everything at high speed, some people prefer taking their time for the good things in life, even in the professional world. This is clearly noticeable. "Slowness as a way to accelerate productivity" appears to gain a foothold in the business world. At least in some more progressive companies.

An increasing number of "resistance movements" against the "disease of speed" have been formed and are trying to make life more beautiful and healthier. "Slowness" is the name of an already long-lasting trend. For the last 25 years people have been looking for an easier and less stressful way of life. "Slow" is not just about causing a more enjoyable and joyful life. It is also about health aspects which have become so important to many people. Currently, everyone is talking about "burnout," the "speed disease" of the fast and furious ones caused by a vicious circle of overwork, stress, and the feeling of being overwhelmed.

In the 20th century the speed of transportation has increased by the factor 102. Social relationships, cultural values and lifestyles are subject to an ever-faster change. Time, pressure and stress are among the basic factors of everyday life; they strongly influence and control our feelings. Really good ideas are rarely created in the flooded river of hustle and bustle.

As the queen in Lewis Carroll's "Alice in Wonderland" said: "In this country you have to run as fast as you can if you want to stay at the same place."

There are alternatives: In St. Moritz, there is a newly built skiing area called "Chill-out Riding Zone" for the connoisseurs among skiers. Over there in that part of beautiful Switzerland, relaxed skiing is a priority: Enjoyment rather than speed.

"Slow Food" is a worldwide movement of conscious connoisseurs and responsible consumers who have made it their mission to cultivate the pleasure of eating and drinking and staying healthy at the same time.

Some businesses and various industry sectors are seen to be rather sceptical when it comes to "work-life-balance." For example, many consider the mobile communication technology as being a main cause of stress. Being able to call anyone at any time, and vice versa being reachable at any time, can put quite some stress on people. Some companies have discovered slowness as a source to increase productivity. Take Montblanc which wants its employees to take a break as long as they want. Slowness is a central piece of its corporate ideology nowadays. Their demanding quality standards require concentration and focus at a top level. For them, mistakes are more expensive than granting long breaks.

Some companies even follow the slogan "good things need time." Think of the - fortunately still existing - little pastry shops in many countries in Europe which manufacture their cakes and pastries carefully by hand. Or craftsmen who produce only three musical instruments in one year. Why? Because - like making chocolate biscuits by hand – it is a meticulous and detailed work which "takes time." There are even a few shoemakers left who do their job so well and in such an artistically detailed way that they can produce shoes without seams, so-called "one piece shoes". And, of course, giving them the right to charge a fortune. There is a cheese maker in the lovely Southern German region "Allgaeu," which "grants" his cheese two years of maturing before even considering selling it.

Ever heard of "Slow Cow", a relaxation and slowness drink? It is marketed in an opposite direction to the trendy Red Bull drink. Slow Cow, the proud "anti-energy drink," is supposed to create feelings of peace and serenity. A key component of the beverage is its amino acid L-theanine, which has a calming effect without making drinkers tired. It also helps to reduce stress, and to improve concentration and the quality of sleep.

For many people it was - and still is - possible to be professionally successful by powering their way ahead. Full steam. Neither looking to the left nor to the right. Good on them. Often, however, when trying to lead a fulfilled life, they fail, mostly because they lack a concrete vision of life. They've just taken on too many tasks, roles, and responsibilities over the years. They've forgotten to design their personal plan of life. They were too fast and got mixed up in everyday life. They have not taken enough time to cherish their body and mind. They have not yet understood that if you are in a hurry you should slow down.

The higher the (individually perceived) pressure of acceleration becomes, the broader and stronger a counter-trend towards slowing down will further evolve. The general awareness that faster is not always better will increase over the next few years – and will lead to "time rebellions" of the masses. This will put increased pressure on "high-speed" companies and products.

At the same time it'll offer an ocean of opportunities to introduce sophisticated products and services which help people to slow down, to enjoy life and still be at the innovative forefront of human evolution.

Chapter 3

EXPLORE!

Tomorrow's top leaders have a strong passion to learn, to question, to dive deep, and to be misunderstood. Relentlessly.

Their interest goes far beyond their own organizations and industries. They absorb whatever comes across their way and catches their interest. With curiosity they try to figure out what a new watch from Apple might mean for them, what implications it could have when Mark Zuckerberg starts his own reading club, when Artificial Intelligence is nominated by a company as a board member for the first time ever, when Airbus builds an electric plane (and not Tesla), how Puma could compete with Nike and Adidas (or not), when Disney bids farewell to the movie star, or if Microsoft might be cool again.

They are both clear about which countries offer competitive and attractive investment conditions and how to rock content marketing to differentiate their offer and brand. Thanks to content marketing, tomorrow's top leaders will attract and acquire new customers without having to spend big bucks. They will use content more than ever to cover webinars, blogs, forums, podcasts, search engines, how-to videos, innovative mobile apps, and much more. They will completely embrace that Marketing is about telling the world that you're a rock star, but Content Marketing is showing the world you are one.

32. NEW APPLE WATCH - HOT OR FLOP?

On Monday March 9, 2015 at 10.00 a.m. Pacific Time, Apple's CEO Tim Cook will officially present its first wearable to the world – the Apple Watch. Tim is expected to announce final details like pricing and most likely confirm its shipping date in April.

One key question remains: Will the Apple Watch become the industry's much anticipated catalyst to ignite the global smartwatch and wearables market by offering true killer features? Or will consumers make it go down in tech history as the world's most redundant gadget?

Apple fanatics are convinced that it'll be a tech hit; others argue it's just a lovely accessory and at best a fashion gadget. Another group of people still have no clue why they would need it in the first place. Some even wonder why they should go retro and buy a watch when they could just use their iPhone... And tech liberals are frustrated that to pair with an Apple Watch, you'll need at least an iPhone 5 or 6.

Both earlier iPhones and other phone platforms like Android are excluded. Well, my dear friends, don't forget this is an iPhone-owner's product!

So, will you buy one? Before you answer, please continue to read and find out more about Apple's new watch and what you might get for your bucks (and what not):

What The Apple Watch Really Is

It's some sort of digital grab bag: A fitness tracker, a music player, a communications device, a handheld portal to other apps, a virtual wallet making payments via Apple Pay, a remote control for Apple TV, an electronic key to open doors, and a smart control device to manage your house. It boasts swipe-to-glance features, voice-activated controls, and mail functionalities. It charges via a combination of magnets and inductive charging.

What we can expect from the Apple Watch

Premium Pricing

It's known that the Apple Watch will start at $349 in the US for the aluminum and glass Apple Watch Sport. Higher-end versions might easily cost up to $1,000 and beyond. Its flagship, the 18-karat-gold Apple Watch Edition, will certainly be prized in the vicinity of a Cartier, Tag Heuer, or Breitling. The Apple Watch – following the company's tradition - will be tried being positioned as a Veblen good, i.e. using higher prices to make it even more aspirational and preferable.

Premium Quality

Although Swatch and some other Swiss watch makers have finally woken up and started developing their own smartwatches at full speed, the overall Swiss watch industry should expect some disruption and shake up. Since Apple hired Paul Deneve, the former head of the high-end French fashion brand Yves Saint Laurent, and Patrick Pruniaux, the former VP of Sales and Retail of TAG Heuer, it's clear how serious the otherwise design-obsessed Cupertino-based company is about superior design and top quality for its Apple Watch.

Unique Personalization

Apple's watch will be all about personalization. It comes in two case sizes: 38mm and 42mm, both of which can be set up to work on either your left or your right wrist. There will be three "collections": *The Watch, Watch Sport* and *Watch Edition*. They all will come with the same rectangular design with rounded off corners and will be divided by different build materials: There will be six band types and 18 colors. The band types will be easily interchangeable thanks to a unique slide-out locking mechanism. Each watch comes with a variety of faces, from traditional designs to playful characters. Faces are extensively customizable: you can change colors, choose design elements, and add functionality. So one Apple Watch can have literally millions of different appearances.

Dedicated Ecosystem of Apps

The success of Apple's watch will strongly depend on the apps the third-party developers will launch. Here are some apps which are known already:

Of course, there will be own Apple apps like Maps, iTunes, Siri, Apple TV control, etc., News apps (Yahoo News, Feed Wrangler), Social networking apps (Twitter, Facebook, WeChat, Instagram, etc.), Traveling apps, Productivity apps, smart home apps, and entertainment and leisure apps, etc.

Fitness will be a central element of the Apple Watch. Apple will offer its own fitness apps as well as third-party apps like Nike Plus, Fitness Spades, WaterMinder, Slopes, and many more. Four sapphire lenses on the back of the Apple Watch will measure heart rate by using a combination of infrared and LED technology. In a nutshell, the Apple Watch has the potential to become your preferred personal fitness trainer, tracking your everyday activities, proposing a workout plan, and monitoring your caloric burn.

So, Will the Apple Watch be HOT or NOT?

There are forecasts stating that Apple will ship anything between 15 and 20 million units in 2015. If we assume an average retail price of $700 per watch (which is even on the conservative side), the Apple Watch could generate between $10.5 and $14 billion of the company's sales this year.

Apple's first-generation watch will not be perfect; it'll miss some top apps at launch, its rather poor battery life will be an issue, and pricing of its top models might be a stretch for many consumers. Also, the wrist feel will be crucial, i.e. will consumers perceive it as a nice and comfortable feeling when wearing the Apple Watch? Will they consider the watch's fit and finish as elegant and refined?

On the other side, there is an army of loyal Apple fans waiting for the next big thing. The latest huge success of the company's iPhone 6 range has significantly broadened the hub base for the new watch.

Apple's popular brand, its cool marketing campaigns, its sophisticated personalization strategy, its very loyal fan base, its broad and deep retail presence, its pretty good apps ecosystem, and the well-chosen "timing" of the launch will guarantee a strong uptake for the Apple Watch. At least in first few months.

The ultimate question to be asked is not if you NEED the new Apple Watch, but how desperately you WANT it and how well Apple makes you believe in it!

What do you think? Do YOU want one? Will YOU buy one? Or will YOU skip it and wait for the more advanced second generation of the Apple Watch?

33. ZUCKERBERG IS NOT OPRAH

"My challenge for 2015 is to read a new book every other week - with an emphasis on learning about different cultures, beliefs, histories and technologies." That's what Mark Zuckerberg posted on his Facebook site on January 2, 2015.

Back then – and still today – I think that Zuck's idea is a beautiful one. Promoting regularly reading a stimulating book and using his popularity to get people motivated to read and discuss books is brilliant! It's exactly what we need in a world where many people have forgotten about the beauty of words, the power of their own thoughts, and the magic of eloquence. Consequently, all of us – and not only the publishing industry - need to give a big hand to everyone who tries to make reading more popular, especially in times when books compete with apps, online games, music streaming, movie subscription services, etc.

What happened after his Announcement?

Well, what a surprise! When someone like Zuck invites his 31 million plus followers in the age of the omnipresent digitalization, immediately the Internet reacts frenetically. Indeed, within a few days after his post became public a quarter of a million people liked his newly created page, "A Year of Books." His first book pick "The End of Power" by Moises Naim magically transformed overnight from a rather unknown book into a bestseller. Many journalists predicted that his "book club" – which he had never explicitly founded or announced as such – would become a big market shaper in the future of books. Other "experts" even dubbed him "the new Oprah."

What else has happened?

Unfortunately not a lot. When Zuck together with Moises Naim finally hosted a Facebook Q&A session to discuss the book, only a few hundred people showed up. Having read their questions and comments – several requested a pirated PDF of the book and others posted ads to promote their businesses – I dare say that not even half of them read the book. Which is a pity, since it's a thought-provoking book that explores how the world is shifting to give individual people more power that was traditionally only held by large organizations and institutions.

So, what has not (yet) happened?

It seems that there's no "literary connection" (yet) between Zuck and his army of followers. Whilst Zuck seemed happy with the Q&A and went on to post, "Btw, thanks for doing this Q&A. I really enjoyed reading your book. It was a great way to start off my year!", the Q&A session only showed 1,484 likes, 167 comments, and a mere 101 shares. What went wrong?

First of all, Zuckerberg is Zuckerberg and not Oprah. And that's good. He's a gifted programmer, addicted to data and numbers, an astute tech entrepreneur who created a great company. Oprah – the soul lady – is an entertainment genius who has built over many years a media empire which is founded on her personal brand. Although both are in the "people business," the Oprah approach is the one most of us can relate to far more easily. And reading a book is still a personal and often emotional thing to do. Oprah is accepted as a tastemaker, Zuck as a business maker.

In addition, in today's hyper-competitive and noisy world you need to shout loudly to promote your products and services. Even if your name is Mark Zuckerberg and especially when you do something which you're not well known for. It's crucial you structure your outreach: Promoting content the right way means targeting multiple sites, adequate blogs, and forums, as well as exchanging with various key influencers and opinion leaders to keep your story going and building up. Personally, I only heard about the Q&A when it was already over. What about you?

Also, and it's very crucial, there's a technical challenge to overcome with the Facebook site. Based on its filtering and ranking algorithms, comments, questions, and answers are neither ordered chronologically nor ranked by community votes (as it is on Reddit, for example). That makes it difficult to follow and to get involved.

Finally, the book – although as previously mentioned a stimulating read which is well-reviewed, is challenging and time-consuming. I'm not reasoning that shallow books should be chosen moving forward. Possibly, and mainly to start such a journey in a more effective and smoother manner, you might want to begin with smaller and easier steps.

What Else Will Happen?

Actual involvement with the site has been limited so far. That's a fair statement. Still, and that's more relevant, it's encouraging and motivational that Zuck has started the reading initiative. It demonstrates that there are still many things we all can do for books and the promotion of reading and discussion. I'm sure he'll find ways to further encourage people to stronger participate at future Q&As; to read more broadly, and to trigger off good conversations.

By the way, Zuck has already made his next book pick, having chosen Steven Pinker's "The Better Angels of Our Nature." It is a widely discussed book (832 pages!) that argues that violence has decreased in modern times: "Recent events might make it seem like violence and terrorism are more common than ever, so it's worth understanding that all violence — even terrorism — is actually decreasing over time. If we understand how we are achieving this, we can continue our path towards peace..." Zuckerberg writes.

34. APPLE AND ITS NEWEST CHALLENGER

According to the International Data Corporation (IDC), smartphone manufacturers shipped a total of 327.6 million units during the third quarter of 2014, resulting in 25.2% growth compared to the same quarter of last year.

Xiaomi – The Strong New Kid on the Smartphone Block

New smartphone releases and an increased emphasis on emerging markets, which are still growing at more than 30% collectively, drove global smartphone shipments. A driving force behind the record smartphone volume was the combined effort of the vendors trailing market leaders Samsung and Apple. Among those there is one clearly protruding challenger.

4-year-old Chinese company Xiaomi, both its country's largest mobile phone maker and the fastest-growing in the world, achieved 5.2 percent of the market share which had put it in third spot behind established leaders Samsung (23.8%) and Apple (12%) before Lenovo completed its acquisition of Motorola some days ago. Xiaomi, having displayed an incredible rise since its first smartphone launch in September 2011, makes Android phones with high-end specs qualitatively in-line with Samsung's Galaxy S5 or the iPhone 5S. All of that for just half the price. Its latest flagship model is the Mi4 smartphone with a sharp 5-inch screen and powerful specs for $320 in China (less than half the price of the iPhone 5S) which still is by far the company's biggest market.

Xiaomi has just moved into the other huge Asian market, India, by allowing the e-commerce site Flipkart exclusively selling its phones. When at the beginning of October Flipkart put 100,000 of Xiaomi's Redmi 1S smartphones up for sale for $98 (5,999 rupees) a piece, they were sold out within four seconds. Xiaomi is planning to enter Brazil and Mexico in a next step.

The Company's Success Factors

In China, the company succeeded to build high brand loyalty via a strong fan base by offering low-priced phones with the latest technology and hip merchandise. It sells mostly online, spends very little on traditional marketing (instead being a smart social media marketeer), keeps almost no inventory on hand - which means it regularly runs out of new phones quickly (which stimulates demand and makes it a cool brand with rare and aspirational products), accepts rathorzin margins by pricing its devices just slightly above cost, executes a one market at a time expansion strategy by concentrating on poorer emerging markets, and in parallel goes slowly upmarket in its established Chinese market with the launch of the Mi4. Last, but not least, the company recruited top executives from leading tech companies; e.g. ex-Googlers Lin Bin as President and Hugo Barra leading its international expansion.

More than Just A Copycat?

Despite its success, Apple aficionados especially comment that Xiaomi is just another Apple copycat, since its devices look a lot like Apple's iPads or iPhones. Businessweek called the Mi 4 an "iPhone-esque smartphone."

It doesn't help either that Xiaomi's CEO Lei Jun, dubbed the Steve Jobs of China, most recently ended a presentation with a slide that stated Apple's hallmark "One more thing…." This over-shadows its innovation attempts and successes by having evolved the user interface for its Chinese demographic, for example. Xiaomi's phones are distributed with a strongly modified version of Android which enables almost infinite customization. Multiple pundits rate the company's own application marketplace as one of the best Android ones.

Although currently only being available in a handful of countries, Xiaomi is quite a success story and already sells more phones in China than Apple and Samsung do. The company's expansion strategy targets big emerging markets like Brazil, Mexico, and Russia. Right now, there are no immediate plans to enter Western Europe or the U.S. In my opinion this will change once they reach the required level of economies of scale to afford doing so.

A New Breed of Chinese Companies

With Alibaba and Xiaomi, more and more Chinese technology companies are coming to the rest of the world. Can they master the challenge of ever-increasing production linked with demands in regards to excellent quality and execution? Can they come up with their own design and unique features to avoid costly intellectual property rights lawsuits? Can they create impactful marketing and strong branding initiatives? How quickly, if at all, can they get out of a copy-mode-approach? Can they get to the top, although currently almost completely unknown outside of China? Are their pockets deep enough to compete with the gorillas?

Coming from nowhere today, Xiaomi generates approximately $5 billion with smartphones versus Apple's more than $60 billion in this category. Although this is still rather tiny, it seems that they're about to challenge both Apple and Samsung in smartphones and very soon also in other categories like tablets, TV streaming, etc. Their strategy of offering high-end specs at low prices might well pay off in many Western markets.

35. HOW TO ROCK CONTENT MARKETING

Thanks to content marketing, today, many companies and small businesses are in a position to attract and acquire new customers without having to spend big bucks. It's no longer about paying tons of money on traditional marketing and ads. Instead it's about open-mindedness, creativity, an understanding of technology, a passion for new media, and the will to take risks and to keep testing.

"Content marketing is a marketing technique of creating and distributing valuable, relevant and consistent content to attract and acquire a clearly defined audience – with the objective of driving profitable customer action" (Content Marketing Institute).

Content may cover webinars, blogs, forums, podcasts, search engines, how-to videos, innovative mobile apps, and much more. Effective content can drive the rest of a successful marketing campaign and can assist in reaching your audience's audience. In the words of Robert Rose:

"Marketing is telling the world you're a rock star. Content Marketing is showing the world you are one."

Read on and get to know 20 impactful and proven content marketing principles that you can implement to successfully differentiate yourself and your products:

Set targets and define a strategy – That's where everything starts. There are three prime objectives for content marketing: reach, engagement, and conversion. Publish everywhere to get reach, and publish specifically to get conversion, i.e. be bold to also focus on niches. Content needs to be linked with both brand and SEO targets, e.g. brand reputation, conversion, retention goals, etc. Creating content comes afterwards.

Define key metrics for each content target - Goals should be set in a measurable way to see if they deliver required ROI levels. Remember what Peter Drucker once said: "If you can't measure it, you can't manage it."

Monitor beyond financial KPIs – Monitor your brands online reputation. Use services like Google Alerts, Tweet Alarm, or Social Mention to broadly monitor your and your competitors' reputation.

Source and generate relevant content – It certainly is about quantity. Even more, however, it's about quality. Re-use your best content once in a while. Have each piece of content promote another one.

Treat your content like a product - Ask yourself if your content offers the quality, if it delivers the value, and if it satisfies the needs, wants, and expectations of your target group.

De-complicate your content - You need different content for various levels in the buying cycle. But be careful. Not for every level of the buying cycle! That would be too complex. Instead consider just three to four main stages of the buyer journey and create content only for these.

Structure your outreach - Promoting content the right way means targeting adequate blogs, forums, and publications as well as exchanging with key influencers and opinion leaders.

Interact with your audience – Do not just post and think that's it. Interact with your audience in a consistent and regular manner, and answer their questions quickly and clearly. If you want to promote your content then you should spread the campaign over months or weeks rather than several days.

Treat your audience with respect – Content marketing is not advertising. Forget about running a campaign. Content marketing is a conviction and a commitment. It should be simple, transparent and straightforward.

Build trust first, sales will follow - Focus on helping and giving and not on getting. Content marketing is about your audience and building relationships. It's not about you.

Do more than storytelling – Telling stories is good. We all know it by now. However, it's not enough. Storytelling should be combined with a call for action to motivate buyers to take action and to buy your products.

Apply a conversational communication style – A good way to generate engagement is to ask your audience questions which could be answered by most of them. Ask them for their opinions, experiences, and tips. Create content that is relevant, important, and emotional.

Be in the top social sites – Analyze the communities and geographies where your audience is. In most Western countries you would need to be on Facebook, Twitter, and Instagram. Depending on your business, you also need to be on LinkedIn, Pinterest, and Youtube. In other countries, like China, sites and services like Sina Weibo, RenRen, or Pengyou should be covered. Don't rush into every new social network.

Channel Your Communication – Feed your communication in all relevant channels. However, only optimize it for 1-2 of the absolutely most important ones. They are your pillar channels and are most relevant to your target group.

Get visual whenever possible – Use photos and videos. They are more likely to create engagement and get clicked.

Create an impactful headline – Use the news or a strong statement. Make it relevant to your target group. Although long titles sometimes work, the rule is still valid: The shorter and crisper the title the better.

Integrate social sharing buttons - Your audience and your readers love to share good content.

Be Mobile – Your thinking, strategy, site, and technology. Messages and graphics look different on a small screen of a smartphone than on a tablet or laptop.

Have a person in charge – Call her director of content, curator of amazing stories, etc. The title doesn't matter. Relevant, however, is that she's empowered to design the content marketing strategy, that she owns a budget, and that she knows how to create and share exciting content with limited resources.

Final Principle: Comprehending the spirit and endless possibilities of content marketing is like singing the chorus lines of the enthralling song *All Star* by Smash Mouth:

"Hey, now, you're an All Star get your game on, go play
Hey, now, you're a Rock Star get the show on get paid
And all that glitters is gold
Only shooting stars break the mold."

36. INTERNET 2025: WHAT IT COULD LOOK LIKE

When 25 years ago Sir Tim Berners-Lee, today known as the father of the World Wide Web, proposed in a paper the creation of an open "information management system," not many would have anticipated its mind-boggling impact on mankind. Once he had released the code for free to the public in December 1990, nothing could have stopped any longer the conquest for global connectivity.

In a recently released survey, the Pew Research Center and Elon University had asked thousands of experts to make their own predictions about the state of digital life by the year 2025. Interestingly there is a strong consensus among them with regards to technology change: effortless Internet access in all regions of the world, omni-present and invisible computing networks ("like electricity"), smart sensors and software, augmented reality technologies and devices, artificial intelligence-enhanced cloud-based information storage, intelligent databasing and analytical mapping, to name the most common ones. Many of the experts also noted that the Internet will continue to strongly revolutionize most human interaction, and predominantly affect work, politics, economics, education, health, entertainment, and social life.

Although a majority of experts believe that the Internet of Things will be mainly positive in 2025, quite a number of them are concerned about data security, ethics, surveillance, crime, and terror. The expert predictions can be grouped into fifteen theses, eight of which are being classified as 'hopeful', six as 'concerned', and another as a kind of 'neutral'. They are listed below based on the Pew report:

More-Hopeful Theses

1. Information sharing over the Internet will be so effortlessly interwoven into daily life that it will become invisible, flowing like electricity, often through machine intermediaries.

2. The spread of the Internet will enhance global connectivity that fosters more planetary relationships and less ignorance.

3. The Internet of Things, artificial intelligence, and big data will make people more aware of their world and their own behavior.

4. Augmented reality and wearable devices will be implemented to monitor and give quick feedback on daily life, especially tied to personal health.

5. Political awareness and action will be facilitated and more peaceful change and public uprisings like the Arab Spring will emerge.

6. The spread of the 'Ubernet' will diminish the meaning of borders, and new 'nations' of those with shared interests may emerge and exist beyond the capacity of current nation-states to control.

7. The Internet will become 'the Internets' as access, systems, and principles are renegotiated.

8. An Internet-enabled revolution in education will spread more opportunities, with less money spent on real estate and teachers.

Less-Hopeful Theses

9. Dangerous divides between haves and have-nots may expand, resulting in resentment and possible violence.

10. Abuse and abusers will 'evolve and scale.' Human nature isn't changing; there's laziness, bullying, stalking, stupidity, pornography, dirty tricks, and crime, and those who practice them have a new capacity to make life miserable for others.

11. Pressured by these changes, governments and corporations will try to assert power — and at times succeed — as they invoke security and cultural norms.

12. People will continue — sometimes grudgingly — to make tradeoffs, favoring convenience and perceived immediate gains over privacy; and privacy will be something only the upscale will enjoy.

13. Humans and their current organizations may not respond quickly enough to challenges presented by complex networks.

14. Most people are not yet noticing the profound changes today's communications networks are already bringing about; these networks will be even more disruptive in the future.

15. Foresight and accurate predictions can make a difference; 'The best way to predict the future is to invent it.'

Without doubt the Internet will become more deeply embedded in people's lives. For good or bad.

37. FIRST TIME EVER: ARTIFICIAL INTELLIGENCE NOMINATED AS A BOARD MEMBER

In May 2014 Hong Kong-based Deep Knowledge Ventures appointed for the first time ever Artificial Intelligence (A.I.) as an official and equal board member.

Yep! Not a joke! You're not in Star Trek nor experiencing another sequel of Terminator or an encounter with Optimus Prime and Megatron of The Transformers.

Although robotics and A.I. are already popular in manufacturing, finances, and the military, this marketing stunt makes you wonder, how and when A.I. will further develop and become more and more part of our lives. Scary? Exciting? Both?

In this case, A.I. is a sophisticated machine learning program capable of making investment recommendations in the life science sector dubbed VITAL (Validating Investment Tool for Advancing Life Sciences). It basically uses machine learning to analyze financing trends in databases of life science companies and predicts successful investments. Aging Analytics, a UK research agency providing life science market, licensed VITAL to Deep Knowledge Ventures. VITAL will report its findings to the board. In addition, it will have an own equal vote in the company's board when making important investment decisions. The company expects that its opinion will be considered as the most relevant one.

In a press release, Deep Knowledge's senior partner Dmitry Kaminskiy expressed: "The variables involved in the long-term success of a biotechnology company are many and complex. We were attracted to a software tool that could in large part automate due diligence and use historical data-sets to uncover trends that are not immediately obvious to humans surveying top-line data.

We plan to incorporate new information from prospective investments into the databases to compare the outcomes against our selected investments."

So, that sounds more like an algorithm-based software which can quickly and accurately analyze huge quantities of data to identify trends and calculate various business scenarios and options. Aging Analytics claims that its long-term goal is to develop VITAL to a point where it can operate "autonomously." That's why now, it already acts as a board member. Fortunately, lacking human intuition and emotions... at least for the time being.

In a recent article, Stephen Hawking stated:

"One can imagine such technology outsmarting financial markets, out-inventing human researchers, out-manipulating human leaders, and developing weapons we cannot even understand. Whereas the short-term impact of A.I. depends on who controls it, the long-term impact depends on whether it can be controlled at all."

I still struggle to imagine a board room full of flesh-and-blood directors sitting next to a rather clumsy robot which tries to give explanations and recommendations. Saying that, how close is it already?

38. THE WORLD'S MOST COMPETITIVE COUNTRIES

IMD, a global business school based in Switzerland, in May 2014 announced its annual world competitiveness ranking. As part of its ranking of 60 economies for 2014, the IMD World Competitiveness Center also looks at perceptions of each country as a place to do business.

For the past 25 years IMD has been measuring every year how well countries manage all their resources and competencies to increase their prosperity. The overall ranking reflects more than 300 criteria, two-thirds of which are based on statistical indicators and one-third on an exclusive IMD survey of 4,300 international executives.

In a nutshell: The US leads, Europe recovers, and big emerging markets are struggling.

Highlights of the 2014 Ranking

The US retains the No. 1 spot in 2014, reflecting the resilience of its economy, better employment numbers, and its dominance in technology and infrastructure. Europe fares better than last year, thanks to its gradual economic recovery. Denmark (9) enters the top ten, joining Switzerland (2), Sweden (5), Germany (6) and Norway (10). Italy (46) and Greece (57) have strongly fallen. Japan (21) continues to climb in the rankings, helped by a weaker currency that has improved its competitiveness abroad. Elsewhere in Asia, both Malaysia (12) and Indonesia (37) make gains, while Thailand (29) falls amid political uncertainty. Singapore is at rank 3, just ahead of Hong Kong.

Most big emerging markets slide in the rankings as economic growth and foreign investment slow and infrastructure remains inadequate. China (23) falls, partly owing to concerns about its business environment, while India (44) and Brazil (54) suffer from inefficient labor markets and ineffective business management.

The Importance of the Countries' Images Abroad

Seven of the top 10 countries in the overall ranking for 2014 are also in the top 10 for having an image abroad that encourages business development, according to a survey of executives based in each of these countries. In general there is a strong correlation between a country's overall competitiveness ranking and its international image as a place to do business.

Executives in Singapore are most bullish on their country's overseas image, while Ireland, Chile, Qatar and South Korea are all far higher on this criterion than in the overall ranking.

By contrast, executives in the US, France, Taiwan and Poland are far gloomier about their countries' international image. The US results may reflect international conflicts and domestic political gridlock, while perceptions of France continue to be colored by slow reforms and the country's negative attitudes toward globalization.

It seems that while economic performance changes from year to year, perceptions are longer-term and shift more gradually. They can also lead to a virtuous circle of better image and even better economic performance.

In other words, and as stated by IMD: How executives feel their country is being perceived is a potentially useful guide to future competitiveness developments there.

39. THE ELECTRIC PLANE: INSPIRED BY TESLA. BUILT BY AIRBUS

Is Tesla dominating electric transportation? Well, if at all, then maybe in cars.

Whilst Tesla's founder, Elon Musk, still ponders about his latest vision of designing an electric supersonic airplane, with the ability to take off and land vertically, members of the Tesla Motors Club are already broadly involved in discussing the most recent and successful maiden flight of Airbus Group's new green plane.

As a matter of fact, in April 2014 Airbus unveiled its all-electric E-Fan 2.0 prototype electric aircraft, which has two motors with ducted fans powered by a lithium-ion polymer battery. The two-seater, which has been tested since the beginning of March near Bordeaux, is built of carbon fiber and can fly for about half an hour at 110 miles (177 kilometers). It has a wingspan of 31.2 feet (9.5 meters) and weighs 1,212 pounds (550 kilograms).

It could be the aircraft maker's next step in trying to enter (via hybrid electric powered engines) the market for regional jets (70-90 seats). According to Airbus, this might take anything between 15 to 20 years. Such a hybrid regional airliner could slash fuel consumption by 70-80% based on current technology and it could significantly cut noise levels.

Consequently, Airbus and its partners are aiming to perform research and development to construct a series version of the E-Fan and propose an industrial plan for a production facility close to Bordeaux Airport.

Certainly there is a place for electric and hybrid concepts in civil aerospace. However, the challenge will be to manage the high electrical loads on-board and to have enough power storage to fuel large jets. In addition, batteries need to be stable and highly resistant in any context and given situation, something Boeing struggled a lot with on its 787 Dreamliner. Lately, it's also been rather quiet about Boeing's once very popular SUGAR Volt concept: A hybrid aircraft which would use two hybrid turbofans that burn conventional jet fuel when taking off, then use electric motors to power the engines while flying.

Indeed, currently it appears that the rather clumsy and bureaucratic Airbus group is at the technological forefront of electric airplanes—not Boeing or Tesla.

By the way, if you were to consider getting your own E-Fan 2.0, you might be interested to know that it'll be priced in-line with similar-sized planes at around $300,000.

40. LOVE AFFAIR WITH A HITCHHIKING ROBOT

Remember Will Smith in iRobot? Or, Spike Jonze's film "Her" in which the hero Joaquin Phoenix falls in love with Samantha, his phone's Siri-like operating system huskily voiced by Scarlett Johansson.

Now there is a new guy in town: hitchBOT! A trivia-loving, wellington-wearing, tweeting humanoid robot which is currently hitchhiking across Canada. It left Halifax, Nova Scotia on July 27, 2014 and is on its way to Victoria, British Columbia, more than 6,000km away. And people have been falling in love with its wit and charm ever since.

hitchBOT was first conceived in 2013 as a collaborative art project between Dr. David Harris Smith of McMaster University, and Dr. Frauke Zeller of Ryerson University. Together with researchers in communication, multimedia, and mechatronics, they developed a robot to explore topics in human-robot-interaction and to test technologies in artificial intelligence and speech recognition and processing.

Developed as a sociable robot, hitchBOT's creators are encouraging Canadians to pick it up (as it cannot walk) should they see it on the roadside during its hitchhiking tour, and plug it into the car's lighter for power.

Hitch On Tour

hitchBOT is able to communicate with those who pick it up; drivers can ask the robot about its creation and personal history, and ask about its family. The robot relies on people to get around, including being strapped into a car seat belt. hitchBOT, described by its creators and parents as an outgoing and charismatic robot, is using artificial intelligence (AI) and user interface (UI) design, including speech recognition, speech processing, and social media and Wikipedia APIs.

You can follow hitchBOT's journey on Twitter and Instagram. If you see the little fella by the side of the road, don't be afraid to pick it up. Just buckle it up!

Usually, we as human beings are concerned with whether we can trust robots. This project, however, asks: can robots trust human beings? It's somehow an inversion of mankind's ultimate fear that eventually, one day, machines will take over and rule the world as stipulated by movies like Terminator, etc. Robots which will have transformed humans into servants as they'll have outsmarted their creators, having developed their own independent intelligence and having decided that it would not be enough for them to work in car plants, to deliver parcels, and to fight wars in the name of humanity any longer.

Well, at least hitchBOT seems to be charming and trustworthy enough as it's very close to its final destination already after 2 weeks of hitchhiking.

41. SENSE AND NONSENSE OF DAVOS: DO WE REALLY NEED A WORLD ECONOMIC FORUM?

"The Reshaping of the World: Consequences for Society, Politics and Business" was the thematic focus of the 2014 World Economic Forum Annual Meeting.

No doubt, it is the premiere gathering for elite businesspeople, leaders, well-known academics, celebrities, and international bureaucrats. Still, I'm wondering more than ever if the world really needs such a giant networking event where 2,500 plus so-called leaders gather to possibly visit one or more of 250 sessions to discuss the world's problems. Aren't there more effective and inclusive ways in today's world?

Founded in 1971 by German-born Klaus Schwab, then professor of business policy at the University of Geneva, over the last 20 years the Forum has evolved beyond business to a global sphere, stipulating that political, business and civil society leaders must work together to address the challenges of a globally interconnected world.

Participation in the Annual Meeting is by invitation only for CEOs of the Forum's 1,000 member companies (typically global enterprises with more than five billion dollars in turnover; and paying membership fees), political leaders (usually from the G20 countries), heads of international organizations, technology pioneers, spiritual and cultural leaders, and some more carefully chosen ones.

Before coming across as too skeptical, let's have a look at the 2014 highlights of the Forum:

- Hassan Rouhani, President of the Islamic Republic of Iran, delivered a speech that combined themes of conciliation, moderation and investment US Secretary of State John Kerry spoke about diplomacy in the Middle East

- Israel's President Shimon Peres accepted an award

- Bono talked capitalism (the only Davos Man whose tough love other delegates crave)

- UN Secretary-General Ban Ki-moon and former US Vice President Al Gore discussed climate change

- German Finance Minister Wolfgang Schaeuble had harsh criticism for EU Economic and Monetary Affairs

- International Monetary Fund Managing Director Christine Lagarde said that euro zone inflation is "way below target," making deflation a potential risk

- Brazil's President Dilma Rousseff brushed off Soccer World Cup worries

- Japanese Prime Minister Shinzo Abe took the chance to remind everyone that Asia has become the growth engine of the world

- American actress Goldie Hawn explained if she would return to acting or not

- Mexico's president expressed hopes to expand federal presence to combat drug cartel violence

- Audi's CEO announced that the company would invest €22 billion in the coming years in technology and new innovations (especially driverless cars)

- London mayor Boris Johnson flew in to Davos in search of investors. By the way, it is the same Boris Johnson who once dubbed the Forum as "a constellation of egos in an orgy of adulation."

So, what exactly were the precise topic and specific action points? Hm...

Don't get me wrong. I think it's excellent and permanently needed looking at the causes of global instability, climate change, growing rates of youth unemployment, poverty, nationalism, privacy concerns and other pressing problems.

In addition, I also like the ambivalence of such gatherings, i.e. influential people discussing and trying to resolve the world's issues (among themselves). And by doing so becoming more visible as leaders. Certainly the Forum offers its participants a great opportunity to meet and learn from a huge variety of personalities, encounters, and workshops within a trustful environment.

Saying that, the sheer size and ambitious scope of the event makes you wonder how thoroughly topics can be worked upon. Instead we're hearing a lot of populist speeches, bold promises, and not seeing approachability, transparency, and actions. Personally, I can't recall any major and successfully implemented initiative coming from the Forum which would have had a positive impact on the world's prosperity.

And whilst those leaders at the Forum might exchange rationally and emotionally and – sometimes – during fabulous parties, the world's elite have twisted laws in their own favor, undermined democracy and created inequality across the globe.

42. HOW PUMA CAN COMPETE WITH ADIDAS AND NIKE

Puma, a distant third in the sporting-goods industry behind giants Nike and Adidas, announced in November 2013 that it would like to return to its sporting roots, led by its then new CEO Bjoern Gulde. The struggling brand's profits crashed 70 percent in 2012 and its sales declined by 2.5 percent in the first 9 months of 2013. The turnaround plan abandons the company's efforts over the past two decades under former CEO Jochen Zeitz to focus on fashion-led consumers.

But taking on the dominance of Nike and Adidas, which have annual sales of €18.5 billion ($25 billion) and €14.8 billion ($20 billion) respectively, against Puma's €3.5 billion (€4.7 billion), will be quite a challenge. Is it possible at all?

A colorful Past – The two Brothers who started Puma and Adidas became bitter Enemies

The two brothers Adolf (nickname *Adi*) and Rudolf (nickname *Rudi*) Dassler originally were partners in the *Dassler Brothers Sports Shoe Company*, in the small German town of Herzogenaurach. They convinced legendary track star Jesse Owens to wear their shoes as he competed and won four gold medals in the 1936 Olympics.

There are various rumours about why it eventually came to a split between the two brothers in 1947, with Rudi forming a new firm called Ruda (from Rudolf Dassler, which he later rebranded Puma) and Adi Dassler founding *Adidas* in 1949. Elderly residents believe the brothers split because Adolf slept with Rudi›s wife and their wives loathed each other. Of course, there are more of those entertaining rumors and stories going around in Herzogenaurach.

Fact is, while Rudi had the sales staff and was better at moving product, Adi had the technical know-how and better relationships with athletes who provided excellent brand exposure. As a result, the scales tipped in favor of Adidas with Puma permanently playing catch-up. As they were concentrating so vehemently on each other, both companies woke up far too late to the arrival and surge of Nike.

Today's Competitive Environment

Nike: The world's largest sporting-goods maker reported 2013 revenue of €18.7 billion ($25.3 billion, up 8 percent). The company said it would have €22.2 billion (€30 billion) in annual revenue by the end of its fiscal year 2015. Nike's sales forecast equates to a compound annual sales growth rate of more than 9 percent over the next few years. Its annual sales growth rate was 10 percent in the past three years. Nike, a true growth company, is the clear leader in North America, very well positioned in apparel, basketball, running gear, and women›s products. It expects strong growth coming from its Converse subsidiary and new, innovative products such as the Fuelband (an activity tracker that is worn on the wrist).

Adidas: The world's second-largest maker of sporting goods realized a revenue growth of €14.6 billion in 2013 and is aiming to reach a target of €17 billion euros ($23 billion) in annual revenue in 2015. As such, growth will be slightly behind Nike, although significant revenue increase is expected next year, boosted by sales of national team shirts and official balls for the soccer World Cup in Brazil. Adidas cut its 2013 profit forecast last month because of Russian distribution difficulties, a weak golf market and the strength of the euro.

The Little Dangerous Ones: Last, but not least, there is increasing competition from newer brands like Lululemon, Under Armour, and smaller specialist players like Asics, Mizuno, Brooks, and others.

How a beleaguered Brand should behave

Focus on the brand's DNA and heritage: In Puma›s case this is performance and its sporting roots in soccer and athletics – fashion must come after sports. Finally the company has realized and developed a new mission statement: "Forever Faster".

The statement and a new tag line will be launched to consumers in 2014. (Remember its old one: "Puma has the long-term mission of becoming the most desirable and sustainable sports lifestyle company.")

Build on the brand's biggest and most promising category and strive for category leadership: For Puma this is footwear. Precisely the running sub-category. With Usain Bolt as brand ambassador this should be a clear objective and a non-negotiable one.

Heavily invest in innovation and in parallel cut Opex: Technological-driven innovations in its core categories (running and athletics) must drive growth and margins. Sports should serve the fashion-side of the business, not vice versa.

Focus on a few selected marketing campaigns and make them as big and as exciting as possible: Fiercely promote existing brand ambassadors and at the same time get new top ambassadors (the new Arsenal London deal will not be sufficient) to build brand recognition.

Maintain transparent and trustworthy relationships with main stakeholders: Re-build trust with key retail partners, with employees and with French parent company Kering (which owns 84 percent of Puma).

Strengthen the distribution network: Gain back lost share of space and share of mind at key retailers. Establish a holistic multi-channel distribution strategy with a key emphasis on e-commerce (both on its own site and on key e-retailers' platforms).

Manage expectations: Bringing Puma back on track will require a comprehensive turnaround and change management program, something which can take anything between 12 to 24 months until the first significant benefits might appear. Senior management would be well advised to pro-actively explain that to all stakeholders.

Do your financial homework and clean up the balance sheet: Quickly execute one-off charges and write-offs which are typical in crisis situations. Future financial results will look more encouraging and will help to stress that the company is on the right path. It is expected that Puma will book approximately €130 million one-off charges in the fourth quarter of 2013, mainly for the closure of a development center in Vietnam and for relocating staff from London to Germany.

Appreciate the past and set the team's focus on conquering the future: The leadership team needs to re-inject self-confidence into staff. They need to show appreciation and at the same time constantly raise the bar. A mindset of innovation and Execution in Excellence should be established and lived by everyone. Existing talents and high performers need to be rapidly developed and empowered whilst new external talent should be recruited to bring in some fresh ideas and drive.

The leader is key: A beleaguered brand needs strong leadership - someone who is very close to the business, who is in the relevant details himself and is able to develop together with key stakeholders a lasting vision and compelling strategy. He needs to be a convincing communicator and motivator, being able to inspire the team in an honest way and in parallel to deliver quick wins. He should display a positive Can-Do-Attitude, a very high level of resilience and energy and manage his teams based on Tough Empathy (giving the teams what they need and not necessarily what they want).

A Company's ability to innovate

At the heart of any successful business lies its ability to compete. The ability to compete is dependent on its ability to differentiate from competitors. And its ability to differentiate, in turn, is stemming from its ability to innovate and communicate with consumers. Question: Have you perceived Puma as an innovative company for the past 2-5 years?

Instead, Puma tried to be everything by pursuing a so-called multi-category strategy when it aimed at being a sports and fashion company at the same time. Sadly it ended up being nothing. Why? Because it did not take as much pride in what it didn't do as what it did. In other words: It missed a clear positioning and it lacked focus; two marketing and branding mistakes you shouldn't commit. Puma lost its shine when it morphed into a copycat of Nike and Adidas.

Can the cat successfully return and attack again? Or is it already too late for a comeback?

43. DOES DISNEY BID FAREWELL TO THE MOVIE STAR?

Has Disney lost its sparkle for film enthusiasts after movie theater audience numbers have been stagnating or even dropping in many major countries over the last few years? Has the end of the traditional movie theater arrived? Has it already started without us realizing it? Will Disney and its film *The Little Mermaid* put an end to how we've used watching movies in theaters whilst munching popcorn and sipping at our Coke? The way how we identified ourselves with the stars on screen? How will it impact our future media consumption, us, and our society?

Well, indeed we might be close to nothing less than a(nother) media and electronics revolution. This time it goes almost unnoticed. Or do you know that Disney is explicitly asking cinema visitors for today's re-release of The Little Mermaid to forget about the old rule and warning to turn your mobile devices off before the movie starts? Yes, for a special *Second Screen Live* showing of Disney›s *The Little Mermaid*, it's going to be very different as moviegoers are encouraged to use their iPads for an augmented experience while the film is showing on screen in select theaters. The stars are not any longer in the movie. The stars – and main actors – are watching and interacting with the movie! That's what I call a revolution!

Officially, of course, it's nothing to be concerned about that Disney has created an app which allows viewers to interact with the movie in select theaters. Visitors will be able to play games, compete with fellow audience members, watch behind-the-scenes video, and sing along with the movie (*Mama Mia* and *The Rocky Horror Picture Show* are sending their best wishes!). The app is free, but Android tablets are not supported. Disney and Apple have had a long-running and close relationship, with Steve Jobs having taken a seat on Disney›s board of directors and become the company›s largest individual shareholder when Disney acquired Pixar in 2006. Disney president and CEO Bob Iger joined Apple›s board late 2011 after Jobs› death. You're getting my drift?

The Little Mermaid edition is the first that works in theaters, which could prove very interesting. Especially for family movies it might be more of an enhancement than a distraction and maybe also for specific niches (e.g.

midnight screenings). Most likely, it's also interesting in general for popular re-releases when the plot is already known. It is Disney's first public use of the technology after a trial run last fall alongside Tim Burton's *The Nightmare Before Christmas.* According to the mouse-house, the audience reacted quite positively back then.

Consequently, if it works – then Disney will be doing this with all their re-releases – and then on their main features, leading to other companies starting to think about it.

However, while it could be seen to be as fun as the "Rocky Horror Picture Show" experience, many people just go to the movies to watch the movie, not wishing to be surrounded by tablet and smartphone screens glowing brightly and distracting them from the movie. For them, myself included, a movie theater is a place of tranquillity, personal stimulation, and indulgence. For sure it seems to be a splendid idea for home video. Saying that, you might wonder about the impact on society in general and on kids in particular if it were to become the norm in movie theaters.

Should we as a society further demystify going to see a movie by introducing our children to the notion that it's fine playing with their tablets and smartphones during movies? Is it okay to not pay attention, not concentrate, and not use one's own imagination any longer? Do we really want to define "watching a movie" as "playing with your tablet in the theater?"

True, weak ticket sales have also been caused by the poor economy, rising admission prices, online streaming services like Netflix, and the ease of illegally downloading movies. Often, however, they were also triggered by a lack of blockbuster movies and a backlash over poor remakes and boring sequels. Over the years the studios responded with new technologies such as widescreen color images, stereo sound systems, and in the most recent past again with 3D films (which have quickly disappeared) to lure visitors to the movie theaters.

That's not to say that Hollywood & Co. should not try to smartly incorporate some interactive media tools into certain movies. I'm just wondering if expensive tablets (which are not available to everyone) are the best way to get moviegoers more involved and to stimulate engagement, fun, and imagination. And how to do it without bothering regular visitors.

44. A SERIOUS THREAT TO APPLE

Finally, rumors were confirmed when at the end of August 2013 Samsung revealed that the launch of its much anticipated Galaxy Gear smartwatch would take place at their own event at the IFA consumer electronics fair in Berlin on September 4, 2013

Although it's known that both Apple and Samsung had been working in the smartphone category for quite some time now, it's kind of a surprise that in the end Samsung won the race. That might have major consequences for the communications and electronics market. Most of all, it will probably change the dynamics between Samsung and Apple.

It was the first time that Samsung takes the lead in entering a promising new product category. And it came at an awkward point in time for the California-based electronics giant. Apple's last quarter sales and profits were again rather weak; it has not launched any break-through innovation for many months, it is distracted by activist investors Carl Icahn and David Einhorn (most likely there are many more of them behind the scenes), it's involved in multiple legal battles over patent infringements, and it is not clear if Apple has a convincing strategy to cater to the lower end of the market without diluting its premium image (which experts argue is needed to fully succeed in emerging markets and to fight off cheaper Android devices in many markets in the world).

Likely Features of the Galaxy Gear smartwatch

In theory, so-called smartwatches have been around since the 70s (remember Hewlett-Packard's HP-O1 LED calculator watch released in 1977?). When Samsung, however, will launch its Galaxy Gear smartwatch it is expected to try to redefine the market.

It will feature a powerful dual-core processor, a built-in camera, small speakers on the clasp of the watch, and is designed to pair up to devices with Bluetooth 4.0. A built-in accelerometer may allow users to turn on the screen by moving their wrists toward their eyes. The OLED touchscreen seems to be square-shaped and will measure roughly 2.5 inches diagonally (and 3 inches including the case). This would make Samsung's smartwatch larger than the ones of other niche players like Pebble which already operate in this market.

Extremely interesting is the rumor that Samsung would use its own app store to take advantage of the watch hardware. That most likely means if you want a Samsung Galaxy Gear smartwatch, you'll need a Samsung Galaxy phone or tablet. If Samsung does require the use of its own app store for the Galaxy Gear, it'll be the company's biggest attempt yet to take control of Android. If the South Koreans really should have a go at creating a walled-garden approach of its own (like Apple did), many Android fans might not like such an approach.

How Apple is Expected to Respond

Besides significantly ramping up its marketing efforts by using its huge financial power, Apple must quickly come out with some promising new products on its own. Those are very much needed as in the last one to two quarters Apple did not release any new breakthrough devices. On top of this, the new 2013 MacBook Air received only lukewarm reviews. The company will need to speed up launching the following five initiatives before the end of this year to drum up excitement, to accelerate growth, and not to fall behind Samsung. What we can expect:

iPhone 5S and 5C - Market observers expect that we will see the new iPhone 5S probably around September/October. That will position it against rival Samsung, who will introduce the third generation of the Samsung Note, the Samsung Note 3 at IFA in September. It seems now almost certain that the iPhone 5S will be accompanied by the cheaper and more fancy-free iPhone 5C.

iPad5 and new Mini iPad - Let's also not forget that Apple is the leader in the tablet market. It is expected that at the beginning of October, i.e. shortly after the iPhone 5S and 5C launches, the Californians will release two new iPads:

iPad 5 (slimmer, lighter, more powerful) and a new iPad mini, the first with a high-resolution screen, i.e. using its Retina display on which for sure many eyes will be fixed on.

New iOS 7 Software - Around the same time Apple will come out with the new iOS 7 software. The beta versions of iOS 7 show a significant break from the past. Although a bold move, it is expected that people will like the changes overall, which makes the software more intuitive and fun. The new software will help drive new phone buyers and increase the loyalty of existing users.

iWatch as Major Launch - More than anything else, Apple will try to get its smartwatch on the market as soon as possible. Clearly a matter of honor, now more than ever. Apple is even doomed to deliver a new wrist watch that many are calling "iWatch." It has been hiring people with adequate expertise for many months now. Most recently it recruited an ex-Nike staffer, Jay Blahnik, who worked on Nike's Fuelband which is already used by 18 million people worldwide. As such, Apple's smartwatch might be more of a band versus Samsung's Gear watch. It'll sync to other Apple devices, will offer lots of health-related apps and features, plus other helpful communication tools such as email, clock, etc. It is expected to be launched just in time for the holidays and, for sure, Apple will play it big. Think iPhone, iPod, and iPad!

Implications for the Consumer Electronics Market

Being first-to-market means that the stakes are high for Samsung. The South Koreans will have to prove that not only they can develop a new category, but also be capable of launching a bulletproof device which does not suffer from connection drops, user interface challenges and other issues found in prior smartwatch and smartphone efforts. Saying that, many believe that the Galaxy Gear might be a winning device, coupled with Samsung's strategic vehicle of trying to take more control of Android. The device will most likely require an app provided through the Samsung dedicated app marketplace in order to work. As such, it will be an accessory exclusive to Samsung's own smartphones and tablets.

According to Samsung, the Galaxy Gear is primarily targeted at "young trendsetters." Having obviously designed a device which aims both at "early adopters" and at "fashion-oriented" consumers (which most of us are in a certain way), Samsung will want to take its new "electronic accessory" mainstream as quickly as possible. If it were successful with such a move (and chances are not bad), Samsung might be perceived as a company and brand which is about to take Apple's nimbus away of being the most innovative and trendiest electronics company in the world. That indeed seems to be the main threat. That's what entering the smartwatch market is really all about for both of them.

And there is another sure thing: Niche players like Pebble, The Hot Watch, Sony's Live View wearable or Motorola's MotoACTV will need to fight hard to survive once the two electronic giants enter the smartwatch arena.

45. WHAT THE FITCH IS GOING ON AT ABERCROMBIE?

Abercrombie & Fitch's 2013 first quarter results sharply missed already low expectations: Sales slipped 8.9% to $838.8 million and shares fell by almost 10% last week, trading at the bottom of the S&P 500. In its home market – the US, which accounts for more than 60% of total revenue – sales dropped by 17%. Luckily, international sales increased by 10%, mostly coming from new store openings, to spare the company even more dramatic figures.

Due to a double-digit slump in same-store sales, the company issued a pretty cautious view for the remainder of the year. The company cited tighter inventory controls, the softness in the women's business as well as weakness in Europe as the official reasons for its significant shortfall and caution. Are those, however, the true source of worries at Abercrombie?

Already in recent quarters the company had been showing weaknesses. It seems that its fashion is failing more and more to resonate with teens and young adults. Or should we better say with "cool" teens and with "cool" young adults? Ever since its CEO Mike Jeffries stated in a 2006 interview that he doesn't want "not so cool" kids wearing his company's clothes, Abercrombie has been in the public spotlight.

Besides a recently weaker assortment policy, the company's pseudo selective marketing strategy now seems to backfire. For the last few weeks the company has been (again) under severe attack as it is said to have offended customers with its "thin and beautiful" shopping policy. Abercrombie "succeeded" in a really "cool" manner to withstand two weeks of high-profile backlash against its divisive sizing policies: it was accused of purposefully excluding plus-sized customers earlier this month ("plus" meaning for Abercrombie anything above women's size "large" and trousers size 10).

According to the market research company BrandIndex, as a result, Abercrombie & Fitch skidded to its lowest perception with young people since October of last year. At the same time, both H&M and American Eagle – Abercrombie's strongest competitor – have seen a small rise in their perception scores.

A&F, which prides itself on employing "good-looking people", obviously only wants "cool" people wearing its clothing. This is supported by a Salon interview from 2006, where its CEO explained:

"...we hire good-looking people in our stores. Because good-looking people attract other good-looking people, and we want to market to cool, good-looking people. We don't market to anyone other than that... A lot of people don't belong [in our clothes], and they can't belong. Are we exclusionary? Absolutely."

One might argue that Mr. Jeffries and his management team should better recall what Confucius already knew:

"Everyone and everything has beauty, but not everyone sees it."

Obviously Jeffries is under the false illusion that (today's) teenagers are only cool if they are thin and beautiful. It's irritating that a high-profile business executive – someone who is supposed to act as a role model – tries to define beauty by wanting to squeeze young people into the smallest possible clothing sizes.

Even worse, with such an attitude, Jeffries is obviously sabotaging diversity and social integration in a weird attempt to market Abercrombie, Hollister & Co. as what he thinks a selective brand is expected to be.

Jeffries seems to have forgotten that successful marketing is built foremost on the principle of "respect" for customers and that selective brand positioning does not mean offending people. As a reminder, what "respect" stands for as defined by the Oxford dictionary: "A feeling of deep admiration for someone or something elicited by their abilities, qualities, or achievements."

Of course, a brand that tries to appeal to everyone will likely appeal to nobody. With such provocative and exclusionary comments, Jeffries wants to sharpen the brand identity of A&F, trying to portray its customers as a chosen group of good-looking and popular people. Being attractive only to a certain target group of consumers is a legitimate business and marketing endeavor. It should be achieved, however, by applying the right product mix, the right pricing, and the right distribution policy. And not by executing an offensive, shocking, and discriminating communications policy. It is a very thin line Jeffries and Abercrombie are balancing on. Already, many years ago the Italian fashion company Benetton had to learn and to "respect" that consumers are not willing to accept extremely polarizing and ethically questionable forms of communications.

It's not encouraging news for A&F when even celebrities like Ellen DeGeneres and Kirsty Alley have started to challenge the company's "sizeism" issue. Ms. DeGeneres, for example, in making a point to address the children watching her show, said that in her eyes beauty is not physical: "What you look like on the outside is not what makes you cool."

A Change.org petition was signed by 70,000 offended customers. Furthermore the blogger Jes M. Baker addressed the issue in an open letter to Abercrombie's CEO and created a series of mock Abercrombie & Fitch ads, titled Attractive and Fat.

Despite potentially alienating customers, last Friday Mr. Jeffries simply explained on the company's Facebook page that Abercrombie & Fitch "is an aspirational brand that like most specialty apparel brands, targets its marketing at a particular segment of customers."

As a reaction, my two young daughters – who based on their clothing sizes fit very well into Abercrombie's target segment of customers – decided that they would stop wearing and buying the company's products from now on. That's what they referred to as being "cool". And most likely with H&M, Zara, and many other trendy brands available to them, they might not miss it one bit.

46. IS MICROSOFT COOL AGAIN?

A recent Reuters/Ipsos poll – conducted between February 5 and 19, 2013 – found that almost half of 853 respondents between the age of 18 and 29 thought Microsoft is cooler now than it was a year ago.

Twitter scored 47 percent, just below Microsoft's 50 percent. Facebook received just 42 percent of the same response rate like last year. Google's Android achieved 70 percent - the highest score. Although lately not so popular with financial investors, Apple came in second with 60 percent of young adults questioned.

It's argued that part of Microsoft's lift appears to stem from a well-coordinated marketing blitz around its all-new Surface tablets. They have revamped the familiar Windows interface with a tile-based, mobile app-friendly look and feel. Also, its Xbox gaming console and "Kinect" accessory, which can respond to gestures and voice commands, seems also to have positively influenced its coolness image among younger consumers in the past year.

Possibly, consumers also appreciate Window's more open and more consumer-oriented approach versus Apple's closed and interwoven ecosystem of products and applications. But can Microsoft really take advantage of Apple's latest weakness, especially among young customers? It's true that young smartphone shoppers' appetite for Apple iPhones have been steadily decreasing over the past few months. Apple dropped several spots or remained flat on various teen brand opinion polls.

Although Microsoft's past is littered with not so successful attempts to conquer the consumer gadget marketplace, from clunky early tablets to the Zune music player, it seems that Microsoft's efforts are finally somehow starting to pay off. Of course, it still has to be proven that it's increase of the coolness factor will translate into gains of sales and market shares. Gartner estimates that Microsoft sold fewer than 900,000 Surface tablets in the fourth quarter, a fraction of the 23 million iPads sold by Apple. Windows phones now account for 3 percent of the global smartphone market, far behind Google's Android with 70 percent and Apple with 21 percent.

Regardless that both definition and impact of "coolness" remains disputable, consumer perceptions are pivotal in determining the longevity of products, particularly in the fast-moving consumer electronics industry.

47. WHERE I WORK - IN A REAL FANTASY

When sitting in my office there are some real things I'm seeing — and some not so real.

Is this reality?

It's always been very important for me to enjoy what I'm doing. Of course, often this is not automatically the case. It might take hard work, creativity, courage and drive to put things the way you want to have them. Not in an egotistic manner, but in such a fashion that all other key stakeholders also feel involved and respected.

And our team members are true artists. Excellent and highly committed to satisfying our customers' needs and wants in the most beautiful way. They are always on stage and ready to perform at a world-class level.

Let's listen to them! Just sit back, relax and enjoy the show.

Were you suddenly "watching" your team, "seeing" them performing and listening to their very unique style of "music"? To music that makes your heart go faster and makes you feeling so alive and proud?

Back to reality, at least for a short moment. My office is in lovely Munich in the wild South of Germany, an incredibly lovely part of Germany where people speak with a very strong accent. Looking out to the other side of our offices, I'm seeing a splendid and illuminated Ferris Wheel every evening.

Wishing you a successful, imaginative and great week at YOUR place of work... wherever it might be!

48. THE WORLD DID NOT END ON DECEMBER 21, 2012

Towards the end of any year - and also back then when the world did not end on December 21, 2012 - it's a good time to reflect on "Green Sustainability" and "caring about our environment."

For many companies and for many of us, these are popular buzz words and concepts. If you want to do "the right thing," you better still use the word "sustainability" at least 5-10 times in a good presentation or impactful speech.

Of course, we know by now that the concept of sustainability has lost some of its past sexiness as it was put by many corporations onto their daily agendas. Some of its aspects – like conservation of resources – are widely accepted these days.

The question remains, however, of how to keep it a focus for all companies and for all individuals to improve every-day-life. And, equally important, it should be reviewed if sustainability is treated just in a superficial way – since it's en vogue – or if CEOs are really serious about it and willing to invest big money to push through major sustainability initiatives.

Let's have a closer look at three main macro trends which drive sustainability into the business cultures. This will be followed by six company examples from Apple to Nike. And finally, we will discuss five resulting key questions which we should address to better understand the possible future state of the sustainability concept.

By doing so, I will refer to an excellent article written by Andrew Winston who is the author of Green Recovery and an advisor to some of the world's biggest companies on environmental strategy.

I. Macro Trends

1. Historic drought and Hurricane Sandy sweep away (some) climate denial

For many people this year, climate change moved from theoretical to painfully real. Mega weather took many lives and cost over $120 billion in the U.S. alone ($50 billion for the drought, $71 billion for Sandy). After Sandy raged across the eastern coast, Businessweek blared on its cover, "It's Global Warming, Stupid." New York Mayor Bloomberg, a Republican, endorsed President Obama in the election, titling his open letter, "A Vote for a President to Lead on Climate Change."

As bad as Sandy was, the relentless drought across the middle of the country may prove more convincing in the long run. Corn yields per acre fell 19%, food prices rose, and water disappeared — the Mississippi River may soon struggle to support commerce. Individual companies are feeling the bite: analysts at Morningstar estimate that input costs at Tyson Foods will rise by $700 million — more than its 2012 net income.

Over one-third of the world's largest companies surveyed by the Carbon Disclosure Project are already seeing the impacts of climate change on their business. So with life-and-death consequences and vast costs, we must have moved quickly to tackle climate change, right? Sort of...

The year ended with the failure, yet again, of the international community to come to some agreement on climate change. But country-level and regional policy moved forward: Australia passed a carbon tax, South Korea approved carbon trading, and California just began its own trading experiment.

Many countries also committed serious funds to build a clean economy: Saudi Arabia pledged $109 billion for solar, Japan declared that a $628 billion green energy industry would be central to its 2020 strategy, and China targeted $372 billion to cut energy use and pollution.

In the U.S., a backdoor approach to climate policy took over. The Obama administration issued new standards to double the fuel economy of cars and trucks, and the National Resources Defense Council (an NGO) proposed using the Clean Air Act to reduce emissions from power plants by 25%.

2. The math and physics of planetary constraints get clearer

Arithmetic had a big year: Nate Silver's nearly perfect predictions of the election gave him the oxymoronic status of rock-star statistician. The math and physics of sustainability got some serious attention as well.

Writer and activist Bill McKibben wrote a widely-read piece in Rolling Stone about climate math — how much more carbon emissions the planet can take — and followed it up with a national awareness-building tour. Based on similar numbers, both McKinsey and PwC UK calculated how fast we must reduce the carbon intensity of the global economy (PwC's number is 5% per year until 2050).

And on the resource constraint front, Jeremy Grantham, co-founder of the asset management firm GMO ($100 billion invested), continued his relentless numbers-based assault on the fallacy of infinite resources. In his November newsletter, he demonstrated exactly how much of a drag on the U.S. economy commodity prices have become.

Nobody can really deny that, in principle, exponential growth must stop someday. Grantham, McKibben, and many others are making the case that someday has arrived.

3. The clean economy continues to explode

The rapid growth of natural gas production (the biggest energy story of the year) and the high-profile failure of one solar manufacturer (Solyndra) have confused people about the prospects for clean tech. In reality, the clean economy is winning. The share of U.S. electricity coming from non-hydro renewables doubled to 6% in the last 4 years. On May 26, Germany set a world record when it produced 50% of its electricity needs from solar power alone. In a mini political tipping point, six Republican senators publicly supported an extension to the wind production tax credit in the U.S. (which will expire in days), and got an earful from a Wall Street Journal editorial.

It wasn't just energy. One auto analyst declared 2012 the "Year of the Green Car," with more high-MPG models, 500,000 hybrid sales in the U.S., and plug-in sales up 228%. To cap the year, the pure electric Tesla Model S was selected as the Motor Trend Car of the Year.

II. Company Stories

This year, there were countless eco-efficiency stories about companies saving millions of dollars and developing new tools to make buildings, fleets (Staples and UPS, for example), and manufacturing much leaner. Aside from that overall theme, the following stories grabbed me because of their connection to larger trends.

1. The green supply chain gets some teeth: Walmart changes incentives for buyers

This year, Walmart finally added a key element to its impressive green supply chain efforts. The retail giant's powerful buyers, or merchants, now have a sustainability goal in their performance targets and reviews. For example, the laptop PC buyer set a goal that, by Christmas, all of the laptops Walmart sells would come pre-installed with advanced energy-saving settings.

It was by no means a hiccup-free year on sustainability issues for Walmart, with deep concerns about corruption in its Mexican operations. But the subtle change in buyer incentives is a big deal.

2. Transparency and tragedy raise awareness about worker conditions

Early in 2012, Apple took some serious heat for the working conditions at Foxconn, the giant company that assembles a huge percentage of our electronics. Later in the year, tragedy struck Dhaka, Bangladesh when a fire at the Tazreen Fashion factory killed and injured hundreds of people. The company that owns the factory serves Walmart, Carrefour, IKEA, and many others (but in fact, some companies didn't even know that Tazreen was a supplier). It's unclear if any of these human and PR disasters will affect the companies' downstream, but transparency and knowledge about the lives of the people who make our products will continue to rise.

3. Data gets bigger and faster: PepsiCo and Columbia speed up lifecycle assessments

The rise of Big Data was an important theme in business in general this year, but especially in sustainability. And nowhere is good data needed more than in the onerous and expensive task of calculating a product's lifecycle footprint. PepsiCo has had great success with the method, finding ways to reduce cost and risk for key brands, but execs wanted to apply the tool across thousands of products. To make the exercise feasible and affordable, they turned to Columbia University, which developed a new algorithm for fast carbon footprinting. This isn't just a wonky exercise: As PepsiCo exec Al Halvorsen told me, "The real reason you do an LCA is to improve the business, to put more efficient processes in place, and innovate in the supply chain."

4. Sustainability innovation opens up: Unilever, Heineken, and EMC ask the world for help

This new world of social media, where everyone has a voice, can be tough on companies. Consumers can gather around a green issue and pressure companies to change their behavior. Some notable change.org campaigns this year challenged Universal Pictures (about its green messaging around The Lorax), Crayola (recycling markers), and Dunkin' Donuts (Styrofoam cups). But companies can also use "open" innovation tools to generate new ideas and invite the world to solve problems together.

Unilever, which has my vote for leader in corporate sustainability right now, held an online discussion or "jam." Then the company posted a list of "Challenges and wants" and asked for ideas on solving big issues such as how to bring safe drinking water to the world's poorest regions. Unilever has received over 1,000 ideas and is "pursuing 6 to 7 percent of these with internal teams." Other notable open innovation models this year included Heineken's $10,000 sustainable packaging contest (which yielded some very fun ideas like a roving tap truck) and EMC's eco-challenge with InnoCentive on e-waste.

5. The economy gets a bit more circular: M&S, H&M, and Puma experiment with closing loops

On the heels of Patagonia's "Don't Buy This Jacket" campaign (one of my top 10 stories from last year), British retailer M&S began a program called "Schwop" that asked customers to bring back old clothes every time they bought new ones.

This month, H&M also rolled out a global clothing collection and recycling effort.

Puma, after making last year's list with its Environmental P&L, kept the momentum going and announced a new "InCycle" collection with biodegradable sneakers and shirts, and recyclable jackets and backpacks. Remanufacturing has been around a long time, but closing loops is getting more popular every year.

6. Dematerialization gets sexier: Nike's knitted shoe shows off sustainable style

Keeping the apparel theme, um, running, check out Nike's new shoe with FlyKnit technology. The upper part of the shoe is constructed from a single strand, which greatly reduces waste and lightens the shoe dramatically. It's a great thing when a more sustainable design also coincides perfectly with customer needs. Enough said.

III. Five Questions For The Future

Some other promising stories are in the "too early to tell" stage, but bring up some key questions:

1. **Can we standardize sustainability**, which some smart folks began to do around rankings (GISR) and accounting (Sustainability Accounting Standards Board)?

2. **Will we find a way to value externalities like ecosystem services and internalized, intangible benefits?** (A focus of some of my work as an advisor to PwC US). For example, Microsoft launched an internal carbon tax and some major companies (Coca-Cola, Nike, Kimberly-Clark, etc.) pledged to value natural capital at Rio+20.

3. **Will government get in the way or help**, like when the U.S. Senate allowed the military to keep investing in biofuels?

4. **Hertz and B&Q (Kingfisher) have delved into collaborative consumption** (see WWF's Green Game-Changers report), but will the sharing economy make a dent on sustainability issues?

5. **Finally, how much will we challenge the nature of capitalism**, and what will that mean for how companies operate? (This is the focus of my next project.)

What do you think about the above-listed driving forces, company examples, and the questions that were raised?

49. MORE IPADS AND CONDOMS SOLD IN TOUGH TIMES

Treat yourself is the name of the game during tough economic times. At least from a consumer's perspective.

Research shows that for some industries, like sweets or cosmetics (at my former employer we used to call it the "lipstick effect"), sales are going up as it is getting more challenging for consumers in an economic context.

It's then all about how "to treat yourself" properly. Although life might have gotten more demanding, still consumers want to enjoy the good things and indulge themselves.

The slogan is something like "Me (and my family) are worth it!"

Chapter 4

GROW!

Tomorrow's top leaders believe that you will what you want and that there are no limits to personal growth. They avoid the 12 irrational ideas that limit personal success. They are what I call "Realistic Optimists," i.e. being both optimistic and realistic. As such, they combine the two into one behavioral style that creates a unique sense of open-mindedness, attention, and focus. This high level of awareness and focus allows them to see things many of us do not notice while we're too busy with problems and ourselves.

They are masters at succeeding professionally and personally by following certain principles to better navigate their lives and to concentrate more on establishing sustainable and precious relationships to guarantee success without personal regrets. They are clear about what they want to achieve in life and about the price they have to pay for it. They have reframed the notion of work-life-balance as they've realized that work and life are irrevocably interlinked. They have found smart ways to integrate the two of them efficiently and effectively. They don't consider workaholism as a virtue; they believe in managing up and pushing back if necessary.

Happiness is a growth priority for them. They define happiness not as daydreaming or as seeing the world through rose-tinted glasses. In fact, they consider happiness and the well-being of people as a fundamental human right, well aligned with, and not hiding behind, economic growth and social responsibility. They know what numerous studies have shown – happy people are healthier, more confident, more productive, more satisfied, and more resilient.

Successful future leaders are willing to give, share and support and not just take or receive. They listen more than they talk and enjoy being a sounding board. They admit mistakes and present a plan of how to get back on track. They comprehend that it's okay not to know everything and not to try and be too professional. Instead, they prefer to stay authentic, human, and vulnerable. As a result they are more approachable and likeable.

50. HOW TO SUCCEED PROFESSIONALLY AND PERSONALLY

When I was working in my first leadership role as a director of key account management at L'Oréal - and having been highly committed to manage a challenging business and a talented team - our baby daughter was diagnosed with craniosynostosis. To avoid possible brain damage an immediate head surgery was required. As every parent would, my wife and I discussed with doctors and medical experts to find the right hospital and treatment.

When I sat there one evening whilst our little one was crying in her rocking cradle, I was contemplating the upcoming surgery and her future. I was sorrow-stricken and regretted the long hours I used to spend in the office, the countless business trips I had made, and not having been at home as often as I should have been. Of course, all of that was with the very best intentions - to earn sufficient money for a good living, to finance our own home, to secure a pleasant lifestyle, to be successful, independent, and respected.

My beautiful wife has always been very understanding and supportive. And whilst this eliminated some of my guilty conscience, back then I started to realize and appreciate the true value of affectionate and caring relationships founded on love and mutual respect. And most importantly, it dawned on me that to safeguard our family I would have to permanently strive for spending as much time as possible with my loved ones, not allowing my work and ambitions to take over our personal lives and destroy our relationships and bonding; the actual source of our energy and happiness.

Now, almost 15 years later, besides my regular job at Amazon I'm working in my spare time as an executive coach to assist my clients - mostly ambitious, hard-driving executives – to cope with similar challenges and conflicts. They've all received multiple and often similar advice which they rationally understand: To spend more time with family and friends, to do more sports, to learn how to avoid stress, how to plan your tasks, how to delegate, etc. All very useful concepts which can be found in various excellent books.

Still, many of them struggle in finding the good balance and in investing enough time for non-work-related activities, mostly because they're not infusing enough time and efforts in building lasting relationships from which they would receive backing, encouragement and relief. There is neither a magic formula nor a silver bullet to resolve this dilemma; especially for people in demanding positions. However, what I can offer is a different perspective, i.e. providing proven principles to better navigate one's life and to concentrate more on establishing sustainable and precious relationships to guarantee success without personal regrets.

Be clear about what you want to achieve in life. What do you want to be known and famous for once you have passed away? Do you want to bequeath a big bank account to your offspring or do you want to be remembered as an affectionate and loving parent, partner, friend, or mentor?

Be realistic about work. It's okay to work hard if you like it and if it gives you satisfaction. At the same time you need to acknowledge that you cannot do everything. Otherwise, the results are likely to be personally adverse and also not in the best interest of the company.

Don't seek perfection. Mankind is not perfect. You are not perfect. Your family, friends, and colleagues have their shortfalls and make mistakes. And that's good! Recognize that from time to time you and others miss targets. Don't hold yourself nor others to ridiculously high standards. Instead, aim at continuous improvement initiatives.

Forget about the work-life-balance. You better start reframing that notion. Work and life are irrevocably interlinked. Find smart ways to integrate the two of them efficiently and effectively. Don't waste any energy on trying to rigorously separate them.

Live in the moment and be in the moment. When you are with your loved ones and friends give them all your attention and be present with all your senses. Only be there for them. Switch off any work-related devices and thoughts. Practice mindfulness.

Be willing to give, share and support. And not just take or receive. Listen more than you talk. Try to listen with more than two ears. Enjoy being a sounding board. Be proactive and establish yourself as a useful resource.

Admit mistakes. Apologize for them and present a plan how to get back on track. It's okay not to know everything and not to try being too professional. Stay authentic, human, and vulnerable. That makes you approachable and likeable.

Be tolerant and learn to like people. You can't love everyone, but you can teach yourself to like others. Especially those who are different to you by being willing to open your mind up to different opinions and change, and by being generous and forgiving.

Make it personal. Appreciate others. Don't praise yourself. Instead, never forget who got you where you are. Express thanks and gratitude as often as possible to friends, colleagues, business partners, clients, and customers.

Be transparent and encourage constructive criticism and honest feedback. Be brave enough to comment and to suggest improvements whenever you feel doing so.

Walk your talk. When you say you're going to do something, then do it. Meet your deadlines. Always be a reliable partner. As such, eliminate (bad) surprises. That builds trust.

Set up an easy, non-complicated system to ensure that you connect with your contacts on a more or less regular basis. Sometimes it might only be writing one short mail. Maybe even one sentence or one short SMS. There's no reason that you have to write a two page letter to stay in contact with someone.

Look after yourself. Only if you are happy, satisfied and in-sync with yourself you can establish well-functioning and sincere relationships. Spend enough time on whatever gives you this special kick: sports, a drink with former college buddies, enjoying a relaxing spa and/or beauty treatment, reading a good book, etc.

Don't take yourself too seriously. You are replaceable. So am I and so are all of us. Enjoy yourself and show those around you that you know how to have fun. It only takes a few muscles to smile. Humor – including the ability to laugh about oneself - is a great teacher!

Living a happy and fulfilled life comes from being willing to work sedulously on building mutually beneficial relationships with family, friends, colleagues, and business partners. Without having them, it's impossible to be successful without regrets.

Don't forget: Everything what we can achieve in life is with and through other people. Be generous with others and help them achieve their own success in any way you can. Then they will help you.

51. YOU WILL WHAT YOU WANT – LIVE YOUR DREAM!

Let me tell you today the true and amazing story of an incredible woman, a marvelous ballet dancer, an ultimate fighter, and a hard-working pursuer of her dreams who has become a role model for many people.

Someone who believed they deserve better. Someone who has never given up. Someone of true talent and relentless determination. Someone who chose her own path, who set her own standards, and who shaped her own destiny by not allowing others to define her.

This remarkable person is Misty Copeland, who became only the second black soloist in the history of the most prestigious American Ballet Theatre by the age of 24. What makes it even more impressive is the fact that Misty comes from a family who saw three marriages fail, had to move through the country as a very young child, and with her three older siblings often experienced situations where the family almost run out of money and food. Misty did not begin dancing until she was 13. This is many years after those who become professionals usually get their start. Although already some months afterwards her exceptional talent and immense will became obvious, her perceived body physics - bigger feet, very muscular legs, larger breasts - kept her out of many prestigious dance programs.

And still, Misty did not give up. Indeed, the contrary was true. As a girl who fell in love with ballet, an art and sport that has traditionally included very few people of color, she was convinced of having to dance as a ballerina. Misty, now 31, has not only become a famous ballerina, but also served as a judge on the TV show "So You Think You Can Dance," wrote a popular memoir at the beginning of this year, and is currently performing in a beautiful ad for the sports apparel company Under Armour as part of their "I Will What I Want" campaign.

This is a campaign that portrays people who had struggles but persevered while not conforming to the typical mold. In the Under Armour spot, Misty is warming up, while the voice of a young girl reads real rejection letters that Misty received. And yet we see her flying through the air and spinning across the stage in elegant determination and with inspiring grace. At the end of the spot the viewer understands the payoffs by reading that Misty indeed is a soloist of the American Ballet Theatre.

The Beautifully Gracious Misty Copeland

Kudos to Misty for having followed her dreams and having turned into a remarkable and modest role model. Well done Under Armour for not having aired a campaign with sweaty football players, but an elegant and emotional TV spot (and yes, we understand that there also is a commercial background to it).

It's an inspiration for many of us to vigorously insist on living our dreams and not accepting any limitations and obstacles. That's what makes the world spin around!

52. MAKE HAPPINESS YOUR PRIORITY

Did you know that March 20 was the International Day of Happiness which was established by the United Nations in 2012. It's supposed to be celebrated throughout the world every year on this same day.

Hmm? Were you celebrating it? Were you, your friends, colleagues, or team members happier, because it was the International Day of Happiness?

Well, unfortunately, most likely many of us were not. And one might also wonder if there aren't more important things the UN and other institutions should focus on. Have those happiness preachers not realized that today's world is confronted with more serious topics: Wars, civil conflicts, income disparities, social inequalities, environmental issues, etc. Can we just "smile away" all of those major risks? And what about our own daily chores and challenges? Let's be a little bit happy and all will be good? Are you kidding?

I guess you get my point! We can act sarcastically by arguing against the word and the concept "happiness." Alternatively, and that's more the approach I favor, we can be positive, audacious, and open-minded about its broader meaning and purpose.

The way I'd like to define happiness has nothing to do with daydreaming, trying to escape reality, or seeing life through rose-colored glasses. In fact, I consider happiness and the well-being of people as a fundamental human right. The pursuit of happiness is a beautiful goal to strive for. And it should become one of our main objectives in life. Well aligned with, and not hiding behind, economic growth and social responsibility.

Never Give Up On Your Dreams

The International Day of Happiness should remind organizations and individuals to look for ways to raise awareness about the importance of happiness. And to assist yourself and others in becoming happier.

Governmental and non-governmental organizations as well as every one of us should make a contribution through education, training, coaching, or awareness-raising activities. It's worth it! Numerous studies have shown that happy people are healthier, more confident, more creative, more dynamic, more productive, more satisfied, more powerful, and more resilient.

As such, creating happy and meaningful lives does counteract depression, fear, ruthlessness, frustration, and crime.

Recent research proves that a vast majority of people would prefer to live in a society with the greatest happiness rather than the greatest wealth. The Kingdom of Bhutan designed the concept of Gross National Happiness (GNH) to measure quality of life and social progress in a more holistic manner than only the economic indicator of gross domestic product (GDP).

The country's Gross National Happiness Commission is charged with reviewing policy decisions and allocation of resources by putting emphasis on the well-being of its people. Another alternative metric is the Genuine Progress Indicator (GPI), which also takes fuller account of the health of a nation by incorporating environmental and social factors which are not measured by GDP.

How To Make Happiness Your Priority

Below are my favorite techniques to reclaim and strengthen happiness:

Practice Mindfulness: Live your life with more depth, contemplation, and sincere contentment. Focus on yourself and do not compare yourself with others.

Think Happy: Thoughts create feelings. And feelings behavior. Positive behavior and smiling attracts more positivity. This re-stimulates happy thoughts.

Surround Yourself With Happy People And Nurture Relationships: A beautiful trigger of happiness!

Treat Yourself Well: Spoil yourself. Respect and love yourself. Do more of what you really love and spend more time with loved ones.

Catch And Memorize Great Moments: Put the bad ones aside. Slow down to enjoy the joys of life. Write them down and read them whenever needed.

Be Active And Take Care Of Yourself: Go outside, go for a walk, do sports, etc. Learn new things. Stimulate yourself. Challenge yourself.

Set Meaningful, Achievable Targets: Be committed and take one step after another.

Help Others And Be Generous: Practice acts of kindness and learn to forgive.

Your Mission – Reclaim Happiness NOW!

You can start immediately by making yourself and others happy when following the below-listed three, easy steps:

Look through your photos now to find a picture of something that made you happy.

Next time something makes you happy, take a picture to capture the moment.

Inspire others to find happiness by sharing your pictures with #happinessday and/or mailing them to your partner, a friend, colleague, etc. Use your pictures to remind yourself and others of what really matters.

Enjoy e.g. listening to "Happy" by Pharrell Williams.

From now on, celebrate your personal happiness day every day. And help others to get there too!

53. HOW TO BUILD RELATIONSHIPS OF TRUST

Trust is a core ingredient to build successful relationships. Both personal and professional ones. It is a major leadership characteristic. However, you can't take it for granted. You need to work hard to earn trust and to keep it.

Isaac Watts once said that "Learning to trust is one of life's most difficult tasks." If you're not seen as a trustworthy person you can neither form engaged relationships nor high performing teams. And without them you can't become a successful leader and manager. If you are not careful, you can lose trust within days or even hours.

In today's article I'd like to share with you my thoughts and what I consider to be the most important principles to build, regain, and sustain trust.

Walk Your Talk. Mean what you say and keep your word. Deliver your committed tasks and duties on time and in full. Be consistent and reliable. Arrive promptly to meetings. If you might risk missing an agreed timeline, proactively communicate and explain it, apologize and come forward with a new proposal. Try not missing it a second time to protect your reputation. Lead by example and permanently demonstrate that you deliver on your promises and that others can count on you.

Communicate Frequently And Openly. Direct, quick, accurate, and honest communication builds trust. Share regularly with others. This underlines that you have no hidden agenda. Address possible trust issues within a team in an open and prompt manner. In this context it's also crucial to develop and possess good active listening skills.

Tell The Truth And Take A Stand. Be honest and don't lie. This is not as easy as it might sound. Of course, we wouldn't admit it, would we? Anyway, it's key not leaving out relevant facts, figures, and opinions when discussing and arguing. Even, and especially, when it's awkward and painful. People will appreciate it. Also, be willing to say no. You can't be everything to everyone. Taking a stand based on sound arguments - well and politely articulated - will earn you respect and trust.

Be Transparent And Unite. Share your objectives, strategy, agenda, and values. People want to know what you think and believe and to understand how they might fit into the picture. This gives them security and confidence in you and your intentions. Create a common identity and establish a sense of companionship.

Show People That You Care About Them. Be out for others and not primarily for yourself. Appreciate all people you're dealing with. Show sensitivity to their interests, wishes, and needs. Value them and thank them. Express sincere gratitude two times too often rather than missing it just once. Do it from the heart.

Empower Others. Show people that you trust them. Grant flexibility, stimulate initiative- taking, and ask for regular feedback. Have faith in others' skills and capabilities. Be willing to let go and to share power. "The best way to find out if you can trust somebody is to trust them," (E. Hemingway).

Focus On The Positives. Don't punish mistakes. As they can happen, think and speak about them in a results-oriented and forward-looking way. Jointly look with others for solutions and implement actions to avoid them happening again.

Coach And Train Others. Guide people around you and assist them in finding their way and the right solutions for themselves. Don't tell them what to do. Instead ask them for their opinions. Support them in becoming great and outstanding.

Follow High Ethical Standards. Do the right things. Even, and especially, when it might be hard. People will like, respect, and trust your integrity.

Admit Mistakes And Weaknesses. Fortunately, you're only human. So, when you don't do the right thing, admit it. Be transparent, authentic and willing to talk about your mistakes and faults in a constructive manner. When you are vulnerable and have nothing to hide you radiate trust. That's what people love.

Establish Long-Term Relationships. Trust is usually not the result of short-term actions and profits. It's stemming from deeper values, ethics, and fundamental principles. Take your time and don't rush. Be willing to let trust evolve and flourish. The best trust fertilizer is to "give without any strings attached." Don't always expect something in return.

54. 12 IRRATIONAL IDEAS THAT LIMIT PERSONAL SUCCESS

Last week, at an advanced coaching training course I attended, we spoke a lot about the human growth potential and possible factors holding it back.

In this context we also discussed in depth the *Rational Emotive Behavior Therapy* (REBT), which was created and developed by the American psychotherapist and psychologist Albert Ellis. REBT is a practical, action-oriented approach to coping with problems and enhancing personal growth. It places a good deal of its focus on the present: on currently-held attitudes, painful emotions and maladaptive behaviors that can sabotage a fuller experience of life.

One of the fundamental premises of REBT is that humans, in most cases, do not merely get upset by unfortunate adversities, but also by how they construct their views of reality through their language, evaluative beliefs, meanings and philosophies about the world, themselves and others.

REBT argues that the following 12 core irrational ideas, which have been observed and analyzed over many years, are at the root of the most self-limiting thinking and believing factors:

- The idea that it is a dire necessity for adults to be loved by significant others for almost everything they do — instead of their concentrating on their own self-respect, on winning approval for practical purposes, and on loving rather than on being loved.

- The idea that certain acts are awful or wicked, and that people who perform such acts should be severely damned — instead of the idea that certain acts are self-defeating or antisocial, and that people who perform such acts are behaving stupidly, or ignorantly, and would be better helped to change.

- The idea that it is horrible when things are not the way we like them to be — instead of the idea that it is too bad, that we would better try to change or control bad conditions so that they become more satisfactory, and, if that is not possible, we had better temporarily accept and gracefully lump their existence.

- The idea that human misery is invariably externally caused and is forced on us by outside people and events — instead of the idea that it is largely caused by the view that we take of unfortunate conditions.

- The idea that if something is or may be dangerous or fearsome we should be terribly upset and endlessly obsessed about it — instead of the idea that one would better frankly face it and render it non-dangerous and, when that is not possible, accept the inevitable.

- The idea that it is easier to avoid than to face life difficulties and self - responsibilities — instead of the idea that the so-called easy way is usually much harder in the long-run.

- The idea that we absolutely need something other or stronger or greater than ourselves on which to rely — instead of the idea that it is better to take the risks of thinking and acting less dependently.

- The idea that we should be thoroughly competent, intelligent, and achieving in all possible respects — instead of the idea that we would better do rather than always need to do well and accept ourselves as a quite imperfect creature, who has general human limitations and specific fallibilities.

- The idea that because something once strongly affected our life, it should indefinitely affect it — instead of the idea that we can learn from our past experiences but not be overly-attached to or prejudiced by them.

- The idea that we must have certain and perfect control over things — instead of the idea that the world is full of probability and chance and that we can still enjoy life despite this.

- The idea that human happiness can be achieved by inertia and inaction — instead of the idea that we tend to be happiest when we are vitally absorbed in creative pursuits, or when we are devoting ourselves to people or projects outside ourselves.

- The idea that we have virtually no control over our emotions and that we cannot help feeling disturbed about things — instead of the idea that we have real control over our destructive emotions if we choose to work at changing the musturbatory hypotheses which we often employ to create them.

55. THE POWER OF BEING A REALISTIC OPTIMIST

We all know the common idiom about the glass being considered as either half-full or half-empty. And the related assessment if in consequence someone has an optimistic or a pessimistic outlook on life.

"A pessimist sees the difficulty in every opportunity; an optimist sees the opportunity in every difficulty." (Winston Churchill).

Is it really so simple?

Personally, I favor a third way which I call *Being A Realistic Optimist*. Meaning that in general and for most situations I am (very) positive, i.e. an optimistic thinker. However, in particularly challenging situations (e.g. before and during very complicated negotiations with many unknown and unfavorable variables), from time to time I might apply a more conservative style. As you'll find out below, this has certain advantages.

The Optimist

The word "Optimism" is originally derived from the Latin *optimum*, meaning "best." Being optimistic, in the typical sense of the word, ultimately means one expects the best possible outcome from any given situation.

"There are only two ways to live your life. One is as though nothing is a miracle. The other is as though everything is a miracle." (Albert Einstein).

Research has found that positive, i.e. optimistic thinking can aid in coping with stress, in becoming more resilient, in being more courageous, and in addition it is playing a significant role in improving one's health and well-being.

According to Martin Seligmann, people with a so-called optimistic explanatory style tend to give themselves credit when good things happen; and typically blame outside forces for bad outcomes. They also look at negative events as temporary and atypical.

The Pessimist

The term "Pessimism" is derived from the Latin word *pessimus,* meaning 'the worst'. Pessimism is a state of mind in which one anticipates undesirable outcomes or believes that the evil or hardships in life outweigh the good or luxuries.

"We are all in the gutter, but some of us are looking at the stars." (Oscar Wilde).

Individuals with a pessimistic explanatory style often blame themselves when bad things happen, but fail to give themselves adequate credit for successful outcomes. They also have a tendency to view negative events as expected and lasting.

At the same time, certain studies that examined the consequences of unrealistic optimism have found that greater optimism is associated with less preventive behavior, i.e. that sometimes a negative style might lead to being more focused, better prepared, and more cautious.

The Realistic Optimist

Albert Bandura, one of the founding fathers of modern psychology, argued decades ago that optimism is the basis for creating and maintaining motivation to reach goals. And that an individual's success is mostly based on the fact whether or not she believes she will succeed. The results of his findings have yet to be proven wrong.

Unrealistic optimists (I also refer to them as naive realists), on the one hand, are convinced that success will happen to them almost automatically and that they will succeed effortlessly. Some of them even think (and hope) that only by sending out positive thoughts the universe might reward them by transforming all of their wishes and aspirations into reality.

Realistic optimists are vigorously optimistic, too. They strongly believe that they make things happen and that they will succeed. They have no doubt about it. Saying that, on the other hand, they perfectly know that in order to be successful they have to plan well, to access all necessary resources, to stay focused and persistent, to evaluate different options, and to execute in excellence. Having done all of that, i.e. being well prepared and organized, such a state again stimulates their confidence level and, as a result, their optimism.

"The pessimist complains about the wind; the optimist expects it to change; the realist adjusts the sails." (William Arthur Ward).

Being both optimistic and realistic, i.e. combining the two into one behavioral style of *realistic optimism,* creates a special breed of very successful people. Realistic optimists stay positive and upbeat about the future, even – and especially – if and when they recognize the challenges ahead. As such, realism and optimism are not diametrically opposed. The contrary is true: They're complementing each other in a very powerful manner!

Final tip: In case of doubt - and mostly if you want to achieve something very unique and impactful - the optimist in you should outwit your realist. Why? The realist might be too prone to anxiety. The optimist, however, if stimulated and guided well, will activate your fantasy, imagination, and boldness.

56. HOW TO STAY CALM AND PERFORM UNDER PRESSURE

Imagine you're about to miss your monthly sales targets; you do not get a crucial contract signed within an agreed timeframe; you've forgotten to answer an urgent request from one of your key customers; your boss has called you three times in the past two hours to get a super urgent analysis for his board meeting from you, or something went wrong which seriously affects your business and possibly offsets other stakeholders.

In today's fast changing and highly complex (business) world, this can happen easily.

A coachee of mine, a talented young marketing manager, some weeks ago told me that she had just missed an essential deadline for a major product launch. She and her team had been working extremely hard for many months to prepare a "perfect" launch, but could not make it on time as a third-party supplier let them down at the very last moment. They all were very disappointed and frustrated, but still, they did not want to give up and tried not to waste any time. They rapidly got on their feet again, and everyone was busy doing anything with any kind of apparent activity. In retrospect, many of those activities – she admitted - did not make any sense.

Headless Chicken Syndrome

My friend described those days to me as a period of collective disorientation and non-coordinated hyper-activity. For her it was a complete new experience. Pushed by her line managers to deliver immediate results, she lost her usual impressive capability to see the big picture. She "forgot" to contemplate, to analyze the status quo, and to calmly discuss possible solutions with her team. Instead she got nervous and became more worried about how her boss would think of her than about how to draft together with her team a solid alternative plan.

She suffered from what I call *Headless Chicken Syndrome*. Have you ever watched a headless chicken jump and flap around as if in search of its lost head? My friend was acting just like a headless chicken. She had entered *Headless Chicken Syndrome* without realizing it. She was overwhelmed by the situation. She and her team created more and more to-do lists, started non-coordinated initiatives, and generated a disconnect between the various teams and management. All with the best intentions, but unfortunately without simply sitting still and thinking through the problem.

Strategies to Stay Calm Under Pressure

The most important task of any manager in very stressful, high pressure and extremely demanding situations is to keep calm and keep one's shirt on. It's not about finding quick solutions in the first place, it's about avoiding chaos, about stabilizing the situation, and re-injecting self-confidence into the organization. And only afterwards looking for adequate solutions.

To get around the risk of facing stressed leadership I'd like to present two formulae which help me to stay even-tempered and focused during critical times and crisis. They are straightforward in concept and, with repetitive practice, also in execution:

The START Formula – This is a preventive concept, i.e. knowing and applying it assists in minimizing the risk to encounter possible headless chicken situations.

The SWITCH Formula – Once you find yourself in a situation where you are about to lose your head you better exercise this method to stay on course and keep your cool.

The *START* Formula

If you live by the START formula you significantly reduce the risk of being dragged into situations where you might lose your temper and head.

S - Stand Up
Make your point and explain your strategy and action plan. Don't allow others to push you around. Don't be afraid to say no, especially if you've already got too much on your plate.

T - Trust
Trust in yourself and others.

A - Action
Action your strategy and plans. Push back if needed. Eliminate all possible distractions like unnecessary meetings, phone calls, etc.

R - Respond
Be responsive and responsible. Keep your line managers, peers, and all other stakeholders always informed and regularly ask for their opinions. If you need help, be brave enough to ask for it.

T - Take It Easy
Don't take yourself and your tasks too seriously. We are all replaceable. Don't give in to stress or anxiety – no matter how far behind you are or how badly you've messed up. Relax.

The *SWITCH* Formula

Once you find yourself in deep and unknown waters, applying this method will help you to keep your wits and stay calm.

S – STOP
Stop running and chasing your tail. Sit down. No further movements.

W – Wait
Make sure you allocate yourself as much downtime as necessary.

I – Inhale
Inhale and breathe. It clears your head. It'll balance the analytical processes of the mind with your emotions and gut.

T – Think
Contemplate the situation you're in. Try to understand the root causes and interdependencies. Important: Always allow more time than you think you'll need.

C – Calculate
Calculate and plan. Set yourself and your team clear goals. Break them down into monthly, weekly, and daily milestone targets. They should be

specific, measurable, actionable, realistic, and time-bound (SMART). Leave a sufficiently big buffer between every task.

H - Head and Proceed
Once you are clear about your objectives and your action plan, and only then, move on and execute.

Final Thought

We all know that the more we rush, the higher the chances are we fail. Still, often we do it with or without realizing it. In consequence we often create more waste and churn, trigger unnecessary activities, put too much pressure on others and make them feel uncomfortable, and fail to spot real problems or real opportunities to improve.

57. ARE GREAT LEADERS GREAT COACHES?

In the last two decades coaching has become increasingly popular. With change in life and business still accelerating - and coaching being a highly effective methodology which assists in working with change - it is one of the most powerful communication and leadership instruments. Unfortunately it's not being practiced yet by many managers and leaders. Only a smaller group of exceptional business individuals has realized its relevance and power to develop team members and companies.

Although there exist mental coaches, stress coaches, career coaches, conflict coaches, family coaches, executive coaches, team coaches, success coaches, health coaches, and many more, in the corporate world coaching still seems to belong to a more exclusive domain of top executives and a few chosen ones. In addition, in Europe, for a long time and only until some years ago, coaching has been considered as a "special" development effort granted (prescribed) by the company to successful and simultaneously difficult managers who would need to get their rough edges softened a little bit in order to be turned into real corporate superstars.

Today, however, there is a need that leadership coaching (the coaching of current and future leaders) becomes a given component in organizations to assist executives, managers, and employees in their personal and professional development. As most companies have understood that highly motivated and fulfilled team members enjoy what they are doing and as such are more effective, coaching should be chosen as a key leadership option (among others; depending upon the situation the manager/leader is confronted with).

This article aims at assisting managers and leaders to apply a so-called "coach approach" adapted to various settings by focusing more on their people skills, their emotional and personal intelligence, and as such more on the holistic development of their teams with the objective to help their employees to achieve the results that matter, to live accordingly to their values, to develop their own vision and objectives, and ultimately to lead a fulfilled life.

Definition Of Successful Coaching

Coaching is a model, a set of skills and a technique as well as a relationship and communication approach which aims at accompanying a coachee (=client) to realize his self-defined wish for change and development.

Coaching is not about solving problems in the first place (although eventually they will be solved). It's about actively listening, asking the client powerful questions, stimulating his awareness and curiosity, helping him to obtain new perspectives and options, encouraging the client to find his own solutions and answers, supporting him on his path of change, challenging and re-assuring him, and helping him to discover that he already possesses all resources needed.

As such coaching, is a Co-Operative relationship in which the coach and coachee are two active equals for the purpose of meeting the coachee's needs and wishes.

Assumptions Of Successful Coaching

The Coachee is capable, resourceful, and already has the answers – The coach fully trusts in the know-how, competencies and capabilities of the coachee. A coach may propose a course of action, but the coachee himself will need to make decisions in the end.

The Coach is not a hand-holder. Instead she's a catalyst – Since the coach assumes that the coachee is resourceful, capable, and creative, she's a fan of the coachee. As a catalyst the coach is a main piece in the coaching process by assisting in speeding up the process of change.

The Coachee is the one working and being accountable within the coaching process –The coach lends a hand by creating a framework and process for the coachee. Like building a wooden frame for a painting. However, the coachee himself needs to take the brushes in his hands and needs to start drawing the picture he'd like to paint of himself and his life.

The Coach enjoys assisting the Coachee in achieving his higher purpose – The coach loves to live and to display passion, commitment, and sincere interest for the coachee. By doing so it's not only a job for her, but a mission.

The whole coaching process is built on trust and confidentiality – To hold all coaching conversations confidential certainly is a main criteria for successful coaching. Trust is also expanded by respectful, open-minded and honest exchanges among coach and coachee.

Coaching is about what the Coachee creates – As such, the coachee requires sufficient space for himself to think, feel, experiment, dream, visualize, and to be able to embrace different thinking patterns, models of the world, and perspectives to possibly come up with new ideas and/or solutions.

Characteristics Of Successful Coaching

A coach understands that coaching is not just a form of good communication with the coachee/client. Instead, coaching is seen as moving to a deeper level of human interaction and connection.

The coach considers herself as a peer-to-peer communicator, i.e. she's not following an authoritarian communication style, but a cooperative communication pattern concentrating on opportunities and new ways of thinking and feeling.

The coach respects being only in charge of the process and the structure. Not setting the agenda nor leading the discussions. She would only take charge if it were to serve the client's agenda; e.g. if the coachee were getting side-tracked by non-relevant topics.

Another two key qualities of a good coach are "Active Listening" and "Asking Powerful Questions." **Active Listening** means that the coach is very present, asks questions to clarify when she has not fully understood, listens in search for direct and indirect information about the coachee's vision, values, attitudes, and objectives. She tries to get the story behind the words and demeanor while not thinking of her own agenda.

If the coach asks a Powerful Question she would phrase an open-ended question (versus a yes-no-question) to stimulate clarity and to receive new insights by having followed the client's lead. The two techniques want to invite the coachee to see his issue, life, objectives, etc. from different angles to present new perspectives and to possibly arrive at new conclusions. The coach could further elaborate on it by applying a reframing statement (by taking the original information of the client and interpreting it in a different way).

In addition, during the first stage of the coaching process, the clarification and discovery stage, the coach might need to assist the coachee in clarifying his situation, topic, and desired outcome by using powerful questions, reframing, etc. Coaching goals should be set and possible actions and timings should be discussed to keep the coachee focused during the whole coaching process.

An effective coach should also be emotionally detached from situations described by the coachee (in order of not becoming an active participant in the coachee's plot). She should be honest and respectfully direct (e.g. if the coachee were to start kidding himself), and she should request the coachee – based on his agenda - to take care of certain tasks in order to forward the coachee's action (e.g. asking him to write a coaching diary that might include homework, observations, etc.).

Finally, a successful coach would enable the coachee not only to achieve his originally defined objective, but in addition enabling him to put it into a broader context. She would have realized the inter-connectivity and inter-dependency with other aspects of the coachee's life. She would try to assist the coachee in seeing the bigger context and variety of options. She would encourage and induce transformation.

Final Considerations for Leaders and Coaches

As a leader and line manager you're always wearing multiple heads. That's okay. You just need to be aware of it and to be clear with your coachee. As a line manager you're having the right – if the situation demands it – to impose your agenda on the employee. As a coach, however, you are following the coachee's agenda. Full stop. You would need to change your head and your attitude in many situations if you are a more directive leader and if you were serious about applying a coach-driven leadership style.

Still, it's acceptable, if you possess valuable and relevant expertise and information which would help the coachee to accelerate his development process, that you share these with the coachee even when you are wearing your coach head. In such an instance you would act as a "consultant" and you would need to ask the coachee for permission in order to be sure that he really wants to hear it. Also be clear about offering it without any strings attached.

Most importantly, as a coaching-driven leader you will need to be able to build trust with your employee to accept your coaching leadership style. Creating a safe and highly confidential coaching environment is key. The coachee must feel respected, reassured, and being in good and trustworthy hands to talk freely and to open up.

Coaching is a complex and at the same time very rewarding, exciting communication medium with specific rules and techniques. It's built around mutual respect, listening, asking, clarity, relying fully upon the coachee's own resources, opening up new perspectives, and the absolute willingness to address challenging conversations and situations. Coaching assists people to achieve the results which truly matter in living a successful and fulfilled life.

58. SIX WAYS TO AVOID THE HUMAN RAT RACE

It's not only since the recent news of the suicides of two top Swiss executives and the death of a young "highly dedicated" German intern at Merrill Lynch's London office that we know that increasing workloads, hectic schedules, and huge stress levels get many people exhausted, unhappy, and desperate.

Stress, emotional exhaustion, and a reduced sense of personal accomplishment often result in burnout and depression.

What about You?

Are you often stressed out? Do you have the feeling that your life is sometimes out of control, that you're running from one task to another, and that you do not know how to reconcile your multiple responsibilities? Do you have enough downtime? Are you able to balance your professional and private lives? Are you making a difference between the two of them at all?

6 Actions Stopping You from Human Rat Racing

Without any doubt – first and foremost – companies are responsible for all of their staff being put in a position where they are able to cope with their increasingly demanding roles. They need to ensure that enough resources are provided and that targets, even if set in an ambitious and demanding way, can be achieved by applying reasonable efforts. In addition, if team members are struggling, certain trainings should be offered, from time management and organization skills to stress management trainings (e.g. autogenic training, relaxation techniques, meditation, energizing hypnosis).

Secondly, and even more importantly, it's the individual's responsibility to take ownership of one's life and to lead it in a holistic manner, i.e. not living to work, but working to live. As you can't add days to your life, you should focus on adding life to your days.

This is how to do it:

Be Fully Dedicated to Managing Yourself: It's about self-management and taking full responsibility of yourself. You can and you must pro-actively organize and live your life. No one else can do it for you.

Managing Your Life is Much More than Career Management: Work (career, wealth) is just one aspect of life. There are other crucial areas which need to get adequate and regular attention in order to lead a fulfilled life: social areas (family, friends, recognition), health areas (sports, relaxation, diet, well-being and fitness), and spiritual areas (fulfillment, religion, love, philosophy).

Write Down Your Personal Vision and Mission of Life: Ask yourself what's really important for you, what you would like to achieve, what you are really good at, what your values are, and what you want to look back on at the end of your life.

Formulate Your Life Goals: Determine and write down what you'd like to achieve in each of your life areas. This allows you to anchor your personal life vision in your ongoing schedule. At the same time it will add meaningful content to your life.

Weekly and Daily Priority Planning: There will always be external tasks and deadlines which you will need to comply with. It's a fact of life. Still, in order to master your life, you will also need to set your own priorities in order to concentrate on your important professional and private goals. You need to control your day in order to control your life.

Conduct Regular Life Quality Checks: Make sure that once or twice a week you put 10 to 15 minutes aside to review whether your daily activities and your weekly schedule are consistently aligned with your overall goals. If not, change your agenda to reflect back to what you really want to achieve in life. In case of doubt, just look at your personal life vision and mission statement. It will always give you the reassurance you might need from time to time.

59. IT TAKES TWO TO TANGO: THE NEED TO MANAGE UP

Only a very few companies might be ready to embrace concepts such as holacracy in a serious and all-encompassing manner and to dance to this new rhythm. And although being around for about 10 years, holacracy still has to demonstrate its effectiveness on a broader and a sustainable manner.

As such, managing up is as important as managing down or cooperating with peers. It's part of a holistic and participatory management approach. Based on mutual trust and respect it takes the perspectives of all stakeholders into consideration and truly empowers and challenges employees to proactively take part in organizational decision making and learning.

Managing relationships upward, either only by yourself or jointly with colleagues and/or your team is not about promoting self-interests or political maneuvering. Instead it's a needed skill to obtain the best possible results for your organization, your team, your line manager, and also for you. In addition, the way you interact with your line manager is influencing the relationship the two of you are having. It's like dancing the tango.

Although, depending on the particular setting, in general when approaching the relationship with your boss with an attitude of open-mindedness and cooperation, you have much better chances to become a more effective manager and person.

I suggest to take the following main principles into consideration:

Understanding The Nature Of the Relationship With Your Boss

Remind yourself that you and your boss are mutually dependent on one another. You should be part of the same team by having very similar objectives. She needs your support to progress with certain tasks and you need your boss to benefit from her assistance and guidance to do the right things the right way. As such, it's an equal relationship on eye level and based on mutual respect and appreciation. The relationship and the communication with your line manager is always a two-way street.

Managing Your Interests and Your Career

Without doubt, it's one of your line manager's most important tasks to assist you in your development. Still, you should also look after yourself. It's what I call the "Principle of Self-Responsibility and Self-Accountability." It means that you're also in charge of your life and, of course, your career. It's up to you to actively influence the development of things and the relationship with your boss as good as possible. You should view yourself as the subject and not as an object.

Organizing Yourself and Your Work

You need to be organized in order to be able to become proactive and to have sufficient time and space to manage up. Be clear about your targets, clarify priorities, and constantly differentiate between important and urgent topics. When being trapped in the human rat race there's no way you can discuss constructively and thoughtfully with your boss. Recognize your needs, strengths, and weaknesses and align them in an appropriate manner with those of your line manager. Jointly define realistic expectations and targets (incl. deadlines, costs, etc.). The magic words are "together" and "realistic." Don't set expectations too high. This might discount your credibility in case you don't achieve them. However, don't intentionally set them too low. The two of you should feel comfortable with them.

Comprehending The Personality Of Your Boss

You should try to adjust your style and to adapt to your line manager's modus operandi as good as possible. Example: If your boss is an analytical type of person you would need to have sound data at hand when discussing with her a project or business initiative. You should also be able to categorize your boss's behavioral style, her pet peeves, and her likes and dislikes. Does she prefer taking her time before making decisions? Is she satisfied by getting the whole picture or does she usually require all key details?

Putting Yourself In The Shoes Of Your Boss

Try to understand the situation and context in which your boss is. Does she have to finish budget preparations; is she organizing a key meeting; about to meet very important customers? What is her immediate task and what are the objectives she has to deliver?

Being Transparent

Building trust by being trustworthy is a crucial element in managing up. If things are getting complicated, go to her first. If the two of you can't resolve a serious issue, you might have to go over her head. This should be a last resort and you should tell her beforehand. To secure your general "independence" you should try having a mentor or coach.

Over-Communicating and Avoiding Surprises

Very good communication skills are the basis to successfully managing the relationship with your boss. It can be verbal or written. If you want to be heard by her, then make it as convenient as possible for her, i.e. adjust to her communication style. If you're not sure, ask her and get confirmation by requesting feedback. Also don't wait for your annual review to find out what your boss thinks of you and your work. Whenever you receive feedback handle it in a rational manner. It's very helpful if you respect agreed commitments, project deadlines, etc. Either way (i.e. even if you were to miss a deadline), the best method is always honest and forthright communication. Provide early heads up and don't hide information. Bad news doesn't get any better with age.

Focusing On Solutions And Not Problems

Without doubt, sooner or later you, your boss, and your projects will encounter problems. Actually nothing better can happen, since such situations separate the wheat from the chaff. By quickly coming forward with possible solutions you can demonstrate that you have given the problem some thought and that you care. When you share a problem timing is critical, i.e. discuss the issue within an appropriate situation and not in a "hit and run" setting. Your boss will appreciate being informed about a delay of the most important project well before entering the board room and meeting with the exec team.

Disagreeing And Committing

Of course, it's okay to disagree with your boss. It should be based, however, on a sound analysis, solid arguments and – if possible – some precise examples. She will respect you for that. Even more so if at the end you will support a decision taken by various company stakeholders and her, even if the final outcome was not your preferred option.

Raising Your Concerns and Speaking Up

Raise your concerns clearly and stand firm, if needed. If you're doing the best job you can do, keep your head held high and don't give in too easily. Rather ask questions, seek to understand, and work to deactivate a difficult setting instead of suffering in silence or responding in anger. It may not always change the situation or the final outcome, but at least you would have given it a try. And if done in a rational, respectful, and well-articulated manner, it will earn you the respect of your boss. By the way, every good line manager will appreciate when you approach him with good and challenging ideas and a genuine desire to make things working better. Usually this kicks off a new level of cooperation and trust between you and your boss.

It Takes Two to Tango

At the end, however, it is crucial to stay true to yourself, to stay authentic and not to violate and to ignore your relevant core principles. You should not give up on your essential beliefs and convictions to get along and to work well with your line manager. If your boss is not listening to you, not being vocally self-critical herself, and not willing to also adjust from her side and to respect your opinion and needs, then there exist fundamental miss-alignments between the two of you.

In such instances you're well advised to rather try changing your job (and boss) within the company or to leave the company. You should not regret anything if you tried hard and if it still did not work out. For sure you have learned a lot (even and especially with such a boss) and you know that they do not deserve you. Others will appreciate your talents!

60. HOW TO CHANGE YOURSELF FOR GOOD!

At one time or another, wanting to change and better yourself is a great thing. Just think about how many people set a New Year's resolution at the beginning of 2014. Unfortunately, it turns out that most of our good change intentions fail and that they are not being successfully implemented.

Why Is that? Three Main Reasons

Often, we have not precisely analyzed the underlying cause and true necessity of our intention to change. Secondly, we have not developed a thoughtful plan of action (incl. not having thought about possible consequences in advance). Thirdly, and most importantly, often we remain stuck with resolutions and good intentions. Meaning, we're not able to really change our habits and, as such, our behavior.

So, how to systematically plan your own change and – in order of attaining lasting personal change - how to teach an old dog new tricks?

What has worked for me in behavior change, and what I've seen functioning very well for others, is reflected in the following principles:

Assess If There Is A Need For You To Change At All

Before you'd like to storm ahead with any change initiative, make sure that it isn't the opinions of others making want you to change something. It should be you who has a clear reason for change in order to eventually succeed with your efforts. You are in charge of your life and you set your personal agenda of change. Try to find out the reasons why you'd like to change something by asking yourself questions from multiple perspectives. Don't be irritated if you were to arrive at the conclusion that you do not want to change in the end, and that instead you only had the perception of wanting to change. It happens sometimes!

Identify What Exactly You Want To Change

Start writing down what you're really good at and what you like about yourself. Maybe you decide to change in such a way as to make your strengths even stronger. And only in a second step tackling your dislike areas and/or your areas you'd like to improve on. Then write down your flaws and prioritize them. State what you want to change in one precise and positive worded sentence. As you'll write your sentence(s) in an increasingly concrete manner, you'll almost naturally find the good starting point of your change process, e.g. I want to run 5 miles every day before going to work (instead of I want to do more sports). Tip: Analyze everything you've thought about to change and pick the one thing that's most important for you.

Visualize How It Will Look And Feel Once Having Successfully Changed

Examine and speculate about what kind of person you would like to become. Typically you would ask questions that challenge your most deeply held assumptions about who you are. "What if" questions are vital here: What if I stop being a self-centered, egotistic, and superficial manager? What if I no longer worry so much about only achieving quantitative targets? What if I no longer feel personally guilty of having missed certain objectives? What if I begin to tell the truth to myself and to others? Other helpful contemplation and imagination-stimulating techniques are meditation, yoga, and hypnosis.

Determine How Much You Want To Change And How Quickly

Best is to start with an easy to manage personal change project. If it's a bigger one, chunk it down into small bites. Take one chunk after the other, i.e. take small baby steps. Keep in mind that often the initial effort is the hardest. Afterwards, it usually gets easier. The best time to start with the actual change process is as soon as you're clear about your objective. And not one second later. It won't get easier if you were to postpone it. The contrary is true; it will get harder and harder and you will end up with having less time to make the change. So, get your act together, define what and how much you want to change and get started. Now! One more advice: Set a deadline and create milestones to encourage more effective behavior.

Consider How The Change Will Impact You And Others

When personal change occurs, we need to take into account the wider consequences of that change for the overall system in which we operate. Making a change can end up to be disastrous if you don't take time to step back and evaluate the impact of the change before making it. You should evaluate the future as though the change were made to see if there are any negative, harmful, or unnecessarily expensive results caused by its implementation to you, your family, colleagues, etc. Questions you could ask are: Does the outcome of the change enhance my life? Does it give me better opportunities? Does it limit me or any other relevant person in any way? Does it empower or dis-empower?

Stay Realistic and Be Prepared For Anything

Set a realistic goal that you believe is achievable. In addition you should also honestly acknowledge that on your journey to change most likely you will encounter a multitude of hurdles to overcome, setbacks to cope with, and various people trying to distract and demotivate you. It's normal. Don't worry; don't blame anyone (neither yourself), but expect obstacles and be prepared. Also, do not anticipate to change overnight. It's not a switch; it's a transformational process!

Make The Change Become Part Of You

As you are exploring possibilities for a better way of being, behaving, etc., you have also learned new modes of thinking. You interrupted the flow of repetitive thoughts that had occupied most of your waking moments. Letting go of these familiar, comfortable habits of thought, you assembled a more evolved concept of whom you could become, replacing an old idea of yourself with a new, greater ideal. Based on that, get out of your comfort zone and develop habits of this new person you're becoming.

Doing things that put us on edge incite new emotions and thought processes. New thought processes lead to new and different opportunities, resulting in change. Chose something related to your goal. If you want to be more convincing, seek occasions that force you to discuss and argue with people. Through repetitive practice you'll make a habit out of it. Ongoing real-life practicing will stimulate the brain to put new neural circuits in place and to make them an integral part of your evolved personality and character.

Establish Ways To Reward And Motivate You

Start slowly and increase the rate of difficulty and speed over time. Go for the low hanging fruits first. Make sure you'll have your moments of glory. Measure, recognize, and celebrate your progress with pride, positive emotions and outside treats: A nice dinner with your partner, a short vacation, a visit to the theater, etc. When doing so, take into consideration not to use rewards which are counter to your objective. Example: If your aim is to stop smoking, you should not celebrate a week without having touched any cigarette by enjoying a cigar and a glass of bourbon (the bourbon is okay). You'd better treat yourself solely with a splendid glass of an old Pappy Van Winkle's Family Reserve Bourbon (which has an exquisite taste).

Keep Going And Stay Relaxed

If you feel and realize you're not on track although you've tried hard, then stop, look for new options, adjust, and start all over again. It's not uncommon that from time to time you might need to fine-tune your goals. Replace unpleasant and negative thoughts with positive ones. Find like-minded people and collaborate with them. Group spirit helps to overcome potential obstacles and is a beautiful source of motivation and inspiration. If you were to fall back into old habits, find out the reasons, write them down and define immediate actions of how to get back on track (e.g. change something in your environment which might represent a distraction or an obstacle to you).

Once you've reached your desired result, still keep the focus and the momentum. Continue to ingrain your new habits and to make them part of your character. It's a never-ending story. Also make sure you stay healthy. Take up sports, eat well, have sufficient rest and plan enough time for things you love. Being healthy means being positive and having more energy and strength. And finally, take it easy. Give yourself time, be generous with yourself, and enjoy to learn and grow by changing.

61. 10 PRINCIPLES FOR PERSONAL AND PROFESSIONAL GROWTH

Besides having studied business management and business administration at university about two decades ago, having visited dozens of various business and management trainings afterward, some years ago I started to take intensive and comprehensive training in coaching, mentoring, NLP (Neuro Linguistic Programming) as well as in hypnosis and hypnotherapy. This was not to gain additional master diplomas, but instead to further develop my leadership skills and to broaden my personal horizon.

Neuro Linguistic Programming (NLP) is a communication and personal development approach created by Richard Bandler and John Grinder in the US in the 1970s. It claims a connection between the neurological processes (neuro), language (linguistic) and behavioral patterns learned through experience (programming), and that these can be changed to achieve specific goals in life.

The purpose of this article is not to discuss NLP itself (possibly in one of my next articles). I understand and respect that NLP might not be an easy concept to grasp; one reason being that its original idea and techniques have often been abused in the past by so called "experts" without any proper education and know-how... and even by one of its founders.

For myself, however, it has had a very significant and extremely positive impact, both on my personal development as well as on my professional career.

Coming back to the purpose and the topic of this article: I'd like to share with you the 10 most important principles of NLP. These can be also considered as generally valid recommendations for successful management, leadership and personal growth, regardless of whether you identify yourself with the original philosophy and concept of NLP or not.

Over the years I have found them to be extremely useful:

The map is not the territory. We do not respond to the world as it is, we act in accordance with our own mental map of it. We have a much better chance of getting what we want if our map is continually revised to take account of the territory. Doing this is much better than trying to bend the world to fit your map.

Mistakes do not exist. We do not criticize any behavior. We should only give feedback. As objectively as possible.

There is no right or wrong model of the world. It all depends on experience, context, point of view, intentions, beliefs, values, culture, etc.

People already have all the resources they need. From our storehouse of memories, thoughts, and sensations we can construct new mental patterning designed to provide the outcomes we want.

People are always making the best choices available to them. We make choices based on experience. More and better experiences allow for more choices.

Underlying every behavior is a positive intention. Look behind what people do to find their positive intentions.

For every form of behavior there is a context in which it is meaningful.

Resistance coming from your partner/client/associate means a lack of flexibility in yourself.

The meaning of your communication is the response you get. People receive information filtered through their mental map of the world.

If what you're doing isn't working, do something else. Do anything else. You'll only get the same results if you do what you've always done.

So, these are my 10 key life leadership principles coming mostly from the NLP arena.

Which are yours?

62. DON'T BE AFRAID OF BEING YOU!

This article of our very popular "Rethink for Success" series will be the final part.
I'm sorry. Sorry, because it was refreshing and exciting to write it, having read the book on which it's based upon, and most importantly, having received several hundreds of comments on the various articles in total.

In My Last Article I presented the following Advices:

(1) Interruption is the Enemy of Productivity

Interruptions break your workday into a series of work moments. You can't get meaningful things done when you're constantly going start, stop, start, stop.

Advice: Your day is under siege by interruptions. It's on you to fight back and create and protect your alone zone. Try to get into the alone zone instead. Getting into that zone takes time and requires avoiding interruptions like instant messaging, phone calls, e-mail, and meetings. Just shut it all up and get to work.

(2) The worst Interruptions of all are Meetings

Often they are not well-planned, not well-conducted, not followed up and as a consequence not productive and effective. Also, they're bloody expensive. Advice: 1) Try avoiding having meetings, if possible. 2) If you really can't avoid having one, then stick to simple rules: set a timer, invite as few people as possible (weak managers would do the contrary), have a clear agenda, start with the objective/issue/problem, discuss real things and real solutions, end with a solution, define precise next steps, allocate responsibilities, implement ASAP, follow up.

Time To Move On With Today's Final Thoughts And Tips

Take a deep Breath

When you rock the boat, there will be waves. After you introduce a new feature, policy, or remove something, knee-jerk reactions will pour in. That's normal. Resist the urge to panic or to make rapid changes in response. Ride out the first rocky week, and things will usually settle down. Let people complain for a while. At the same time, let them know you are listening:
Show them you're aware of what they're saying. Let them know you understand their discontent, but explain that you're going to let it go for a while and see what happens. You'll probably find out that people adjust eventually.

Finally: Sometimes you need to go ahead with a decision you believe in, even if it's unpopular at first.

Sound like you?

What is it with business people trying to sound big? The stiff language, the formal announcements, the artificial friendliness, etc. These managers and companies talk at you, not to you. This mask of professionalism is a joke. We all know this. Yet small companies still try to emulate it. They think sounding big makes them appear bigger and more "professional." But it really just makes them sound ridiculous. There's nothing wrong with sounding your own size.

Don't be afraid of being you. Talk to customers the way you would talk to friends. Explain things as if you were sitting next to them. Avoid jargon or any sort of corporate-speak. Forget rules. Communicate!

63. RE-INVENT YOURSELF

Question: Can you hear the current noises around you? For example, the sound of cars passing by your office or by your home? Are you hearing the voices of colleagues? Can you hear the hum of your laptop or of any other electrical device close to you? How about your heartbeat? Can you hear and feel your heart beating? Just pay attention, focus, and listen for a few moments!

How aware and how self-aware are you as a person and as a leader? What can you learn from the latest findings of the exciting field of neurosciences in order to grow, evolve, and even re-invent yourself? To truly re-invent yourself!

The Power Of Attention

According to neuroscience, by having shifted and having chosen to modify your awareness some seconds ago, you have changed your brain. It'll never be the same again. Unconscious thoughts that run through our mind daily repeatedly create a cascade of chemical reactions that produce not only what we feel but also how we feel.

As human beings, we have the natural ability to focus our awareness on anything. It brings everything to life and makes real what was previously unnoticed and unreal.

The more often we focus on something and think of it, the more real it will become. As such, we can mold and shape the neurological framework of the self by the repeated attention we give to any one thing.

The Continuous Thinking-Feeling-Thinking Loop

The way we think affects our body as well as our life and, as such, also the lives of our colleagues, team members, family, and friends. You might have heard the phrase "Mind over Matter", meaning that there is a strong connection between mind and body. Your every thought produces a biochemical reaction in the brain. The brain then releases chemical signals that are transmitted to the body, where they act as the messengers of the thought. The thoughts that produce the chemicals in the brain allow your body to *feel* exactly the way you were just *thinking*.

So every thought produces a chemical that is matched by a feeling in your body. Essentially, when you think happy, inspiring, or positive thoughts, your brain manufactures chemicals that make you feel joyful, inspired, and uplifted. For example, when you anticipate an experience that is pleasurable, the brain immediately produces a chemical neurotransmitter called dopamine, which turns the brain and body on in anticipation of that experience and causes you to begin to feel excited.

When the body responds to a thought by having a feeling, this initiates a response in the brain which constantly monitors and evaluates the status of the body. In response to that bodily feeling, the brain generates thoughts that produce corresponding chemical messengers; you begin to *think* the way you are *feeling*:

Thinking creates feeling, and the feeling creates thinking, in a continuous cycle.

This loop eventually creates a particular state in the body that determines the general nature of how we feel and behave. We call this a state of being.

You Are a Work In Progress

How your nerve cells are specifically arranged, or neurologically wired, based on what you learn, what you remember, what you experience, what you envision for yourself, what you do, and how you think about yourself, defines you as an individual.

Forget the notion that the brain is static, rigid, and fixed. Instead, your brain cells are continually remolded and reorganized by external stimuli, our thoughts, and experiences. The organization of brain cells that makes up who you are is constantly in flux. You are a work in progress. Let's have a look at the principles behind these insights.

Neuroplasticity and Neurogenesis

Today, neuroscientists argue that the brain changes in response to every experience, thought, and every new thing we learn. This ability – called *plasticity* – allows the brain to reshape, remold, and reorganize itself well into our adult life.

There was a long-held belief that the numbers of neurons we are born with was fixed throughout our lifetime, and that once nerve cells were damaged they could never be replaced. Recent studies, however, suggest that the normal and healthy brain can repair damaged brain cells and even generate new ones. This process is called *neurogenesis*.

Let's throw another myth overboard! Until recently, scientific literature has led us to believe that we were doomed by genetics. We should have resigned ourselves to the proverbial thinking that an old dog can't learn new tricks. Forget about it! Multiple researches have shown that challenges can be overcome, that we can change ourselves, if our will and determination are greater than our circumstances.

That we can break old habits and characteristics by releasing the encoded memories of past experiences that may be dated and that no longer apply to our current conditions.

The Concept of Hebbian Learning

On a neurological level, every thought triggers electrical impulses in our brain and sends electrical currents to different brain areas. This makes nerve cells (neurons) tie up, form neural networks (clusters of neurons), and communicate. And if these brain circuits repeatedly fire, the connections between them become stronger and more enriched. In neuroscience this concept is called Hebbian learning:

Nerve cells that fire together, wire together.

Various researches have proven that even mental rehearsing alone, i.e. non-physical rehearsing of any task, has significant impact on developing neural networks in the brain. Through ongoing mental focusing we repeatedly fire specific neural networks in particular areas of the brain. We wire those nerve cells together in greater measure. As a result, with proper mental effort we can change and grow the brain just by thinking. The reason is that the brain does not know the difference between mental or physical effort.

The Mind – Brain in Action

The brain in action is called mind, triggered by consciousness which is the invisible life essence that animates the brain. Consciousness can be defined as the aspect of self, both aware and unaware, both conscious and subconscious, using the brain to capture the thoughts, and then coalescing them to create the mind. Our conscious awareness is based in the neocortex: The "crown" of our brain, the seat of our free will. This is the conscious thought center of the brain, where everything an individual learns and experiences is recorded, and where information is processed. You have the ability to be consciously aware of yourself, your actions, your thoughts, your behavior, your feelings, your environment, and your mind, and to express thoughts and ideas.

The Neurological Challenge to Change

To change and evolve is not a comfortable process. Why is this?

Neurologically there is a sound answer for that. We choose to remain in the same circumstances because we have become addicted to the resulting emotional states and to the chemicals that arouse that state of being. We choose to live stuck in a particular mindset and attitude, partly because of genetics and partly because a portion of our brain (a portion that has become hardwired by our repeated thoughts and reactions) limits our vision of what's possible.

By now we know: We can change (and thus, evolve) ourselves and our brains, so that we no longer fall into those repetitive, habitual, and often unhealthy reactions that are produced as a result of our genetic inheritance and our past experiences. We can achieve it with will and determination. By making a conscious decision in our neocortex. How does it work in reality?

A Neurological Roadmap to Personal Change and Growth

Most thoughts are ideas that we make up and then come to believe. Believing merely becomes a habit. Repetitive thoughts might determine our lives – think of computer programs running in the background all day. The good news: Since you are the one who operates the programs, you could elect to change or even delete them. Curious how to do it?

Step 1 – Understand the Notion that "Thoughts are real"

Acknowledge that your own thinking process directly impacts your health, your life, your management style, and your state of being. It is your own thinking process that defines you and that – if it happened – has gotten you into trouble. Nothing and no one else is responsible for it, bar you and your thoughts which eventually have become your reality. To get out of it, you need to systematically examine your life. You need to convince yourself of the necessity to become inspired and diligent about wanting to change and/or to better your life.

Step 2 - Fight against the Notion that your thoughts are uncontrollable

This is the next, crucial insight you should arrive at. Choose to be free and to take control of your thinking. You need to consciously – as such activating your neocortex – interrupt habitual negative thought processes before they could produce negative chemical reactions. You need to be determined to control and manage your thoughts and eliminate ways of thinking that do not serve you.

Step 3 – Start questioning old Beliefs

To begin changing attitudes start to observe your habitual thoughts – especially the harmful ones – without responding to them, so that they no longer initiate the automatic chemical responses that produce habitual behaviour. Within all of us, we possess a level of self-awareness, which can observe our thinking. To your surprise, you most likely will find out that most of your persistent, negative inner statements might not be true. In other words, just because you have thought it does not necessarily mean that you have to believe it is true.

Step 4 – Step out of Routines

It takes awareness, attention, and effort to break the cycle of a thinking process that has become unconscious. First, you need to step out of routines so you can look at your life. Through contemplation and self-reflection, you can become aware of your unconscious script. You will need to modify unhealthy patterns – i.e. destroying old, negative neural networks – in your subconscious in order to achieve new, aspired behaviors in your consciousness.

Step 5 – Speculate and explore

In this step it is all about examining and speculating about what kind of people you would like to become. Typically you would ask questions that challenge your most deeply held assumptions about who you are. "What if" questions are vital to this process: What if I stop being a self-centered, egotistic, and superficial manager? What if I no longer worry so much about only achieving quantitative targets? What if I no longer feel personally guilty of having missed certain objectives? What if I begin to tell the truth to myself and to others? Other helpful contemplation and imagination-stimulating techniques are meditation and hypnosis.

Step 6 – Gather Information

Gathering information is another important step on the path to reinvention. Take what you know about yourself and then reformat your thinking to develop new ideas of whom you want to become. Start with ideas from your own life experiences. Dive into books and movies about people you respect and admire.

Piece together some of the merits and viewpoints of these figures along with other qualities you are contemplating, and use all of this as raw material to start building a new representation of how you want to express yourself.

Step 7 – Rehearse every Day

As you are exploring possibilities for a better way of being and leading, you have also learned new modes of thinking. You interrupted the flow of repetitive thoughts that had occupied most of your waking moments. Letting go of these familiar, comfortable habits of thought, you assembled a more evolved concept of whom you could become, replacing an old idea of yourself with a new, greater ideal. To strengthen and enrich the resulting neural networks in your brain, and as such to follow the Hebbian learning concept, you need to constantly rehearse and practice what this new person would like to be. As discussed before, mental – and afterwards real-life practicing – will stimulate the brain to put these new neural circuits in place and to make them an integral part of your evolved personality and character.

At the end of this process, you will be able to summon these new behaviors at will. After all, our thoughts are created from our memories. Our sequential thoughts are linked together to produce our attitudes. The totality of our attitudes creates our beliefs. Our beliefs, when synthesized, make up our perceptions of the world and determine the choices we make, the relationships we have, the creations we manifest, the behaviors we demonstrate, the leadership style we execute, and ultimately, the life we live.

From willing ourselves to change, to changing ourselves at will, the process of evolving our brain, and as such ourselves, is limited only by our imagination.

64. THE SINGLE MOST ESSENTIAL BUILDING BLOCK OF SUCCESS

There is this one question. This one ultimate question. One question we all ask ourselves. Some of us on a more frequent basis. Others only from time to time. Some of us acknowledge doing so. Others pretend they do not care. Still, we all ask it:

What is THE fundamental building block of success?

What is it that makes an organization or a person succeed whilst others fail? What do we need to carry with and in us that enables us to win the race, to achieve something in the best possible way, to go on when others have already given up, to see the big picture and not to sweat the small stuff, to be inspirational and not to become sarcastic and destructive, to grow and to enjoy and not to regret and to complain?

A myriad of excellent books and articles have been written on this exciting topic. I'd like to highlight three of them:

What we can learn from "visionary" Companies

In *Built to Last,* Collins and Porras - based upon a six-year research project – identified the following six timeless fundamentals of the so-called visionary, and as such successful companies: Make the company itself the ultimate product; Build the company around a core ideology; Build a cult-like culture; Homegrow your management; Stimulate growth through big goals (BHAGs); Embrace the "genius of the and."

What we can learn from "Top" Leaders

Lessons from the Top, written by T. Neff and J. Citrin, describes what makes a great business leader. What qualities do the men and women at the top of the world's best-run companies have in common?

The result is a broad and consistent palette of personalities and philosophies that the authors synthesize into 10 common traits (passion, intelligence, communication skill, high energy, controlled ego, inner peace, a defining background, strong family life, positive attitude, and a focus on "doing the right things right") and six core principles (live with integrity, develop a winning strategy, build a great management team, inspire employees, create a flexible organization, and implement relevant systems).

What we can learn from our "Mindset"

In *Mindset,* Stanford University psychologist Carol Dweck explains why it's not just our abilities and talent that bring us success, but whether we approach them with a fixed or growth mindset. She makes clear why praising intelligence and ability doesn't foster self-esteem and lead to accomplishment, but may actually jeopardize success. With the right mindset we can motivate others as well as reach our own professional and personal goals.

The good news, says Dweck, is that mindsets are not set: at any time, you can learn to use a growth mindset to achieve success and happiness. Her overall assertion that rigid thinking benefits no one, least of all yourself, and that a change of mind is always possible, is welcome.

Resilience - The Fundamental Building Block of Success

According to my experience, the primary difference between winners and losers is how they handle setbacks and how they cope with losing. Without a doubt, even the strongest, cleverest, and most competent ones among us stumble from time to time and do not succeed. Some of these challenges might be relatively minor. Others might be much larger in scale.

The real skill, and as such the main building block of success, is getting back on track again after difficult experiences and losses, and not giving up. Instead, bouncing back to the original, or even into a stronger position than before.

In psychology this characteristic is called resilience: "An individual's tendency to cope with stress and adversity. This coping may result in the individual 'bouncing back' to a previous state of normal functioning, or simply not showing negative effects."

Resilience, however, is not a silver bullet which automatically eliminates all problems. It gives people the strength to directly face problems, to overcome adversity and to move on with their lives (e.g. after a personal loss, sickness, nature catastrophe, etc.). People are able to marshal the strength to not just survive, but to prosper.

Ten Ways to become more resilient

There are people who naturally possess certain personality traits that assist them in coping with setbacks and bringing them quickly back on a good track. Today we know that many of these skills can be learned and trained by anyone. As such, they will help you to tackle past or upcoming problems head-on and to become more successful.

Understand that Setbacks are Part of Life

Life is not always cozy and fun. It is also characterized by complexity and challenges. They belong to life like the night is part of the day. Without night there would be no day. Without pain there would be no joy. While we often cannot avoid all the problems, we can choose to stay flexible, open-minded, and determined to succeed.

Be aware of Yourself and the Environment

Resilient people are aware of themselves, the environment, and their own emotional reactions to those around them. They have understood the importance of evaluating the reasons of their feelings by constantly observing themselves. This enables them to take control of the situation and develop various options of behaving and acting.

Believe and know that you are in Control

If you are a resilient person, then you have a so-called Internal *Locus of Control*. You believe that you can control your life, you do not believe that you are defined by external factors which you can't control. Instead, you feel that you have the power to make choices and take actions that will affect your success rate.

Become a Solution Thinker

When a difficult situation arises, resilient people always think of solutions. They act calmly, review holistically the task at hand, and are able to spot possible solutions. If not, they envision them. Next time you encounter a new challenge, make a quick list of some of the potential ways you could solve it. Experiment with different strategies and focus on developing a logical way to work through it.

Believe in Yourself

You are unique. You are beautiful. You have proven already so often in life that you are an achiever. Remind yourself of your strengths and accomplishments. Believe in yourself and become more confident about your own abilities and strengths.

Set Goals and define manageable Milestones

Difficult situations can be extremely daunting. Resilient people are able to view these situations in a realistic way, and then set reasonable goals to deal with the problem. When you find yourself becoming overwhelmed by a situation, take a step back to simply assess what is before you. Brainstorm possible solutions, and then break them down into manageable steps. Be willing to adapt, if necessary. Remain flexible and embrace change.

Stay optimistic

Keeping a hopeful attitude during turbulent times is another key part of resilience. This does not mean ignoring problems at hand in order to focus on positive outcomes. It means understanding that setbacks are transient and that you have the skills and abilities to combat the challenges you face. What you are dealing with may be difficult, but it is important to remain hopeful and positive about a brighter future. View yourself as winner, not as a loser.

Be brave and ask for Help

Resilient people are mature enough to admit that they can't know everything. They are also strong enough to admit if they feel that their energy level is going down and that they need to re-charge their batteries by receiving outside know-how, advice, support, etc. from any potential source of assistance.

In this respect it helps if you have a good social network, if you can exchange with family, friends, or colleagues in order to gain new perspectives and/ or motivation.

Take it easy

Even the best among us will not be able to achieve everything, even if they are properly prepared, have done their homework, can rely on an excellent support network, are super optimistic, and absolutely committed. There are still factors outside of our control. And, most importantly, often things just need time to evolve and develop. Resilient people understand that sometimes the best recipe of success is to step back and to wait. They know that patience often pays off. They do not get stressed out in such situations. Rather, they relax, re-focus on themselves and get ready for possible next steps.

Nurture Yourself

When you're stressed, it can be all too easy to neglect your own needs. Losing your appetite, ignoring exercise, and not getting enough sleep are all common reactions to a crisis situation. Focus on building your self-nurture skills, even when you are troubled. Make time for activities that you enjoy. By taking care of your own needs, you can boost your overall health and resilience and be fully ready to face life's challenges.

65. HOW TO RESIGN WITH STYLE

How do you not just quit, but resign gracefully and with class? Indeed, being courteous and smart about your resignation and departure guarantees that you've given yourself the best possible shot at future success.

Fortunately, there exist some key principles you can follow. We'll talk about them in this blog article.

The most important rule, however, immediately right now: Never quit and leave on bad terms! You owe it to your employer, your colleagues, business partners, and – most importantly – yourself by being and coming across as a professional and mature person.

Evaluate your Situation - Firstly, verify that resigning is the right decision. Don't quit just to make a point. Understand what the pros and cons of your decision would be. Are there things you can do to improve aspects of the job that bug you? Could you get another job in the company? Have you talked with your boss and does she know that you consider resigning (at least, if you feel there are meaningful reasons for you to stay)? Has she had a chance to address your needs and wants?

Check the Legal Aspects - Carefully study any legal documents you signed when joining or working at your current job. Are there any non-compete agreements? Does your contract require a certain period of employment from you, which is the leave notice your company requires, etc.? By the way, you should also be clear about the financial consequences a resignation might have on your life; especially when not having found another job yet.

Choose the right Timing - In a perfect world try to leave when you're on a high note and not when you are burnt out. In a non-perfect world, which is the case most of the time, don't wait with your resignation too long. After you conducted a thorough situation analysis and came to the conclusion it's best for you to leave, then just do it. You have only one life to live!

Do it personally - Don't chicken out. Request a meeting with your boss. Don't send a resignation email or letter. You need to say it face-to-face. Very important: Tell your manager before anyone else. She deserves it.

Hand in a Resignation Letter - Write it in a professional, i.e. non-emotional manner. It should be a short and polite letter stating your intention to leave and by when. Submit your resignation with sufficient lead time before your planned resignation date. Submit it to your direct supervisor (e.g. whilst you personally inform him about your resignation) and with a copy to your HR department.

Be prepared to answer about your Reasons - Be as honest as you can be. Again, in a tactful and respectful manner. It's a good opportunity giving your boss (and others) constructive feedback. Be fair and mention all factors and try to weight them. Whatever reasons you provide, keep your story consistent. Be prepared and open to receive feedback from colleagues, peers, etc. If your company offers formal exit interviews trying to understand the "real" reasons why you're leaving, take part in it. Again, be conscious not to burn any bridges by saying anything negative or insular.

Anticipate the Reaction of your Boss - If you have a good and professional boss, she will tell you how sorry she is to lose you. In case you already have a new job, she should congratulate you. Most importantly, she should respect your decision. If she reacts poorly, then it reflects badly on her, and not on you. Stay professional, explain your reasons and stress that you will support her and the team to make a smooth transition. Don't allow neither your boss nor your team putting any guilt on you.

Anticipate the Reaction of your Company - How has your employer handled employees who resigned in the past? Is your management grateful to employees who provided long notice, or are people who resign usually shown the door immediately? Be prepared for this scenario by clearing personal files and removing personal information and belongings, and getting your workspace organized. Don't take anything with you which belongs to the company.

On the other side, if you are a valuable employee, be prepared that your employer might present you a counter-offer to make you stay. You should have considered in advance if and under which conditions you might accept it. Personally I advise against accepting a counter-offer as experience shows that it still does not work out. Either way, be primed and clear in your answer.

Take with you what you've earned - Ensure to get a fair settlement and compensation for any outstanding salary, commission payments, vacation days, and to get details on all employee benefits, rolling over your pension plan, etc.

Support a smooth Transition - Do your best to complete all open assignments, have any remaining work well documented and organized in a file. And, if time and the situation allows, assist in training your replacement. Some people even offer to be available for a couple of phone calls with their replacement after they leave. This generates considerable goodwill and is often highly appreciated by the replacement and the company. It is a great way for you being remembered as a committed and highly supportive team member.

Respect Confidentiality - Don't talk about your resignation until it's official. Once you've resigned, don't go spreading the word. Do not mention your departure to anyone before you have discussed these details with your boss. Agree with her when and how to communicate it.

Don't be negative - When you're talking about your resignation with co-workers, try to emphasize the positive and talk about how the company has benefited you, even though it's time to move on. Don't brag about your possible new job. Be modest and appreciate what your company and your colleagues are doing. Also, after you've left the company, don't say anything negative about your former employer, manager, or colleagues.

Be committed and hard working until the very last Day - This point usually separates the wheat from the chaff. That's when you can identify the true professionals. Be as loyal as you used to be. Avoid taking a short-timer's attitude and avoid aligning yourself with any discontented co-workers. Sadly, many who resign suddenly seem to have forgotten about all those years when they've worked hard to build their career in and with the company. In a few weeks or days they damage their former – and often also their future – reputation without realizing it. Don't be stupid!

Inform your Colleagues and Business Partners - After having spoken with your boss, be sure to personally tell other managers or key employees with whom you have worked that you have resigned. Thank these persons for having successfully worked with you and having helped you building your career.

Say Goodbye - Before you leave express a heartfelt farewell. Offer your colleagues, boss, and business partners words of gratitude and appreciation. On your last day in the office organize a farewell drink with some food. Your coworkers will remember it. Try to stay in touch with some of them by exchanging contact information with key people. Send a farewell message by email to those whom you can't personally bid farewell.

Ask for a Reference - Ask your boss, colleagues or business partners if they were willing to give you a reference. Inquire if they were available to give a recommendation via email, phone, or professional network sites like LinkedIn.

The way someone leaves a job tells a lot about a person's character. Handle yourself well. In today's highly connected world it's pretty likely that someone knows someone with whom you've worked with. You may also cross paths again in the future. Or, and this also happens from time to time, you might want to be rehired by a former employer.

In a nutshell: Make sure you leave on the best possible terms and don't burn bridges.

66. INTUITION CAN BE LEARNED BY EVERYONE

Currently I'm indulging myself — as I'm spoiling my mind — by reading various books in parallel. Oh boy, how exciting this is! The books are called: Freakonomics, Super Brain, You Can Heal Your Life, Thinking Fast and Slow, The Enlightened Brain, and Look Who's Back.

I'm reading 10-20 pages daily in each book, i.e. I'm more or less enjoying all of them daily. Recommendation: Try reading multiple different books in parallel; you'll also love it! In my blog article today, I'd like to share with you some thoughts and paragraphs of one of them: Thinking Fast and Slow, by Nobel Prize winner Daniel Kahneman.

In his superb book, Kahneman stresses the notion that our minds contain two interactive modes of thinking: System 1 operates quickly and is unconscious, intuitive thought (automatic pilot), while slower System 2 is conscious, rational thinking (effortful system). I'd like to quote the following incredible insightful ideas and findings about intuition:

"The psychologist Gary Klein tells the story of a team of firefighters that entered a house in which the kitchen was on fire. Soon after they started hosing down the kitchen, the commander heard himself shout, 'Let's get out of here!' without realizing why. The floor collapsed almost immediately after the firefighters escaped.

"Only after the fact did the commander realize that the fire had been unusually quiet and that his ears had been unusually hot. Together, these impressions prompted what he called a 'sixth sense of danger.' He had no idea what was wrong, but he knew something was wrong. It turned out that the heart of the fire had not been in the kitchen but in the basement beneath where the men had stood.

"We have all heard such stories of expert intuition: the chess master who walks past a street game and announces 'White mates in three' without stopping, or the physician who makes a complex diagnosis after a single glance at a patient.

Expert intuition strikes us as magical, but it is not. Indeed, each of us performs feats of intuitive expertise many times a days. Most of us are pitch-perfect in detecting anger in the first word of a telephone call, recognize as we enter a room that we were the subject of the conversation, and quickly react to subtle signs that the driver of the car in the next lane is dangerous. Our everyday intuitive abilities are no less marvellous than the striking insights of an experienced firefighter or physician – only more common.

"The psychology of accurate intuition involves no magic. Perhaps the best short statement of it is by the great Herbert Simon, who studied chess masters and showed that after thousands of hours of practice they come to see the pieces on the board differently from the rest of us.

You can feel Simon's impatience with the mythologizing of expert intuition when he writes: 'The situation has provided a cue; this cue has given the expert access to information stored in memory, and the information provides the answer. Intuition is nothing more and nothing less than recognition.'"

67. ARE YOU A GOLD THINKER?

Are you a "Gold" thinker? Ever heard of navy thinking, copper thinking, jade thinking? And, why should you bother anyway?

Just continue reading the following paragraphs please. I promise you will not regret it. Instead I promise you that your curiosity will get triggered. What a start to a fulfilling weekend!

My last question before telling you various insightful news: Ever heard of Clare W Graves? Yep, you are absolutely right: He is the great explorer of human nature, the father of the Gravesian theory.

These are some of his words: "The psychology of the adult human being is an unfolding, ever-emergent process marked by subordination of older behavior systems to newer, higher order systems. The mature person tends to change his psychology continuously as the conditions of his existence change. Each successive stage or level of existence is a state through which people may pass on the way to other states of equilibrium. When a person is centralized in one of the states of equilibrium, he has a psychology which is particular to that state. His emotions, ethics and values, biochemistry, state of neurological activation, learning systems, preference for education, management and psychotherapy are all appropriate to that state."

How cool is that? Our own, individual psychology and nature is not set and stable for all times. On the contrary: It is flexible and adoptable to the person's evolutional state. It is like an ever emergent open system. Graves discovered eight fundamentally different ways of thinking. Eight different ways of making sense of the world. These thinking systems, he argued, would represent eight distinct levels of human existence. The first level being "Autistic Thinking" and the highest level, the eighth level, being "Holistic Thinking."

This research and thinking model is also central to John Robert's beautifully stimulating book "Igniting Inspiration" in which he proposes a new paradigm for creating inspirational communication tailored to the eight different "target groups."

Robert argues that the seventh level, the Gold thinking level (which Graves called "Systemic Thinking"), gives our species the chance of surviving. Gold, he argues, is the first level of thinking that rises above ideology. The gold thinkers' theme for living is "Express self for what the self desires and others need, but never at the expense of others, and in a manner that all life can continue to exist."

This requires, in his opinion, that people express their individuality while still recognizing and respecting the individuality of others.
Gold trusts in life itself and its own intuitive assessment of other people. Gold is not seeking social approval, personal advantage or a sense of absolute truth. Gold is not seeking anything but an opportunity to contribute. Their faith in life is such that, even when they screw up, they always come away with a valuable lesson.

Representative examples are for Robert the so-called "Cultural Creatives," like Barack Obama, Google, David Bohm, Apple, collaborative innovators and the sustainability movement.

68. WOKAHOLISM IS NOT A VIRTUE

Some thoughts of our Re-Think series (based on a great book):

Workaholism is not a Virtue

Our culture celebrates the idea of the workaholic. It's considered a badge of honor to kill yourself over a project. Not only is workaholism unnecessary, it's stupid. Workaholics often don't sleep enough, become more easily aggressive, and create more problems than they solve. Workaholics aren't heroes. They don't save the day, they just use it up. The real hero is already home because she figured out a faster way to get things done.

Enough with Entrepreneurs

Let's retire the term "entrepreneur." It's outdated and loaded with baggage. It smells like a members-only club. Instead, everyone should be encouraged to start their own business. Let's replace this fancy-sounding word with something a bit more down to earth: Let's call them starters. Anyone who creates a new business is a starter.

Chapter 5

DEVELOP!

TOMORROW'S TOP LEADERS enjoy developing and coaching others. They invest a lot of energy and time in building and maintaining personal relationships founded on trust. Trust is a core belief and value of these leaders which they work hard to earn and keep, e.g. by walking their talk, by communicating frequently and openly, by taking a stand (even if it's not a popular one), by empowering others, and by following high ethical standards.

Tomorrow's top leaders are very active team builders and try to lead engaged employees - employees who take pride in their work, who are committed beyond their usual call of duty, who are emotionally connected with their organization, and who want to succeed. They might integrate elements of leadership approaches such as the Fish! philosophy or train their teams on breakthrough techniques such as creativity.

No doubt, top leaders of the future have something else in common which is of paramount importance to their success – a relentless and passionate focus on talent. They are very intentional and uncompromising about this. They have created high-performing organizations consisting of exceptional talents. Tomorrow's top leaders are what I coin HPCDA persons. Individuals who possess a happy, positive, can-do-attitude.

Last but not least, these leaders will develop a significant amount of resources and time to build a holistic talent management approach. Everything done to recruit, retain, develop, reward, and make people perform is their very personal obsession in order to build as many HPCDAs as possible to strengthen and broaden the organization.

69. THE WINNING FORMULA FOR TALENT MANAGEMENT

It most likely sounds familiar to you what a CEO of a well-known software company told me the other day at a fundraising event: "The only factor that really constrains our company's growth is our ability – or should I better say inability - to hire and develop a superior workforce."

Whenever speaking with executives and managers about their main business topics and major challenges, they would very quickly mention that talent-related issues were among their most pressing concerns - one that even keeps them awake at night. During day-time, however, when those executives are absorbed by meetings, by chasing month-end and quarter-end figures, and by trying to please an army of internal and external stakeholders, they often tend to forget what's at the very heart of lasting business success: Identifying exceptionally talented people, developing them, and retaining them.

In one sentence: Talent management matters more than ever!

What is Talent Management?

Talent management is the science of using strategic human resource planning to improve business value and to make it possible for companies and organizations to reach their goals. Everything done to recruit, retain, develop, reward and make people perform forms a part of talent management as well as strategic workforce planning.

Let's see how to build an exceptional talent management strategy, one which takes the objectives and culture of the company into consideration and at the same time is employee-focused.

Key Elements of a successful Talent Management Approach

Business Strategy Fit – Successful talent management approaches need to be tightly linked with the overall business strategy as well as with the company's mission and values. Talent management should assess the skills the organization needs to implement its strategy to attain and keep a unique market position and to plan for recruiting and managing that critical talent.

HR as a Core Function – How much is your organization investing in HR? How much as a percentage of sales do you spend on training & development? Do you have a large enough HR team to spot top talent in a super fluid labor market, to develop and train them, to increase their engagement and commitment?

Do your HR professionals have enough resources to develop themselves? Are they working closely enough with their internal business partners? Do you have rotational assignments for them; are you bringing non-HR people into the function?

Non-HR Managers to breathe and live HR - For top organizations, every manager is a HR leader. When it comes to recruiting and to people development they don't rely only on the HR department. Every manager is crucial and plays a key role. They participate at recruitment events; they search LinkedIn and other business network sites for top talent; they activate and comb through their own networks; they act as internal mentors or internal coaches; they actively attend candidate interview loops; they challenge their HR business partners to come up with new and better ideas, etc.

Performance Development Planning – This is at the heart of any performance management system process. It enables team members and management to identify and specify both the employee's personal goals and the business goals that matter most. To reflect today's complex and very dynamic business environment, goal setting should follow the "SMART Plus" rule, i.e. applying the traditional SMART formula (Specific, Measurable, Achievable, Relevant, Time-based) *plus* regularly review and adjust the goals. An automated talent management system must need to make this simple (not "simplistic") and practical. The accomplishment of agreed and set goals are the reference point for both remuneration and career path planning. They should be discussed in performance appraisal meetings.

Performance Appraisals – These should be conducted periodically, at least every six months. Better quarterly, and most importantly, not being complex in order to assess the employee's performance and progress in an efficient and effective manner. An appraisal should be based on a running record throughout the year. You might also want to include 360 degree feedback to extend and deepen it. If planned and executed properly, then the spirit of these meetings is open-minded, positive, and rewarding for both the employee and the manager.

Training & Development – The starting point are the company's goals on the one side and the employees' performance appraisals on the other side. Crucial skills and competencies gaps which are relevant for the organization's success should be identified. For those targeted, learning activities are needed. To define the true value of any training it is very important to measure the change in the employee's performance that results from a learning activity. Providing meaningful and relevant training and learning opportunities to employees is key to engaging and empowering people.

Career & Succession Management – There should be some form of a career development planning process and system in place. Possible career paths within the department and across the organization need to be outlined. A modern approach also involves the sharing of information about talented employees with other departments, etc. There should be a central database which matches current and future business requirements with individuals' skills, performance, and goals. In addition, your organization needs to be prepared to replace critical roles and competencies at all times. Therefore, you better follow holistic and long-term succession plans throughout your company.

Generate Employee Push – Leading organizations expect from their team members that develop their own career understanding and that are able and willing to design and push forward their own career. Of course, this can only work if the company's culture is prepared for such a transparent approach. For example, by encouraging team members to change their position every two to three years, making all positions open to internal candidates, etc.

Reward Performers – You need to know which team members can, want, and actually do perform. It's crucial to reward them adequately with salary increases, important projects, enlarged responsibilities, rotational assignments, or expressing your organizational commitment and appreciation in other forms. You have to do it at an ongoing basis and in a very sincere way if you do not want to risk losing top talents and top performers.

Talent has always been important. However, in an increasingly complex, global, and knowledge-based world, it's more relevant than ever for the short- and long-term success of any company.

When it comes to talent development you and your organization should better go beyond the usual call of duty, since successful professionals are also relentless talent development managers.

70. WHICH PEOPLE TOP COMPANIES REALLY SEARCH FOR

What type of people do top companies really look for? Which type of persons do top companies love to recruit? Regardless if they are multinational players or small start-ups.

Countless tales and legends surround these questions. Recently, when chatting with business school students at an alumni meeting of my alma mater I was asked how best to enter a leading and admired company. How someone knows whether or not they are suited for a career in such a company. What do they need to know? What skills do they need to have?

If you have also wondered about how to join a great company and how to become and stay successful there, then continue reading and learn all about HPCDA people.

HPCDA People Are Desperately Wanted

No doubt, companies that lead or challenge with speed, growth, and innovation have something in common: a relentless and passionate focus on talent. They are very intentional and uncompromising about this. The executives who lead these companies have created high-performing organizations consisting of exceptional talents.

In this post I will not present an(other) exhaustive list of all the competency and skill requirements of a leader, or a pass and fail guide as to whether you are management material. This article is more fundamental. It's about the personality base one should possess to be able to build upon relevant skills and competencies to become and remain successful. At any company. At any point of time.

Whenever I interview applicants I review how well they might fit with the leadership principles and core competencies which we're living with pride and dedication at our company.

Most people I've seen who over many years have constantly outgrown their peers and, even more importantly, themselves are what I call **HPCDA** *persons:*

Happy – Positive – Can Do Attitude people!

Being Happy

Being happy is an emotional state, an attitude and the result of something that has happened to someone. Happy people have a certain warmth and radiation of contentedness. Happy people and happy candidates follow a pro-active approach in crafting their own lives.

They do not wait until things come along or just happen to them. Instead they go for them and make them happen. They tend to spend a lot of time with family and friends, they are active and anchored in multiple areas of life (sports, culture, charity work, social life), they appreciate what they have, they live in the moment (carpe diem), and they enjoy life. Often, and that makes them so likeable, they are vocally self-critical and strive for a higher purpose in life without attempting to be the center of it.

Being Positive

Happiness sparks positivity. Positive people maintain an optimistic outlook. Even – and especially – in difficult situations. I dub them *Realistic Optimists*. They believe that they make things happen and that they will succeed. They have no doubt about it. Saying that, on the other hand, they perfectly know that in order to be successful they have to plan well, to access all necessary resources, to stay focused and persistent, to evaluate different options, and to execute in excellence.

Having done all of that, i.e. being well prepared and organized, such a state stimulates their confidence and as a result their optimism and maturity level. During the interview, during their career, and during their whole life.

Possessing A Can-Do-Attitude

Top companies are in search of talents who have a strong sense of ownership paired with an incisive bias for action. They love recruiting doers, makers, and shapers. People who think big, who act like they were made to run their own company, who would never take a "no" as a reason to stop and give up. People who always look for solutions (instead of thinking in problems), who rely both on their analytical and creative skills, who take risks, and who are not afraid of failing (as it's part of becoming successful),

People possessing a strong can-do-attitude have also learned how to handle setbacks and how to cope with losing. They have trained themselves to quickly get back on track again after difficult experiences and losses.

In psychology, this characteristic is called resilience: An individual's tendency to cope with stress and adversity. This coping may result in the individual "bouncing back." Highly resilient and successful people consider setbacks as part of their lives; they are brave and still dare to ask for help when needed. They take it easy and have learned to look for themselves and others.

Final Thoughts

Working for a top company can be very exciting and rewarding in many respects. However, reaching a challenging job and position there does not guarantee big bucks, a corner office, a PA, satisfaction, and fulfillment. The hours are often long, complexity is high, demands are countless, and the pressure rises with increased responsibilities and expectations.

Trying to work for a leading organization certainly is a great opportunity to build one's career and future. Saying that, it might not be the right thing for everyone – it is often based on a person's character, aspirations, and expectations. And that's good, as we are all different and unique. Diversity is key. There are countless other opportunities out there for every one of us. We should look for the right working culture and environment. One which suits us.

HPCDA people have what it takes to be successful at any great organization in today's quickly changing and demanding world. They are in high demand since they excel in many areas of business and life. Based on such an attitude they can acquire multiple skills to succeed and to assist others in succeeding.

71. ELEVEN LESSONS TO LEARN FROM THE GERMAN FOOTBALL TEAM

On July 13, 2014 Germany won against Argentina in a tight match the football World Cup for the fourth time. Oh my god, what a match it was! An excellent fight between two great teams.

Congratulations to both teams for having demonstrated in a superb manner the beauty, dramaturgy, emotions, techniques, and excitement of football!

Germany has been in a world cup final eight times. The last time we (yes, I have this strong feeling of belonging…) won the Cup was in 1990. And now, after 24 years, we have done it again. With the triumph at Rio's Maracana stadium, Germany wrote history as the first ever European side to win a World Cup on Latin American soil.

Already before the final the Mannschaft had stunned the world by defeating Brazil in the semi-finals 7 – 1 through showing superior tactics, movement, discipline, will, and focus. Something which most likely we'll never witness again when such two teams meet at another World Cup. It still leaves many speechless.

With all the euphoria let's not forget that only ten years ago, the Mannschaft was at rock bottom. We had exited Euro 2004 without any victory. The team and the nation was unclear about its football future. Besides, even now the team is far from being perfect which is very good. In addition, there are multiple other teams playing great football. Which is even better.

Still, one might ask, what made the Germans become a winning team after all those years? What can football teams and even businesses learn from the German victories and the underlying patterns at this year's World Cup? Below I've listed the most important lessons that, in my opinion, can be learned from the German football team (I'm very curious hearing about yours afterwards).

Create A Strong Vision And Set A Common Goal

The German team wanted to win this year's World Cup. They've been clear and very passionate about what they wanted to accomplish: Becoming world champions! However, the objective was not only about winning, it was also about making a whole nation proud by playing excellent football and representing our country in the best possible way. To realize this goal, the coach and team defined how many goals they wanted to score per match, how many goals scored against them should be the acceptable maximum, what each player would need to deliver, how exactly they would attack and defend, etc.

Embrace Innovation

This was mostly introduced to the German national team by former head coach Jürgen Klinsman in the years 2004 to 2006. It was Klinsi – with the support of his assistant Joachim "Jogi" Löw - who established an atmosphere open towards innovation and the willingness to play a more offensive, dynamic, and position changing style of football. He showed a lot of confidence, conviction, and resilience when he was attacked by many so-called experts who challenged his modern and forward-looking leadership approach.

Train Hard. Never Give Up

The Mannschaft's success is strongly built on intensive, meticulous training, relentless preparation, discipline, and its fighting spirit. The team never quit. They fought until the last second of each match. They understood that a tournament is a series of matches. One after another. And you need to win most of them to become world champion (all of them in the K.O. rounds). Famous German player and coach Sepp Herberger once said: "After the match, is before the match." These words are engrained in every German football player's DNA. We're not the most gifted team. But we're one of the hardest working ones. The Mannschaft plays with mind, heart, and soul.

Stay Flexible

Although the German team is often compared with a well-oiled machine, it's much more than that. Sure, the team follows a precise strategy and specific tactics. However, that's only the basis to build upon something much more sophisticated: A floating format that allows players to quickly change their positions within the team if needed. Strategy and discipline are considered as enablers of flexibility to establish an open-play system which makes it difficult for the other team to anticipate possible moves. It works best if it can be imposed on the other team by very fast and bold moves. Have the courage to change your plan if it does not work. Löw has changed the starting eleven and kept changing the tactics.

Breed Diversity

In the past 10 to 15 years Germany formed a multicultural national football team which includes highly gifted immigrant players from Poland, Africa, Turkey, and many more countries. Besides having players with a foreign background in our team, German coaches learned a lot from foreign teams which have developed new styles (e.g. Tiki-Taka) and transferred effective concepts, e.g. from Spain, France, Portugal, Holland, and Brazil to Germany. They were adapted to our needs and blended with existing techniques and expertise to form a unique and authentic style.

Balance Experience And New Talents

Jogi Löw has been the head coach for 8 years, although he has not won any major title. He's a coach who has well apprehended the importance of building high performance teams of experienced and talented junior team members. Miroslav Klose, for example, is 35 years old and has played in 3 previous World Cups.

André Schürrle, at the age of 23, has already scored 3 goals during the tournament. There are even 2 players in the team who have just turned 20.

Form A Unified Team

Germany are all about the team. Although there are many talented players in the team, there is no stand-out star like Ronaldo, Neymar, or Messi. Instead, it consists of very talented players who collaborate effectively as a team. The Mannschaft's ethics follow our idea that individuals sacrifice themselves for the sake of the team. Every young German football player knows that you have a responsibility to your team. In this sense a football team sees themselves as a true squad. To sustain and further strengthen this spirit and attitude, Löw spends most of his time teaching, developing, and inspiring the Mannschaft. He conducts regular working sessions and meetings, he keenly creates a strong team spirit, and he addresses and resolves conflicts directly and within the team. The team, therefore, behaves in the same way.

Practice Long-Term Talent Development

Over the past 15 years we have intensively studied and further developed the football academies and schooling systems of Ajax Amsterdam, Manchester United, and FC Barcelona. The German Football Association (Deutscher Fussball-Bund, DFB) is a vivid advocate of long-term career planning and development. There is a high commitment to nurture talent. It all starts with the training of our youth teams, their ongoing coaching, subsequent selection, fast-tracking in our football academies, and integration with various local, regional, and national leagues. Often, the players gain very valuable experience by playing in the highly competitive leagues in England, Spain, or Italy. The sense of common identity and the strong bonds among the players sustain a close network.

Never Lose Focus

Every single player, the management team and the whole staff know exactly what their goal is and how they can get there. When being on their mission they would not get side-tracked and would never stop before the objective is achieved. It's like following a program that assists staying free from interferences in critical situations. The team moves on and constantly tries to improve. It keeps attacking. It plays limitlessly and aims to seize all opportunities.

Execute In Excellence

Successes of the past mean nothing in sports or football (same in business, by the way). With every new match it starts all over again. This is especially true in a tournament like the World Cup. The objective of a great football team is to score goals as quickly as possible while preventing the opponent doing the same. Afterwards you will have to adjust your approach to either a more attacking or defensive posture. Either way you need to ruthlessly build your strategic advantage and try to define the rules of the game by executing in excellence your strategy and actions.

Stay Approachable, Humble, And Have Fun

Closely and regularly interact with teams of your broader organization as well as with other internal and external stakeholders. The German team has always been open for interviews, has tried to spend as much time as possible with locals and has often exchanged with their fans and the public. That earned them respect and support. Something which in return they felt themselves and which strengthened their self-confidence and sense of being part of a higher purpose.

Even after they won against the host country, native support in Brazil has been behind the Mannschaft because they stayed authentic, sincerely comforted the Brazilian team, and stayed humble. They did the same after today's final with the Argentinian team. They showed respect and displayed honest joy in being a part of an amazing sport, tournament, and team. They did not allow anyone to put an unreasonable high level of pressure on them. It would have destroyed their passion and fun.

FIFA's football circus has already left town and will re-unite in Russia in 2018. By then we'll see many changes, new playing strategies, promising teams and talents.

I hope that your favorite team will have kept and/or found its mojo by then and might become the next football world champion. I'll keep my fingers crossed.

72. ATTENTION - THE FISH PHILOSOPHY IS STILL ALIVE!

Yep, there still is the legendary sign saying, "Caution: Low Flying Fish" at a world famous boot at the Pike Place Fish Market in Seattle, Washington.

People from all over the world, myself included, go there to buy fresh salmon and to watch the show when the Pike's Fishmongers toss fish around, expertly wrap it, give it to customers, and the audience cheers. The energy is contagious. The employees love working there and obviously enjoy creating unforgettable shopping experiences.

The fish guys inspired what has become the renowned FiSH! Philosophy. Although developed 15 years ago by John Christensen and his company Chart House Learning, it is more relevant than ever today.

It's centered around the following four ideas: *choosing one's attitude, playing at work, make someone's day, and being present.* It is commonly used to improve what is referred to as the "culture" of an organization.

Four simple and highly effective Parts

Be There

Pay attention. Take care of the person in front of you. Employees who are engaged in their work only focus on the job at hand. They are there to do good work and they are there for someone else. Right now, in that very precise moment.

Play

Have fun at work. Don't take yourself, others, and your work too seriously. Some humor can't hurt. The more you play, the more creative and bold you become. And the more you enjoy yourself, the more you make others enjoy the experience, too.

Make Their Day

Engage your customers. Make them part of the fun. Surprise them. Appreciate them. Excite them. There are unlimited creative and inexpensive ways to brighten someone's day. Start with a smile. Making their day will make yours, too.

Choose Your Attitude

That's the central element of FiSH! You can choose your attitude the same way you choose the pants you decide to wear every morning. Bad things happen all the time. That's reality. However, how we react to them is our own choice. Are you going to laugh or shout about something bad? You can make it better or worse. You gotta choose.

Final Thoughts

Swinging salmon has been elevated to one of the first and most successful global motivation philosophies. The FiSH! ideology and technique makes individuals alert and active in the workplace. As such, it's an ever popular topic. One of the most crucial elements of successful companies and teams.

73. WINNING WITH ENGAGED TEAMS

When I caught up with some old friends from university for a drink the other day we had a highly stimulating (and emotional) discussion about the Super

Bowl... and team engagement: Its significant relevance for organizations, its drivers, and its impact on employee and business performance.

There was a strong agreement that in most organizations – and although people spend a substantial part of their lives working – a vast majority of teams and employees are not engaged at all. And as a result such organizations do not perform at their best.

Let me share with you the main points we touched upon.

The Challenge (and the Opportunity) is huge

According to Gallup's State of the Global Workplace study (covers 142 countries), only 13% of employees worldwide are engaged at work. In other words, only about one in eight workers are psychologically committed to their jobs and likely to be making positive contributions to their organizations.

The bulk of employees worldwide - 63% - are "not engaged," meaning they lack motivation and are less likely to invest discretionary effort in organizational goals or outcomes. And 24% are "actively disengaged," indicating they are unhappy and unproductive at work and liable to spread negativity to coworkers.

What is Employee Engagement and why does it matter?

Employee engagement describes the relationship between an organization and its employees. An "engaged employee" is one who is fully involved in and enthusiastic about his or her work. An engaged employee takes pride in his work, is committed, usually exceeds duty's call, and often takes positive action to strengthen the organization's reputation and interests. He's emotionally connected with the organization and wants it to succeed.

Numerous studies show that an organization with "high" employee engagement – and all else being equal – is likely to outperform those with "low" employee engagement. For example, Gallup's research notes that work units in the top 25% of their engagement database have considerably higher productivity and profitability ratings combined with less turnover and absenteeism.

It is well known that employee engagement and positive business outcomes are correlated. The question often was, however, if engagement would truly lead to better outcomes. Or would successful companies just have more engaged employees (chicken-and-egg-problem)? Or does it work in both directions?

A recent study published in the Journal of Occupational and Organizational Psychology shows that organizational commitment has more impact on business performance than vice versa.

Building a Culture of Employee Engagement

Let's have a look at how leaders can raise the bar on team and employee engagement to increase workplace engagement and to achieve better results:

Understand What Your Employees Think And Want

Use employee engagement surveys or company discussion boards to get an understanding about what your team members think and where the bottlenecks are. Fix a maximum of 2-3 issues at the same time. Focus on "low hanging fruits," which simultaneously make a big difference.

Build A Trust Culture

Trust is the base of employee engagement. Innovation, transparency, cooperation, etc. depend on trust. Treat each employee as a valuable member of your team, give them the autonomy to make decisions, keep promises, and be reliable.

Practice Open Communication

Employees should understand what the company's mission and objectives are and what they're expected to achieve. Listen to employee feedback and encourage it. Get the teams in on strategies and explain to them their roles. Then they will view themselves as an important, and crucial piece of the puzzle.

Provide Clear Career Paths

You should support career path development. For example by providing career development and training plans, coaching, shadowing, mentoring, etc. Assist employees to develop professional goals and to learn from colleagues. Show commitment to growth at all levels, and not just senior leaders. Make sure that there exist regular feedback loops between peers, and very importantly, between employee and boss.

Demonstrate Appreciation For Contributions

Take employee engagement seriously by thanking employees, whether that's through monetary rewards, company awards, promotion, strategic project responsibilities, or other incentives.

Inspire Employees Beyond Turnover

People want to work for great and visionary companies, companies led by managers and leaders who look beyond facts and figures. Employees are motivated by inspirational and honest leadership. You could (and should) engage in social interactions outside work like community support projects. This is a splendid way to strengthen relationships and adds an enjoyable social dimension to work. By the way, no harm at all, if you try making your organization a fun place to work!

Communicate Your Employee Focus

If you are a fun and cool place to work for then make sure people know about it. A strong employment brand that offers clarity on the organization culture and its values ensures that the right people are attracted.

Closing Remarks

Engaged employees are emotionally involved, have a higher identity level with their organization, work longer in the same company, are more productive and strive to deliver better customer service. Both usually lead to better customer satisfaction and create unique customer experiences. As a result customer loyalty goes up. The bottom line are higher sales and better profit margins.

74. HOW TO BECOME A MASTER OF CREATIVITY - ATTITUDE!

Masters of creativity are masters of creativity because they know "how" to think and not necessarily "what" to think. If you really want to become more creative, you can become (significantly) more creative both in your personal and professional life by adopting a specific mindset and applying particular strategies and techniques.

You might not become the next Albert Einstein, but you certainly will become (much) more creative than someone who does not know the contents and methods described in this article. You could even become a master of creativity yourself, if you were willing to work hard enough on yourself.

Aoccdrnig to rsecherach at Cmabrdige Uinvrevtisy, it deosn't mttaer in waht oredr the ltteres in a wrod are, the olny ipmrotnat tihng is taht the frist and lsat ltteer be at the rghtit pclae.

By nature we have the talent to make sense out of these mashed letters as we have the gift to immediately see essential aspects as the human mind looks at things in a holistic manner. The only problem is that as adults we have unlearned and forgotten how to look at things differently and how to think like a child. Pablo Picasso once said: "Every child is an artist. The problem is how to remain an artist once we grow up." In other words: How can we re-learn how to think like a child?

I'm very fortunate having worked in the past for some of the most creative and innovative companies in the world. What I've learned and practiced there in respect of increasing my own as well as others' creativity I'd like to share with you in this article, which was also inspired by the superb books of Michael Michalko: Thinkertoys and Cracking Creativity.

FIRSTLY, you need to follow a specific *creative thinking attitude* as the basis for any sustainable improvements. It consists of three levels (topic of this article). Afterwards, in a SECOND STEP, you can train your creativity skills by *utilizing different techniques and exercises* (topic of my next article when I'll present you my favorite creative techniques and practical exercises).

Level 1 - Acquire and cultivate a creative Thinking Pattern

Thinking without Limits and Limitations

Consider yourself as an active subject rather than a passive objective. Meaning, you're the acting and driving force. You can do, influence, and change whatever you'd like to do. If you believe it, you become this person and the world around you will follow. If, however, you were to limit yourself by believing that you can't do it, then your environment would make you adjust to it. Often, the difference between a creative and non-creative person is that the creative person believes that she is creative and the less creative person believes he's not. A very powerful technique is to repeat to yourself or to write down what psychologists call positive affirmations.

Acting like a creative Person

Once you'll have started visualizing yourself as a creative person by having applied positive self-affirmations, for example, you'll start believing that it's true. And with such a belief it will become true, since naturally you'll focus more on related occasions and own behaviors which will lead to good personal experiences and successes. And success will breed more success. You will begin to be more creative than you would have thought possible at the start. Once you assume with deep and honest intentions the role of a certain person, and if you constantly cultivate her behavior, her modus operandi, her movements and motions, her way to approach topics, eventually you'll become very similar to this person.

Being joyful and positive

Creative people are what I refer to as HPCDA persons, i.e. happy-positive-can-do-attitude persons. They think in terms such as "what is," "how to do it differently," and "what else can be done" instead of "what it isn't," "how not to do it," or "what else is not working."" They would look for various options and would create their own solutions and reality.

Deciding to be happy

If you are negative, you can't be creative. Your thoughts affect your attitude, which in turn affects your behavior. To close the circle, in return your behavior determines your attitude. The good news is that you can change your thoughts yourself with will, energy, and focus. A successful technique is to trigger positive emotions by thinking for some moments about joyful and pleasant social occasions (e.g. gathering with family and friends, great parties, etc.). Another effective technique is to model and mimic happy people: their faces, voices, postures, etc. Unconsciously we'll become happier ourselves.

Strengthening your Resilience Level

Getting back on track again after difficult experiences and losses, not giving up, and instead bouncing back to the original, or even into a stronger position than before, is what we call Resilience. There are people who naturally possess certain personality traits that assist them with coping with setbacks and bringing them quickly back on a good track. Today we know that many of these skills can be learned by anyone.

As such they will help you to tackle past or upcoming problems head-on and to become more creative and more successful. Resilient people never give up until they find a solution.

Being determined to learn

Creativity is like many other personal characteristics - not something which is genetically determined (although many people still believe so and/or would like to think so in order to make things easier for themselves by pretending that they are not able doing and learning it anyway). In reality, there is no secret to creativity. You do not need a magic wand to acquire creative skills. Instead, a strong will and determination is needed to embark on the creativity adventure by wanting to study specific strategies and techniques.

Never accepting the first best Solution

Some people will never become a master of creativity based on one simple reason: As soon as they have found an answer or a solution, they stop thinking and searching. They're happy gobbling down fast food and not willing to wait for a nice steak, lobster, and a salad in a nice restaurant. They are satisfied with the first best solution that comes along. Statistically, however, there is no reason that the first answer is the best one.

Often, as we all know, it would have been better to continue our search, to generate more options, to evaluate them a little bit longer, and then make a more profound and a more creative decision.

Asking, asking, and asking

Have you ever observed a master of creativity? One thing he would do most of the time is ask questions, questions, and more questions. Often, he would write something in his little black book or in his iPad. Like a child he would ignore the irritated faces of grown-ups who have been asked tons of questions by their little ones – or who have in their opinion been asked even too many questions. Instead, the creative mind would indulge himself in satisfying his lust for curiosity by throwing questions at them. It does not take creative genius to ask questions. It takes courage, curiosity, persistency, patience, and sometimes charm, sensitivity, and politeness. Plus, the willingness to listen. An attitude unfortunately not many people are used to practicing any longer in today's hectic times.

Collecting, storing and organizing Information

Masters of creativity love collecting tons of information. Quantity is king for them (rather than quality to start with). They believe that the more information they acquire, the more perspectives they can obtain, and the higher the probability will be to generate proper solutions. Afterwards they store collected information and ideas in order to browse through them over and over again. They judge the value of all information pieces and ideas by having set-up criteria which suit the specific problem (e.g. which criteria are essential, desirable, optional, etc.?). Often they will add their own experience and intuition to judge and rank the ideas. Finally, they will discuss their ideas with other people to get feedback, to refine them, and to further develop them.

Level 2 – Understand the Benefit of changing Perspectives

In the next step you should embrace the concept of altering your perspective when looking at a problem. You can vastly expand your possibilities until you realize something new once you'll have changed your point of view. That's why highly creative people love playing around with changing perspectives like little kids love pretending to be their favorite comic book heroes, sports idols, etc. Masters of creativity constantly try to find new perspectives on an issue by restructuring and re-modelling it in some way. If they are lost or stuck, they would look at it in different ways until they come up with one or various solutions. The more times you express a problem in a different way, the more likely it is that you'll arrive at a new and deeper perspective.

That's how you remodel and reconstruct your Problem:

- Switch perspectives; the more often and more diverse, the better
- Question everything, don't accept anything
- Chunk up (generalize the problem at hand by making it more abstract) and also chunk down (go deeper and deeper to the root of the issue by making it more specific)
- Change the sentences and the words of the problem statement by rephrasing it. Use whatever words you'd like to. There's no right and wrong
- Separate the parts from the whole. Fractionize the problem. Slice it apart piece by piece. Move from one detail to another until you arrive at its origin. Examine all the factors and relationships that may influence the issue

A highly effective Exercise to change Perspectives:

Let's assume you have a great new business idea; you're just at the beginning of wanting to evaluate it and you're not sure about how to undertake next steps to further review it. That's a classic example of trying to look at your idea using multiple perspectives:

- In the first step, write down your business idea from your point of view. Formulate the idea, its USP, etc.

- In the second step, write it from the perspective of potential customers. How would they describe it? What's important to them? What would they possibly like and not like?

- In the third step, formulate the idea from the perspective of other key stakeholders, e.g. possible business partners, employees, investors, relevant organizations, etc.

- Finally, synthesize all perspectives into one all-encompassing idea statement

Having written multiple versions from different perspectives on the same idea, you will have generated different perspectives with different possibilities.

Highly creative people would even go a step further: They would imagine that they represent the problem, that they are the problem or at least part of it (which sometimes is the case in reality). It's what I call being "in the eye of the storm." By trying to see the problem from its own perspective they somehow merge with the problem. As a consequence they often find truly innovative and creative solutions. Imagine you are the product manager at a sporting goods company and you were asked to develop and market the new ball for NFL's next Super Bowl championship game.

Following the "in the eye of the storm" approach you might ask yourself the following questions:

- How would I feel being the new ball?
- How would I like to fly through the air?
- What would I like to achieve?
- How would others like to play with me?
- How could I score best?

Level 3 – Aspire to be a Non-Expert

Many people strive to become an expert of some sort. They often believe that it's needed to get recognition and to build their credibility upon. Masters of creativity, however, have realized that the more expert you become, the more difficult it is to stay open-minded and to produce truly creative ideas.

In this third, and most challenging level towards becoming a creative mind, it's all about not specializing your thinking and not becoming an expert. Experts often put borders and imaginative walls around their thinking. They have a tendency to build their searching strategies on what they know best. As a result they often arrive at repetitive (and useless) conclusions. They fail to investigate the whole issue by only looking at (known) parts of it.

On the contrary, non-experts approach issues with a non-polluted mind. Since they lack expertise – and as such are borderless thinkers – they can pull any problem apart, look at every single piece of it, and often come forward with creative and innovative ideas.

Non-experts get inspired by other non-experts who themselves are full of ideas and imagination. They would talk to and interview people from totally different backgrounds, i.e. being far away from their problem at hand.

75. HOW TO BECOME A MASTER OF CREATIVITY: WORK IT!

In my last blog article about creativity I argued that *Masters of Creativity* are masters of creativity because they know "how" to think and not necessarily "what" to think. If you really want to become more creative, you can do so.

FIRSTLY, you need to follow a specific creative thinking pattern as the basis for any sustainable improvements. It consists of three levels (topic of my previous article on creativity). SECONDLY, you need to work hard to improve your mental creativity skills by utilizing specific techniques and exercises (topic of this article).

In the past two decades I've worked for and with some of the most creative and innovative companies in the world. What I've learned and practiced there in respect to increasing creativity levels - i.e. my favorite creativity techniques - I'd like to share with you in this article. In addition, I strongly suggest reading the superb books Thinkertoys, Cracking Creativity, and Game Storming.

Fundamental Techniques of Creativity

Feed Your Brain

Creative thinkers love to "eat" new information, data, stories, etc. The more, the better. Which book(s) do you currently read? Many creative people would read 4-6 books at the same time and every month up to 3-4 (some even more): Fiction, non-fiction, biographies. Whatever. And by the way, no need to read every book from A to Z. Some tips on reading:

- Start by reading what is of most interest to you, i.e. reading selectively

- As you move on, broaden up your reading spectrum

- Take notes: work with your books, i.e. write marginal notes, comments, etc. into them

- Read magazines on different subjects: Personally, I love sports magazines, fashion and lifestyle titles, magazines on music, automobiles, and traveling

- Read every day 2-3 different newspapers: Scan through all main sections like politics, economy, business, sports, health, etc. They'll provide the latest news which might act as a mental platform for additional, interlinked ideas, which might pop-up during the course of the day

- Read biographies and How-to-books: You'll find a wealth of new and unique ideas in them

- Reflect while you read: Think about possible parallels between your issue at hand and what you read

- Read and study an excellent book about Speed Reading

Besides reading, of course, you can and should absorb new information and stimuli also by other means: Go to the movies, theater, opera (there's nothing like Puccini for me), listen to music, eat different food, travel to various places, discover new locations in the place you live, attend as many seminars, workshops, business conferences, and lectures as you can.

Change Your Daily Routine

You might know some of them: They do the things the way they've always done them. They put the things always exactly in its place. All is nice and clean, lovely folded and beautifully labeled. Those are *Masters of Routine*, rarely *Masters of Creativity*.

Instead, you should consciously try to change at least some of your monthly, weekly, and daily habits. Why not shop at a different supermarket next time? Why not take another route home from work? Why not listen to another radio station tomorrow? Why not change restaurants? Why not try a new drink? Why not brush your teeth with the other arm? Why not take a bath instead of a shower, etc., etc. Got it?

Store and Archive New Information

Some people keep a shoe box, a file folder, a little black book, most recently a tablet, to collect and store data, news, quotes, ads, pictures, designs, ideas, questions, cartoons, etc. There is no right or wrong method of storing and archiving. It should only fit your way of thinking, searching, and reviewing. However, either way, you should possess at least one "idea collector and stimulator" somewhere. And as you'll review your collected "material" periodically, you will stimulate your imagination. You will start to search out connections between collected data and your present situation or challenge.

Warming-Up Techniques of Creativity

The following exercises are well suited to allow group members to open up their minds, to relax, and to start getting creative. The first two of them I like running at the beginning of workshops and seminars.

Symbol

Participants are asked to draw, display, present, etc. a symbol that represents their view about the task and/or problem. It could be anything: a simple drawing, a sketch, a comedy, an advertisement, the moon, a can of Coke, etc. Afterwards, each participant would explain her symbol and what it means to her and how it explains the situation.

Baby Pictures

Before this exercise you would need to ask participants to bring with them a picture of her or himself as a baby. Post them on the wall without labels. Ask everyone to match the pictures with the participants. This is a great icebreaker which guarantees that people unclench, have a good laugh, and start to be eager for more. Alternatively, you could also ask participants to bring a photo of their favorite animal, etc. with them.

Walking in Somebody Else's Shoes

In this striking exercise, people will find out what it's really like to be someone in a different position. One day, for example, I went with some marketing and product managers to work during a day in a drugstore to better understand how consumers were buying our products. We were posing as shop assistants and helped various customers during the entire sales process, recording specific behaviors, questions, particular sentences, etc. Back at our offices, we exchanged experiences, discussed our observations, and talked about ways of improving product packaging and product information material to simplify the buying process for consumers.

Advanced Techniques of Creativity

Reverse Assumptions

Reversing your assumptions broadens your thinking. Many creative thinkers get their most original ideas when they challenge and reverse the obvious. This is how to do it:

- State your challenge
- List your assumptions
- Challenge your (fundamental) assumptions
- Reverse each assumption by writing down the opposite of each one
- Record different viewpoints that might be useful
- Evaluate how to accomplish each reversal. List as many ideas as you can

Deconstruct your Problem

To stimulate new ideas, you should determine and list the different attributes of a given task. Then work on one attribute at a time. Focus on each attribute, describe it, and try to change and improve it. The more you'll do that, the more likely you are to think more flexibly, more fluently and to discover alternative ideas and solutions.

Imagine Different Scenarios of the Future

That's a classic, yet still a very powerful exercise. When you force yourself to think about the future you're automatically thinking about what is happening now and what has already happened in the past. The combination of these three inter-linked time dimensions is extremely powerful. Let's assume that in a first step you have stated a particular business decision that has to be taken. In a next step, you would need to identify the forces that have an impact on the decision (political, economic, social, technological and so on). Based on such an analysis you would build three to four future scenarios incorporating all information available. By varying the different input factors (forces), by changing them and/or combining them, you would develop the scenarios into stories. In a final step, you would need to search for business opportunities within each scenario and for new ideas.

Creativity Boosting Techniques

Analogies

Analogies are comparisons of the similar features of two things. Think of submarines and bats... What do they have in common? Yes! The sonar system, i.e. both emit sounds that bounce off objects in their way. In other words: By making analogical connections between two or more things, you can quickly come up with a number of unconventional ideas. The greater the "distance" between challenge and example (i.e. the stranger the analogy), the better your chance for innovative thoughts.

Janusian Thinking

Also called Paradoxical Thinking, it involves creating a paradox or contradiction by conceiving two opposing ideas as being currently true. Examples are "Winning by losing" or "Disagreeing and committing" or "Setting realistic yet challenging goals." The contradiction and its meanings will generate new insights and ideas.

The Anti-Problem

This (group) exercise helps when people are stuck and are at their wit's end. Meaning the team is already working on a problem, but they're running out of ideas. By asking them to identify ways to solve the problem opposite to their current problem, it becomes easier to see where a solution might be. Let's assume that the problem is to increase sales; in this instance the team would brainstorm ways to get customers to avoid buying products. The more extreme the problem's opposite, the better.

The Disney Technique

No doubt, this is one of the best ones. From the master of creativity himself. An offspring of his vivid imagination to produce truly fantastic(al) ideas. To generate and evaluate new ideas, Walt Disney would have shifted his perspective three times by playing three separate and distinct roles: the dreamer (generating as many fantasies as possible), the realist (working the fantasies into practical ideas), and the critic (poking holes into the idea).

Applying above-listed techniques, tips, and exercises – together with a required mind shift (please see my previous article on creativity) – will help you to open your mind and to discover the beautiful world of creative and innovative solutions. It takes conviction, practice, and hard work. The good news, however, is that everyone can learn it. Everyone can become a master of creativity!

76. THE ART OF BREEDING INTRAPRENEURS

We're living in a world of unreason and high complexity, determined by supersonic speed and omnipresent competitive challenges. What is needed more than ever is a free market *entrepreneurship* within organizations, headed by exceptional individuals willing and capable of leading an organization's business as it were their very own. This would boost both the company's growth and the individuals' creativity, productivity, and satisfaction level.

Companies like 3M, Google, DreamWorks and Facebook have in common that they've embraced the idea of allowing their employees to become inside-entrepreneurs, so-called *intrapreneurs,* and capitalized on new business ideas. These intrapreneurs take new initiatives without being asked to do so. Hence, they focus on innovation and creativity, and transform an idea into a profitable venture, while operating within the organizational environment.

How to create intrapreneurs and what do they look like? Let's first have a look at the required breeding ground to attract and develop existing and potential intrapreneurs. Afterwards we'll review the key characteristics of a successful intrapreneur.

Characteristics of an Intrapreneurial Organization

An Environment for Taking and Rewarding Risks

There needs to exist an environment where employees are willing to take risks. The risk tests and increases intrapreneurial conviction and drive. It binds the corporation in an implied contract not to stop the intrapreneur for any reason other than poor performance.

The Rewards of Success Must Be Shared

Pre-agreed and transparent criteria between the organization and the employee about how to split the rewards of the project are key.

Appropriate Funding

Funding a project must be comprehensive and timely so that the intrapreneur doesn't have to keep running to the board to ask for support for his initiative.

Financial Incentives

The intrapreneur should have the opportunity to build up capital, etc. The successful intrapreneur should earn in addition to his cash bonus complete control of a definite amount of R&D funds, marketing funds, etc. – funds which he would have a completely free hand in investing on behalf of the corporation in his future projects.

Granting Independence

The corporation must let the employee-entrepreneur who has earned his independence, have it. The intrapreneur should be almost untouchable by corporate discipline, thereby allowing the independence of spirit the system was designed to create, to flourish. If he doesn't, he rapidly loses his motivation and competency to run the project.

Characteristics of a Successful Intrapreneur

Turning Opportunities and Ideas into Sellable Products

A successful intrapreneur knows how to spot opportunities, to conduct proper market research, to design products, to acquire needed resources and to organize the business.

Behavioral Aspects

He is naturally inclined to take initiative. He's creative and results-focused. Equipped with a very high resilience level, an extraordinary strong ownership attitude, and driven fierce by bias for action.

Social responsibility

He would ensure that there is an active compliance with the spirit of the law, ethical standards and international norms. If not, even the most promising project will not be sustainable and supported.

Networking

Both entrepreneur and intrapreneur must master this skill, the only difference being that in the intrapreneur's environment, "office politics" play a bigger part. Bottom-line in the corporate environment: you can't get somewhere without a powerful support network.

Organization and Process Management

A successful intrapreneur prefers working with a small number of very good people on key projects – the smaller the better. There should exist a short, straightforward document (up to 3 pages) and/or a simple drawing explaining the project. Required reports should be kept to a minimum, but important work must be recorded thoroughly.

Intrapreneurship is key to successful growth and inspiring change, and offers an excellent opportunity to develop the leadership skills and career perspectives of an organization's top employees.

77. HOW YOU SUCCEED AT EVERY JOB INTERVIEW!

I've been intending to write this blog article for a long time. One reason being that over the years I've seen many candidates who have been very good in job interviews and who got the job they applied for. At the same time, I've also met and interviewed multiple people who did not make it, i.e. who did not get the job in the end.

A second reason is that I've arrived at the conclusion that those who did not get the job might not have necessarily been less capable of fulfilling the role than the ones who got it. Often, they were just not able to communicate or to deliver what was expected from them in the crucial moments of the interviews. Why?

Below I've listed 11 interview principles in order to be successful at your next job interview and to get the job. Some of them you know. Some of them you might have forgotten about. And others, you might not have considered yet.

First, make the "Fit Test": Be absolutely clear with yourself that the role and company you'd like to apply for really fits with your skills, career track, professional and personal objectives, beliefs and experiences. Conversely, check if you might match with the culture and needs of the company you'd like to join. If there's no perceived fit already in this very first step, do not move on and do not waste yours nor anyone else's time by wanting to conduct an interview. Only if you know about, believe in, and feel about such a "fit," you can and you will possess - and as such radiate - a 100% motivation level towards the new role and the new company. And that's what it takes to succeed. Every good interviewer will realize very quickly how passionate you are about her company and how excited you are about the offered position.

Research the Target Company: To be well prepared is half the victory. Still, I'm surprised at how many candidates arrive at interviews, even for senior level positions, without having studied our values, mission statement, leadership principles, products, etc. Why would they have not reviewed our Internet site or not read our latest press releases? Why would they have no idea about what our competitors are doing, what our current and future challenges could look like? Don't get me wrong: It's not about being or becoming an expert about the company and role in question, it's more about having acquired a sound knowledge before the interview to be able to formulate your own, knowledge-based opinion which you'll need to express at the interview(s).

Know Your interviewer(s): Today, it's easier than ever to collect information about your interviewers. Spend 40-50 minutes on Google, LinkedIn, etc. and be clear about titles, roles, careers, etc. of all the people who'll interview you. If not, ask the person who's responsible of organizing the interviews and/or with whom you're in contact to provide you some background information about the people you'll meet. Addressing interviewers with their names and implicitly (or explicitly without exaggerating) showing them that you know (a little bit) about their careers, achievements, etc. is not only polite, but also shows respect and interest. You'd be surprised to hear how negatively it is perceived by many interviewers if you do not know these things. And, on the contrary, how flattered many of them will be, if you are aware of some facts and successes of their professional lives. It's like in real life!

Arrive On-Time and Professionally Focused: It's never a good start if a candidate arrives late based on her or his own fault (e.g. having taken the wrong train, not having taken into consideration heavy traffic at a certain time of the day, not having found the right entrance of the building, etc.). In case of doubt and if you live further away from the venue of the interview, you should consider arriving the night before and staying at a hotel. Good employers will not only reimburse related expenses, but will also appreciate your thoughtfulness and professional attitude. It goes without saying that a fresh mind is a much more focused and a much more confident one. And conducting a successful interview is closely linked with possessing and displaying a healthy level of self-confidence.

Adjust Your Appearance, Style and Tone: Imagine you're wearing a short-sleeved shirt, no tie and a casual pair of trousers when meeting for a job interview with one of the country's top insurance companies? Or, imagine – for the fun of it - you took out your favourite Brioni business suit for an interview with the founder and CEO of the hottest Internet start-up around (who is one of those Harvard drop-outs and who is absolutely not interested in any status symbols). Beyond these more obvious things like appearance and clothing, you should also pay attention to the vocabulary you're using. You should utilize words and expressions which are common in the target company, its markets, and its industry.

Also, when applying for a position as a trademark lawyer, for example, you might want to come across as serious and thoughtful, whereas when going for a sales or marketing position, you need to be prepared to show characteristics of vitality, drive, and stamina (among others). Finally, be aware of the first impression you convey when meeting the interviewer(s) for the very first time. It counts and it will be remembered – consciously and sub-consciously – for a long time.

If you were someone who smiled a lot, if you had a firm hand-shake, a pleasant and clear voice and if you had looked for eye-contact during the moment of making the acquaintance with the interviewer, you will be remembered. It's important to remark that the process of "creating the first impression" often starts even before the interview; e.g. when you meet the receptionist, an assistant of the interviewer, or someone offering you a drink, etc.

The "influence" of such indirect stakeholders is stronger in smaller companies you're applying with.

Know Yourself and The Value You Might be Adding: Before entering any interview loop you would need to make sure that you know your strengths and your areas for improvement. Be realistic and honest about them. Be able to list and explain them by using concrete and short examples and explaining what you mean when you state things like "you are restless and always want to storm ahead by seizing all identified opportunities." You should have a clear understanding about what is looked for at your target company and the job you're applying for. You would need to be able to explain why you believe that you're the one "deserving" the job by generating most value to the company. In the short- and in the long-run.

Anticipate Questions and Possible Areas of Concern: Good interviewers will try to imagine you being in the role they're interviewing for. How do they do it? Pretty easy! They try to match your characteristics, your experiences, examples given by you, the way you talk and behave with their culture, their business and management principles, and with the requirements of the role they're recruiting for. Example: If you apply for head of accounting with a company which prides itself of breeding managers who think big and long-term, you would need to come up with one or two examples when you proved being not only numbers- and detail-focused in your past career, but when you also acted as a visionary and a holistic thinker. Write down possible questions, formulate answers, and even rehearse at least some of them with a friend, confidant, etc. Saying that, stay flexible during the interview and do not try to reply with pre-thought and pre-formulated answers to all questions.

Stay Open-Minded, Positive, And Always Engaged: Regardless of how the interview goes – or how you think it goes (as these two are often dissimilar) – your composure should display interest, engagement, and friendly open-mindedness. Consider the interview as an opportunity to learn and grow. Regardless of the outcome. Whilst paying attention and asking questions, of course, you are allowed to smile. By the way, please do not forget about your body language. Communication often is not only about what is said, but mostly about how something is expressed – verbally and non-verbally.

In this respect, you should not think of the interview as a form of one-way-communication, i.e. only you explaining and answering questions. Don't miss the opportunity to establish a dialogue on a level playing field with the interviewer. If you are curious about something, if you did not understand a statement, if you'd like to receive more explanations on an important topic, then you need to ask your questions. It's what every experienced interviewer would expect from you: You only get out of the interview what you are willing to put into it.

Be Yourself And Do Not Pretend: You should not try being everyone's darling or pretending to be someone else just to get the job. Neither in life in general, nor in an interview in particular. Sure, as mentioned previously, you would need to adapt and show that you understood what the company, the role, and the interview is all about. Saying that, never give your core values and convictions up easily. Be ready to enter a good and constructively-led discussion with different point of views. It's important to recognize, however, to remain tolerant, open-minded and to discuss in an empathic and fact-based manner, leaving out emotions, politics, and any extreme thoughts and positions. One final comment: Even after having done a thorough analysis of the company and the role you're interested in, it might turn out in the interview that some fundamental aspects are not in-line with your expectations or, and this also might happen, the position itself does not seem to fit any longer. Once – and after good reflection – this becomes obvious to you then you should not go for the role nor accept it, if it were offered. Most likely it would be a painful experience and it would not work out.

Finish The Interview In Style: The last part of a good interview usually starts with the candidate asking some smart final questions. For example, questions about the overall strategy of the company, about what the interviewer considers as being crucial for being successful on the job (if not covered beforehand), or – if clarification is needed – about the role and its specifics. Either way, you should have written down a list of both more generic and more specific questions. Three to four are sufficient (if there were still more on your list towards the end of the interview, this might indicate that you were not actively asking enough questions in the interview until this point in time). It is crucial you don't ask your questions in a manner that could be perceived as feeling obligated to have to ask them.

Instead they should be presented in an engaging way and you should be prepared to follow-up on answers which might not be precise enough, or not having the depth you would have expected. You need to take care that all of your relevant questions will be answered during the interview. That's your right and obligation towards yourself. If not, you might lack important information and you might join the wrong company. At the very end of the interview ask about next steps of the interview process. Personally, I also appreciate candidates who ask for a very first assessment at the end of the interview. Most importantly, however, and regardless of how the interview went, it is crucial to express your gratitude for the interview and to politely say goodbye.

Two More Things Many Candidates Forget About

First, there is nothing wrong with sending the interviewers – or at least to the principal interviewer – a short mail after the interview thanking them again for the interviews and mentioning that you would be looking forward to receiving their answer. This should be done, however, in a short and non-hyperbolized manner.

Second, and this is very relevant in case you had not gotten the job, you should contact the company to ask for personal and detailed feedback of your interview and about your performance. This is very helpful in order to improve for the next interview. In addition, you should reflect on the previous interview(s) and go through it step by step, reviewing what went well and not so well. Focus on the improvement areas and write down specific action steps on how to better prepare and execute in the future.

78. JUST 3 RULES FOR SUCCESS - DREAM OR REALITY?

The cover page of the April 2013 edition of the Harvard Business Review certainly drew my attention. Why?

Its lead article, which was very prominently featured on the cover, is called "3 Rules for Success." The authors, Michael Raynor and Mumtaz Ahmed, promise to have studied 25,453 companies over 44 years.

Well, the two gentlemen – since they were not so happy about the lack of scientifically credible data about what factors lead to superior business performance – decided to go ahead and undertake a statistical study of thousands of companies, and eventually identified several hundred among them which they qualified as truly exceptional.

Since the ground-breaking book of "Built to last – Successful Habits of visionary Companies" by Jim Collins and Jerry Porras, not many books and articles came close to their findings and the respective title of their study and book. Drawing upon a six-year research project at the Stanford University Graduate School of Business, Collins and Porras took eighteen outstanding and long-lasting companies and studied each in direct comparison to one of its top competitors. By the way, I would call that scientific and high-quality data.

Raynor and Ahmed, after their monumental quest for reliable data on organizational excellence, finally discovered that great companies were consistent with just three seemingly elementary rules:

1. **Better before cheaper** – in other words, compete on differentiators other than price.

2. **Revenue before cost** – that is, prioritize increasing revenue over reducing costs.

3. **There are no other rules** – so change anything you must to follow rules 1 and 2.

They further noted that with few exceptions, the best companies behave as though these principles guide them through all their important decisions, from acquisitions to diversification to resource allocation to pricing.

Questions

Do we really believe that the success of exceptional companies can be distilled down to 3 factors only? In this case, and being precise, even to only 2? Or, is the outcome, conclusion, and – most importantly – the communication of their study just the result of the latest aspiration of almost every management author to put findings, learning, and recommendations in expressions and titles which foremost draw interest and sound simple?

On the other side, do we think that it might be possible that we have this tendency to make things too complicated, and that in reality, however, it could be so easy and straight-forward?

Chapter 6

IMPROVE & IINNOVATE!

Tomorrow's top leaders are data-driven, process-focused, and permanently in a disruptive mindset.

First and foremost, they are paranoid about the fact that speed matters more than ever in a quickly changing world. Although it's not a new finding that market leading companies need to be fast and agile, they have found ways to realize the concept of speed. They have implemented very powerful techniques such as *Only meet to make decisions, Leave Politics to politicians, Plus one minus two, Learn from successes, Stop presentation cat walks*, etc.

Secondly, they apply new business metrics. Of course, revenue, cost, market shares, profit, etc. remain important. However, they put them into a new context and link them with a modified weighting and time frame. In addition, they will complement them with criteria such as customer engagement, customer excitement, number of disruptive ideas, and the capability to invent new successful business models.

Thirdly, they know that in hyper-competitive times, competition is not just on brand and technological innovation, but also – and foremost – on the business model. Disruption is king for them on purpose, and even if it were to mean being a self-disruptor! They have the ability and willingness to envisage where their customers, industry, and adjacent industries might evolve to in five to ten years. They strive to realize a first mover advantage and to dominate their market. They perceive themselves as active subjects rather than passive objects by imagining the impossible. One of their preferred options is to set up a business model where so-called switching costs can be integrated, i.e.

how they can keep their customers within their eco-system by offering them distinctive, cost-saving, and value-adding advantages.

Finally, exceptional future leaders have soaked up the two fundamental rules of customer obession: (1) They make sure that their organizations do everything to make customers happy, and (2) they put customers first, then brand, then revenue, and then profit.

79. HOW TO BUILD A DISRUPTIVE ORGANIZATION

In today's hyper-competitive times, competition is not just on brand, product, and technological innovation. It's also – and foremost - on the business model.

Surprised? Disturbed? This might be possible, since you're not clear about what your business model and strategy really is, aren't you?

Unfortunately, it is something you will not be able to afford any longer. Neither content nor technology is king... it's disruption! Disruption can be caused by the introduction of products, services, or business models either in new or existing markets in such a way as to shake up the industry and eventually to oust established players.

Remember fixed line telephones? Then remember cellular phones? And afterwards? Not just a next generation of technology. Instead, a new business model: smartphones on the one side, and Skype on the other! And tomorrow... Smart watches?

Well, it's pretty obvious that the old guard, and almost every industry, are being challenged by a countless number of cutting-edge business models. Think Nespresso for example. I like my daily cup of its Lungo Leggero from their famous refill capsules. Good quality plus excellent marketing (thanks also to George Clooney and John Malkovich). That's all? By far not! What Nespresso actually achieved was to lock in consumers (including myself) by having created a new business model which generates repetitive sales and profits.

Three basic strategic Options for Disruptors

In general there are three options for a disruptive and visionary game changer.

Firstly, you develop your own disruptive business model (explained in more detail below). Second option, you develop further the existing business model in the current industry or in adjacent industries and categories. Nestlé, for example, is transferring Nespresso into the tea category with its Special.T concept.

Third option, you take an existing business model - let's say something like the Nespresso business model - and apply it to (completely) different industries. Meaning to deploy existing and proven principles elsewhere. Apple, Google, Samsung & Co. have been doing it already by developing their own Nespresso-like ecosystems.

Designing a disruptive Organization

If you'd like to apply a more entrepreneurial perspective to business modelling and to become someone who wants to create tomorrow's businesses, to find new and innovative ways to excite customers, and to replace outdated paradigms and strategies, then the following principles might be useful:

1. **Understand the business you are in, evaluate, and specify your current business model.** It's an obvious starting point. However, not many would be in a position to give a truly succinct answer to it.

2. **Evaluate where your customers, your industry and adjacent industries/categories might evolve to in 5 – 10 years.** Will your existing business model and associated products and technology still fit? Will a process of continuous innovation be sufficient to satisfy and to excite customers?

3. **Decide to be a disruptor - even a self-disruptor - and take the lead.** Also, and especially, in the new age of disruption, there is nothing as powerful as the traditional first-mover advantage.

4. **Broaden your scope and imagine the impossible.** Look far outside of your current thinking patterns and industry boarders. Future revolutions and competition most likely will also come from what you currently might consider unrelated products, services, and industries. Think without Limits and Limitations. Consider yourself as an active subject rather than a passive objective.

5. **Ensure that the new concept is simple, accurate, holistic, easily understood by all stakeholders**, and at the same time doesn't oversimplify relevant aspects. Be specific about future customer segments (including their volatile needs and wants), your value offer (including pricing and promotions), your customer interactions, your partnerships and alliances (including virtual networks), your distribution and communication channels, and your required key resources.

6. **Try to set up a business model where you can integrate so-called switching cost**, i.e. think about how you can keep your customers within your system by offering them distinctive, cost saving, and value-adding advantages.

7. **Replace cautiousness by bold and strategic consideration.** Disruptive strategies will be driven by speed and audacity. In the short-term they might even cannibalize (part of) the existing business and/or decrease profits, since starting margins might be lower. Apply a long-term perspective and resist short-term focused investors and management.

8. **Apply new business metrics.** Put revenue, cost, market shares, and profit into a new context and link them with a modified weighting and time frame. Of course, they will remain important. No doubt. They will need to be complemented, however, by criteria such as customer engagement, customer excitement, number of disruptive ideas, and the capability and ability to invent new business models.

9. **Establish an entrepreneurial spirit in your organization.** An environment should prevail where employees are willing to take risks. This would increase entrepreneurial conviction and drive. It also binds the corporation in an implied contract not to stop the internal disruptor for any reason other than poor performance.

Final Thoughts

Could Johannes Gutenberg, the father of modern book printing, have foreseen the advent of e-books? Most likely not! However, his publishing successors could have been better prepared if they had applied what Peter Drucker once pointed out: "Eventually every theory of the business becomes obsolete and then invalid."

How else could Apple have transformed from a PC maker to the world's leading music seller?

Although disruption and innovation are similar, disruption goes at least one step further by changing how markets behave, how consumers and customers think, and how we live our lives.

Today's industries and organizations are being transformed with unprecedented scale and speed. Often it's not an evolution any longer, but more of a revolution. Time has come for executives, business owners, academics, and employees to understand the impact and in parallel to successfully address the challenges and opportunities of those new business models.

80. 14 RULES TO BECOME THE WORLD'S FASTEST COMPANY

Regardless if your organization is small or big, online or offline, national or international, selling products or services, there is one thing that is of highest relevance to all of them:

SPEED!!!

Speed matters more than ever in a quickly changing world. Companies that want to survive need to become fast and agile.

This is not a new finding. Still, many managers and business leaders do not know how to make it happen and how to realize the concept of speed.

Based on my experience there are 14 simple rules to become the world's fastest company:

Meet To Make Decisions

Meetings steal time and leave less time to get things done. Therefore: No meetings longer than one hour. No meetings with more than 8 participants. No meetings without agenda and minutes. No meetings with more than 5 topics.

Stop The Presentation Cat Walks

Keep presentations to 15 minutes max. Only one presentation in one meeting. Presentations should be fast and to the point. Not more than 6-8 slides. Avoid the multimedia overkill. Put one idea per slide and do not clutter the slides. Presentations are meant to convince and to reach or to get a decision; and not to impress.

Use One Pagers

If you can't explain it simply, you don't understand it well enough (A. Einstein). In other words: You need to be able to boil down your idea on a single page. State the context, issue and task at hand, objectives/strategy/action plan, resources needed, timelines and milestones.

Don't Breed Workaholics

Work hard and smart. It's a tough world. Sadly some companies go too far by considering it a badge of honor to live the idea of the workaholic. In reality, however, workaholics often are over-worked, cranky and tend to create more problems than they solve. Be a real hero in assisting your teams to get things done quicker and plan for sufficient downtime.

Leave Politics To The Politicians

Keep office gossip, politics, and drama to a minimum. Cultivate an open, transparent, and personal atmosphere. Address tensions quickly and directly. Don't tolerate bullies and backstabbers.

Plus One Minus Two

Whenever you introduce something new (e.g. a new product, service offer, process, KPI, etc.) take out two existing, similar ones. It's like following a healthy diet and working out at the same time. Be careful not to become too lean at a certain point, however. You need sufficient energy to outrun your competitors.

Focus On The Future

It's unbelievable how many companies spend a huge chunk of time analyzing and re-analyzing past results. They have developed all sorts of metrics and often get lost within their cemetery of data. They've missed to define a limited set of relevant and simple KPIs.

Specify Clear Goals

Set SMART goals: Specific (target a specific area), Measurable (quantify indicators of progress), Assignable (define who will do it), Realistic (state what results can realistically be achieved), Time-bound (specify when the results can be achieved).

Transparent And Need-Based Communication

Say what you mean. People can handle it, if respectfully expressed. In times of information-overload keep the volume of circulating data and information to a minimum. Make sure that it is clear when to communicate what to whom. And not everything to everyone at any time.

Dump Non-Successful Products And Concepts

If a plan, etc. does not work although you've put lots of resources into it, change it. If it's still not successful, reduce your efforts and throw less at the problem. More people and more money just makes the problem bigger. Don't hesitate in making the tough calls.

Don't Penalize Failures

Making mistakes is a major element of the learning process. Fact. If employees know that failure will be punished, they will stay on the safe side and will not trial new things. Fact. As a result, the organization will be less creative and innovative. Again, fact.

Learn From Successes

At the end of the day, there is only so much you can learn from mistakes and failures. You just learn what you should not do. Learning from successes is about building upon what worked.

Be Clear About Priorities

Fewer, bigger, better. No more than 3 major initiatives/projects should be handled by any organization at the same time. In parallel, decide and empower the teams to stop non-priority tasks.

Stop Talking And Get Started

Ideas are plentiful and the perfect solution does not exist. What really matters is what you do at the end. Thoughts, words, and plans without actions do not generate sales. The success formula: decide, begin, move on, and execute in excellence. Groom a spirit of action.

81. THE BEST NICHE STRATEGIES TO COMPETE WITH THE GOLIATHS

Yes, still nowadays niche companies, SMEs, and underdogs can successfully compete with the big corporations in this world. The David versus Goliath legend is alive!

At the same time, however, the Goliaths of today's fierce and highly dynamic business world (think Google, Wal-Mart, Apple, Coca-Cola, Procter & Gamble, etc.) have become much more innovative, agile, and aware of the need to enter attractive niches.

This article provides proven strategies and concrete action steps for smaller market players. And, believe it or not, you'll learn what a halitophobic is and how one niche company has built its amazing success story on the concept of halitophobia!

So, embark on our journey of learning and discovering new and stimulating insights!

Mass Business versus Niche Business Approach

While a mass business is about selling to everyone, niche companies focus on a specific segment of consumers (defined, for example, by gender, age, ethnic background, occupation, hobbies, etc.). Musicians, pet owners, wine lovers or teenagers are examples of broadly-defined niches. Once you have defined a niche, you are likely to find many other niches within it (e.g. people who die for Spanish Rioja red wines, small dog owners, piano players, etc.).

You can tailor everything from product features, distribution channels to advertising to that specific market by emphasizing the features and the benefits that appeal to that particular segment. If done well, a niche business requires less money. It also provides the benefit of flying under the radar of your competitors (might be helpful while you establish your niche). Starting in the niche doesn't necessarily mean you have to stay there.

The Internet has made the niche business model easier than ever before. However, the strategy of selling smaller quantities of a wider range of goods and earn higher margins (the so-called long-term phenomenon as described by Malcolm Gladwell in his widely acclaimed book The Tipping Point) will not help smaller companies to escape the fierce mass market competition, unless they have found their unique market sweet spots, i.e. offering products and services to target consumers who are willing to pay above-average prices.

The successful Niche Market Strategy

Based on my experience there are 12 business principles that allow any organization to pursue a successful niche market strategy.

Customer Analysis And Target Marketing

After having analyzed possible target markets and segments make sure that your products and/or services are truly different from existing options and that they meet target consumers' wants and needs in a (much) better way. Try to find out if possible offerings are currently missing, if consumers complain about existing offers, or if you have the know-how and skills to combine various sub-offers into a combined, holistic one.

Innovation

Clearly, niche businesses are not immune to competition, especially from larger market players with huge resources and bigger economies of scale. As such, successful niche businesses will respond with innovation and higher-quality products, rather than cost-cutting exercises.

Proto Labs is a leading online and technology-enabled quick-turn manufacturer of custom parts for prototyping and short-run production. They market their high-quality products to product developers worldwide, who are under increasing pressure to bring their finished products to market faster than ever before. They utilize computer numerical control, or CNC, machining, injection molding, and 3D printing to manufacture custom parts for their customers. You can very easily get a quote on their homepage.

Quality Obsession

The Morgan Motor Company is the last remaining family owned and independent British car manufacturer. Morgan cars are famous for their unique blend of charisma, quality materials, craftsmanship and performance. All Morgan cars are coach built. Prospective owners are encouraged to visit the factory to watch their cars being built, and to choose from a wide range of paint and leather colors as well as optional extras that will stamp their mark on the car and make it their own. Today, the factory produces approximately 1,300 cars per year with 177 employees.

First Class Customer Service

Brands are built through every single experience customers have with them. Especially for niche brands, it is crucial to deliver top-notch customer service.

Ever heard of the world's friendliest restaurant Tim's Place in Albuquerque, New Mexico? They not only serve great food, but also personal hugs to any patron who desires being hugged (the hug counter on their homepage shows currently 42,730 hugs given). Tim and his team strongly believe that people have a huge appetite for being genuinely welcomed, connected with, touched, appreciated, and honestly cared for. Who wouldn't agree?

Cost Control

Financial funds are needed to come up with innovations. As a consequence cost management is very important. Most notably, your R&D, production, distribution, marketing, and HR costs should be kept under control.

In regards of R&D and production costs there are multiple ways to maintain economies of scale, even when producing a relatively wide number of narrowly targeted products. Like in the automobile industry, you could establish a generic product platform. Most golf companies offer their clubs and drivers with hundreds of different combinations (multiple shafts, heads, and angles). They have standardized the interconnections whilst being able to configure the various components based on the players' needs. Bringing distribution costs down is also key. Therefore, think about options such as e-commerce, shared offline distribution (e.g. by using agents and other third party providers), producing only based on order, flexible inventory allocation, etc.

An additional option is to implement an Enterprise Resource Planning (ERP) system. This helps to create a solid infrastructure while maintaining continuous operations. Exact Globe Next and NetSuite are two sample vendors specifically designed for small and niche businesses.

Outsourcing And Crowdsourcing

Time and internal resources might be scarce when running a niche and/ or a small business. Consequently, you might want to outsource non-value adding tasks such as bookkeeping, payroll, IT, and administrative support. Potentially also SEO, social marketing, design, PR, and communications. The best freelance marketplaces and outsourcing portals are oDesk (my favorite!), Freelancer, and elance. Crowdfunding, or collaborative funding via the web, is an excellent option, especially for SMEs to get access to fresh capital and investors. The leading sites are Crowdfunder (for any business), Indiegogo (broad focus, high flexibility), and Kickstarter (especially for creative projects).

Agility And Calculated Risk Taking

Niche players must be agile enough to take advantage of gaps in the market and to adapt. That said, being agile doesn't have to mean being inconsistent. Businesses that are not flexible enough run the risk of becoming outwitted by quicker-moving competitors.

For example, in Germany, successful mid-sized and small companies, often being pure niche players, are grouped into the "German Mittelstand." Leading "German Mittelstand" companies – often also referred to as Hidden Champions - are considered as the most innovative SMEs globally, and are two to three times more profitable than large enterprises. One highly innovative and agile company is Enercon. They have more than 30% of all patents worldwide in wind power generation. And they have exceptional ideas, such as the "E-ship" which uses so called Flettner-rotors to harness the power of the wind.

Networking And Collaboration

Building strong networks beyond the niche company's boundaries should be part of its DNA - regular exchanges with other companies, universities, research centers, etc. in order to share certain cost-intensive projects, to learn from each other, and to assist each other. The Meiko Network Japan, a company dedicated to providing best learning and teaching offers to various targeted customer segments, works closely with specific universities, organizations, franchisees, etc. to leverage know-how and resources.

Personal Branding And Digital Marketing

Traditional marketing campaigns are not suitable for most niche markets; besides, they're too expensive and often not precise enough. Instead, use word-of-mouth marketing (e.g. via niche spokespersons and opinion leaders), consumer-generated content (generated via a consumer forum, moderation of a LinkedIn group, etc.), social, and digital marketing.

Also Be Personal: When in 1989 Annie Withey co-founded Annie's Homegrown, Inc. she put her own address and phone number on each box to encourage customers to connect with her. She wanted to show by example that a successful business could also be socially responsible.

Inspirational examples of excellent digital niche market campaigns are Orabrush (now learn about halitophobia!) and Method which has done an excellent job of taking on global megabrand rivals like Johnson and Johnson with a comparatively tiny budget. A fun blog helps, but the real winners are an interesting newsletter and an entertaining YouTube channel as part of the "People Against Dirty" campaign.

Employee Engagement

Everyone gets a slice of the cake at independent London-based The 7Stars media agency. All departments get together for a weekly Wednesday morning meeting, and staff members take turns in the "company bake-off" to produce a homemade treat afterwards.

Bureaucracy is banned. Nobody has to fill in a holiday form and days off are never counted. The holiday policy is to take as much time off as every employee needs. There's a tenner for the employee whose brainwave is voted idea of the week; the bake-off was one winner, and others have included two annual "donation days" to work for a good cause. Everyone has a personal training plan and financial support for work-related qualifications. Employees keep in good health with free gym membership, monthly visits from a masseuse, and breakfast and fresh fruit provided every day.

Focus And Consistency

That's certainly something smaller companies can and must learn from leading big companies. The biggies are crystal clear about what they are (and what they aren't) and what they want to achieve. They are rigid and consistent. Usually, they think about the long-run and show backbone when facing resistance on their way to achieve their set targets. They would not give-in easily. Instead they would try harder.

Leadership

Managing and leading niche companies is a true entrepreneurial challenge. No doubt! Nowhere else leaders need to encompass two main, and opposed characteristics: *Thinking Big* and *Being Obsessed with Details*. Thinking Big means they need to create and communicate a bold direction that inspires results. They think differently, look around corners for new and alternative ways, and they love serving customers. At the same time they are able to operate on all levels. They enjoy deep diving into small details and audit frequently. No task is beneath them.

82. HELP! I AM CUSTOMER OBSESSED!

Oops! Wait a sec! Actually, I'm not insane. I do not need help, since constantly delivering state-of-the-art customer experience is the single greatest success factor of any organization, isn't it? ABSOLUTELY!

It even goes to the very heart of everything you do. And it shows what you and your company truly stand for. Your customers see, smell, taste, hear, feel, and know that better than you ever will.

So, YOU better help your customers!

This article outlines 5 steps that enable every organization to understand and holistically embrace the art of delighting customers in order to be successful in the long-run, to help your customers, to make them happy, and ultimately to become what I call "*Customer Obsessed:*"

Step 1: Soak up the two fundamental Rules of Customer Obsession

1. Make sure that you do everything to make your customers happy!

2. Customers first, then brand, then revenue, then profit!

Step 2: Embrace the 13 Key Principles of Customer Obsession

Offer A Good And Reliable Product/Service: That's the basis. If not, no need to worry about good customer service.

Put Customer-Focused Thinking At The Center Of Everything: Customer service is not a department, it's an attitude and everybody's job!

Worship Your Customer: He's the boss. He's paying the salaries. Ask, listen, and learn from them. Treat people like you want to be treated.

Top Management Commitment and Engagement: Serving the customer starts at the top. It's the CEO's most important job. A good leader needs to be a good servant.

Train, Excite, And Empower Your Staff: All of them and not only the customer service reps. Treat your employees well, and they will treat your customers well!

Act As Quickly And As Reliably As Possible: Based on demanding and precise KPIs be super-fast, polite, honest, transparent, and concise. Be pro-active!

Use Leading Technology: Customers define the systems and IT structure required to provide outstanding customer service. It is not a cost. It's a critical success factor.

Radiate A Yes-Attitude And Be A Communication Master: Smile whenever you interact with the customer. Treat every customer as an individual. Be respectful!

Constantly Inform And Educate Your Customers: Let your customers know about how your products and services work and how you operate and how to contact you.

Under-promise And Over-Deliver: As a general rule you should provide more than what customers expect to get. Ultimately try to delight your customers.

Never Stop Learning And Improving: Think ahead. Anticipate future needs, wants, and possible problems. Get constant feedback. It's all about the long-term!

Leverage Excellent Customer Service: Don't be too shy talking about the good you do in an indirect way, e.g. by using the power of communities or brand advocates.

Don't Forget The Financials: A world-class customer experience is also about business, hard facts, and figures. All such initiatives need to be self-funding over time.

Step 3: Learn from the World's most Customer-obsessed Companies

The world's leading customer-oriented organizations deliver outstanding customer service and customer experience to become and stay leaders in their industries. They understand that it's not only about customer service and customer experience any longer. For them it's all about customer obsession! They constantly embrace it, live it, and celebrate it.

The following companies constantly rank among the most customer-centric ones of any reputable survey and industry benchmark study. They belong to my personal Customer Obsession Hall of Fame: Disney, Amazon, Ritz-Carlton, Singapore Airlines, Nordstrom, USAA, Harrods, and another handful of world-class companies. To fully understand how they do it, continue to read here.

Step 4: Read the best Books on how to make Customers happy

If you are serious about significantly improving your customer experience, then you need to get your hands more dirty and your mind stimulated. I suggest you read the following 3 books:

Delivering Happines: A Path to Profits, Passion, and Purpose, by *Tony Hsieh*

Zappos CEO Tony Hsieh shares the different lessons he has learned in business and life, from starting a worm farm to running a pizza business; through LinkExchange, Zappos, and more.

Tony shows how a very different kind of corporate culture is a powerful model for achieving success — and how by concentrating on the happiness of those around you, you can dramatically increase your own and be successful at the same time.

Getting Naked: A Business Fable about Shedding the Three Fears That Sabotage Client Loyalty, by *Patrick Lencioni*

Lencioni preaches a business model that may seem antithetical to many, which he calls "getting naked": being unafraid to show vulnerability, admit ignorance, and ask the dumb questions when dealing with clients. His central argument is that by focusing on sales, rather than communication, organizations lose out on valuable long-term client relationships.

Outside In, by *Harley Manning and Kerry Bodine*

Based on many years of research by the customer experience leaders at Forrester Research, the book offers a very comprehensive roadmap to attaining a leading customer experience culture. It contains many relevant case studies, it explains the Customer Experience Ecosystem, policies, processes, technologies, and focuses on the relevance of hard data.

Step 5: Bring it all together

In today's highly competitive and dynamically changing world it is a must to be customer-focused. Top companies go a step further by striving to constantly deliver exceptional customer experiences. A third group, however, the very best organizations, aren't satisfied even with that any longer. They're totally customer-obsessed instead.

Define for yourself in which group you currently are and to which one you'd like to belong to by when. There's all the information you need in this article to get moving and to avoid disappearing from the market one day.

83. HOW APPLE, DISNEY & CO. DELIGHT CUSTOMERS

In one of my previous articles on how to build world-class customer service I arrived at the conclusion that top organizations deliver outstanding customer service and customer experience to become and stay leaders in their industries. We also argued that in the end, it's not really about customer service, it's about customer obsession.

It's about being obsessed to constantly deliver the best customer experience possible, it's about delighting your customers whenever they interact with your organization. It's about value-adding products and services, fair prices, about care, about exceeding expectations, about passion, respect, personalization, attitude, simplicity, staff empowerment, and about a never-ending improvement process.

Simultaneously, however, delivering a world-class customer experience is also about business, hard facts, and figures: On the one hand, if done properly, it increases revenue and decreases costs. And, on the other hand, you need to build your internal business case on facts and figures to get funds for your planned customer experience improvement projects.

You know, most likely also based on various personal experiences, there still exist (too) many organizations which think that they can "fool" their customers by only paying lip service to the concept of customer experience. The good news for both customers and truly customer-obsessed companies: Such an approach will not cut it anymore and those companies are already out of the market (they just have not realized it yet).

If you are serious about significantly improving your customer experience, then continue to read and find out how the very best companies are doing it and what delivering a superb customer experience means to them. These companies constantly rank among the most customer-centric ones of any reputable survey and industry benchmark study. (Please note that below brands are selected by myself out of various studies, my own research, and my own working and customer experience. It's not a complete list as such. You certainly know additional ones. See also: American Customer Satisfaction Index studies, Customer Service Hall Of Fame, Forrester Service customer service studies, Consumer Reports, etc.).

The below companies are the ones which have understood the huge untapped potential of delivering customer experience the right way. Get inspired by what they have to say!

L.L. Bean

While doing business today might differ from doing business in 1912, the philosophy of the company has not changed. A lot of people have fancy things to say about Customer Service, but it's just a day-in, day-out, ongoing, never-ending, persevering, compassionate kind of activity. It goes back to L.L.'s Golden Rule of treating customers like human beings.

Ritz Carlton

We are Ladies and Gentlemen serving Ladies and Gentlemen. Our three Steps Of Service: 1) A warm and sincere greeting. Use the guest's name; 2) Anticipation and fulfillment of each guest's needs; and 3) A fond farewell. Give a warm good-bye and use the guest's name. Our Service Values: I build strong relationships and create Ritz-Carlton guests for life. I am always responsive to the expressed and unexpressed wishes and needs of our guests.

I am empowered to create unique, memorable and personal experiences for our guests. Our Employee Promise: applying the principles of trust, honesty, respect, integrity and commitment, we nurture and maximize talent to the benefit of each individual and the company.

Disney

Our aim should be to always exceed our Guest's expectations. The front-line is the bottom line: The employees in front of the customer are the ones they see. Look after them, teach them well, support them. Every face-to-face interaction is a moment of truth. If a customer interacts with 50 Cast Members (= employees) per day there are 50 moments of truth. If there are 49 great moments and 1 bad, which do you think the customer will remember? We need all moments of truth to be great. You have two ears, two eyes and one mouth, use them in that ratio: Listen to your customer, they are trying to tell you something. It is only when they have told you what they want that you can give them the help they need.

Lowe's

Lowe's exists to help customers improve and maintain their biggest asset-their home. We do this by meeting the changing needs of our customers by providing inspiration and support whenever and wherever they shop. Whether our customers shop in store, online, by phone, or if we're meeting them at their home or place of business, Lowe's is ready to help. We've vowed to "Never Stop Improving" so we can satisfy the ever-changing needs of our customers.

Google

Focus on the user and all else will follow: Since the beginning, we've focused on providing the best user experience possible. Whether we're designing a new Internet browser or a new tweak to the look of the homepage, we take great care to ensure that they will ultimately serve you, rather than our own internal goal or bottom line. Our homepage interface is clear and simple, and pages load instantly. Placement in search results is never sold to anyone, and advertising is not only clearly marked as such, it offers relevant content and is not distracting. And when we build new tools and applications, we believe they should work so well you don't have to consider how they might have been designed differently.

UPS

We focus on building and maintaining long-term customer relationships by treating each customer as if they were our only customer. 'Customer experience' isn't seen as a separate unit or department. It is the rubric under which all other decisions are made. All proposals funnel up to what we call 'customer experience,' and if an idea is bad for customers, it can be killed point-blank. We have to enable our employees to be successful, so they can deliver success to our customers. We have to treat our employees like they're our customers.

Amazon

Our mission is to be Earth's most customer-centric company, where customers can find and discover anything they might want to buy online. We endeavor to offer our customers the lowest possible prices. Amazon has teams across the world working on behalf of its customers at Fulfillment Centers, which provide fast, reliable shipping directly from Amazon's retail websites, and Customer Service Centers, which provide 24/7 support. Our leaders start with the customer and work backwards. They work vigorously to earn and keep customer trust. Although leaders pay attention to competitors, they obsess over customers.

Harrods

At Harrods we promise to offer everything the customer wants, and we can't do that without great service. We make no excuses for setting very high standards and high expectations for our employees to deliver exceptional service as our service is one of defining characteristics of our brand. Giving excellent customer service is at the heart of what we do and it's one of the main reasons why customers choose us, and why they keep coming back. There are many different Harrods customers, but only one type of service... outstanding.

USAA

When you join USAA, you're more than just a customer. You belong to one of the leading financial institutions in the country. And as a member, you'll enjoy exclusive discounts, superior support and it's free to join. We're dedicated to providing our members with top-rated service and personalized advice. Through any stage of life, we're here to guide you. We're revolutionizing how our members keep up with their finances. We're honored when we're recognized by the industry's top publications, but we're humbled by what our members say.

Singapore Airlines

We fly one of the youngest aircraft fleets in the world to destinations spanning a network spread over six continents, with our Singapore Girl as our internationally-recognizable icon providing the high standards of care and service that customers have come to expect of us. We have made a habit of leading the way, and along the way developed a reputation for being an industry trendsetter. In our lounges, working relationships, in the smallest details of our inflight service, we rise to each and every occasion, to deliver the Singapore Airlines experience to all our customers.

Lexus

Unsurpassed Customer Care we call Omotenashi at Lexus. Omotenashi is the Japanese word for hospitality. It implies an insightful understanding of customer wants and needs. In the spirit of Omotenashi, we strive to treat you, our customer, as a guest in our home. Recognizing that each guest has different needs, our goal is to anticipate and personalize each solution to exceed expectations, while recognizing that time is always at a premium.

State Farm

'Remarkable' describes our culture of serving others. It's about how we interact with our customers and how we interact with each other in support of our customers. Every day we have thousands of opportunities to connect with customers. In each of those interactions, regardless of the method of contact, we aspire to provide consistently remarkable experiences. Our customers tell us that they wish to be treated in a personalized, caring, and simple manner. That's important to us, and it's why we embrace the behaviors that make us remarkable. All State Farm associates have a stake in joining together to create remarkable experiences for our customers. It's a demonstration of our mission, vision, and values. It's the way we do business. Our goal is to provide an experience that's both simple and caring.

IKEA

We work hard to achieve quality at affordable prices for our customers through optimizing our entire value chain, by building long-term supplier relationships, investing in highly automated production and producing large volumes. We want to create a better everyday for all people impacted by our business.

We re-invest a majority of our profits in existing and new IKEA stores, as well as in product development, sustainable solutions and by continuously lowering prices to our customers. Our co-workers are essential for our continued growth. We see every person as a talent with the possibility to develop.

Isetan Mitsukoshi

Our first goal is to become the world's foremost solution provider in terms of customer satisfaction imbued with our spirit of hospitality to cultivate excellent relationships with our customers. To this end, the quality of our service, merchandise and stores must always be superb. Customer satisfaction is the mirror image of this quality. In order to maintain a reputation for excellence, we must propose new value exceeding customer expectations and inspiring their immeasurable support. What is original and inspiring today may be taken for granted tomorrow. We always anticipate the direction of evolution in the retail and service industry and act decisively earlier than competitors. Our conviction is that customer satisfaction and employee satisfaction are mutually reinforcing as well as our recognition that empathy with customers is a prerequisite for becoming the world's foremost solution provider.

Trader Joe's

"Value" is a concept we take very seriously. And by value we mean great everyday prices on all of our products — no sales, no gimmicks, no clubs to join, no special cards to swipe. We wear Hawaiian shirts because we're traders on the culinary seas, searching the world over for cool items to bring home to our customers. And when we return home, we think grocery shopping should be fun, not another chore. So just relax and leave your worries at the door. We'll sail those seven seas; you have some fun with our finds at your neighborhood Trader Joe's.

Nordstrom

For more than 100 years, we at Nordstrom have worked to deliver the best possible shopping experience, helping customers possess style—not just buy fashion. We believe fashion is a business of optimism, and in that spirit we continue to grow and evolve. Free shipping and free returns, mobile shopping and exciting new retail partnerships offer us continued opportunities to serve more customers in more ways with a fresh, relevant shopping experience and inspiring style. Fashion changes. Shopping changes. Our commitment to happy customers doesn't.

Apple

We are at our best when we deliver enriching experiences. What we tell all our staff: Approach customers with a personalized, warm welcome; Make sure customers are greeted by a friendly smile; Probe politely to understand the customer's needs (ask closed and open-ended questions); Present a solution for the customer to take home today; Listen for and resolve any issues or concerns: By truly listening and acknowledging the needs of your customers, you make your business an oasis of encouragement, empowerment, and excitement. End with a fond farewell and an invitation to return: There is a direct correlation between how people feel when they leave your business and how likely they are to return or recommend the experience to someone else.

Often, in customer service and customer excellence initiatives, we can get lost in concepts like customer loyalty, customer satisfaction scores, customer satisfaction index, and KPIs like time-to-resolution, etc.

Two simple Rules:

1. Make sure that you do everything to make your customers really happy!
2. Customers first, then brand, then revenue and profit

84. BUILDING WORLD-CLASS CUSTOMER SERVICE

Every year you and your company certainly put many relevant topics on the agenda.

There is one topic, however, which should be at the very top of your list:

Improving and Exceeding at Customer Service. Really exceeding at it!

Why?

It separates good companies from the best ones. And in times of turbo-speed, full transparency, and highly demanding customers, it's more important than ever!

If you provide great customer service, you'll receive great rewards in the form of loyal customers who will even bring their friends with them.

Or as expressed by Doug Warner from the opposite perspective: "In the world of Internet Customer Service, it's important to remember your competitor is only one mouse click away."

How to create and maintain an exceptional customer service culture in your company

Offer A Good And Reliable Product/Service: That's the basis. If not, no need to worry about a good customer service. What your product can't deliver your customer service will not be able to make up for. The best way to reduce customer complaints and to improve customer satisfaction is to provide high-quality products and services. Be willing to change/adjust your offered product(s) and service(s), if needed. Possibly even your business model.

Put Customer-Focused Thinking At The Center Of Everything: Customer service is not a department, it's an attitude and everybody's job! It needs to be at the very core of the company's DNA. Practice it every day. Do not just talk about it. Instead, show and prove it every day, every hour, and every minute by assisting your customers. Celebrate customer service-related achievements and successes. Make them visible throughout the whole organization.

Worship Your Customer: He's the boss. He's paying the salaries. Ask, listen, and learn from them. Treat people like you want to be treated. However, only respecting them is not enough any longer. Instead, improve your product/service based on their feedback. Even a complaining customer represents an excellent opportunity for more business. Treat all your customers with the same high level of sincere respect and make your customers feel important and appreciated. Treat them as individuals. This will create good feelings and trust.

Top Management Commitment and Engagement: Serving the customer starts at the top. It's the CEO's most important job. A good leader needs to be a good servant. He should lead by example and demonstrate how customers should be treated. He should know by heart the company's products and services. If your company wants to be world-class in customer service, your CEO needs to act as Chief Service Officer (CSO).

Train, Excite, And Empower Your Staff: All of them and not only the customer service reps. Develop a holistic customer service approach, specific procedures, a rewards and compensation scheme with your staff. Based on detailed product and customer know-how. Get them involved. Let them develop, agree, and commit. Respect their opinions. Give every team member enough information and power to make small customer-pleasing decisions. Employees are your internal customers and need a regular dose of appreciation. Treat your employees well, and they will treat your customers well!

Act As Quickly And As Reliably As Possible: This is a very visible, and as such a very important part to your customers. There need to be ambitious and tightly-managed KPIs in place for answering the phone, responding to mails, calling back customers, etc. Rule: Be super-fast, polite, honest, transparent, and concise.

Use Leading Technology: If needed, tailored to your unique business and customer needs. Customers define the systems and IT structure required to provide outstanding customer service. Not the other way round. IT is not a cost. It's a critical success factor. It certainly costs much less than delivering bad customer service.

Radiate A Yes-Attitude And Be A Communication Master: Smile whenever you interact with the customer. Immediately deal with the highest priority complaints, be results-focused, know how to sincerely apologize (and try not to put the blame on the customer) and how to treat every customer as an individual. Keep customers pro-actively up-to-speed.

Constantly Inform And Educate Your Customers: Let your customers know about how your products and services work and how you operate. Also inform them about how easily they can exchange with you and whenever needed. Make it simple for customers to complain and value their complaints. Always deliver on promises. No exceptions.

Under-promise And Over-Deliver: Although this gap should be small (in order to not risk losing credibility), as a general rule you should provide more than what customers expect to get. Also be helpful even if there is no immediate benefit or profit for you.

Never Stop Learning And Improving: Think ahead. Anticipate future needs and wants (and possible problems) of your customers. Many might be emotional and not only rational. Always go a step further. Get constant feedback. You are much better prepared if you know your customers and if every day you try to make the customer experience a little bit better. It is a beautiful and never-ending activity. It's all about the long-term!

Leverage Excellent Customer Service: Don't be too shy talking about the good you do in an indirect way, e.g. by using the power of communities or brand advocates. Two rules you should follow: 1) Do not boast. 2) Only do it if you are very good from your customers' perspective, i.e. only if you really built a great customer experience.

At the end, the customer doesn't know, doesn't care, and shouldn't need to care about what the reasons of his product concerns and dissatisfaction might be. He has the right to receive a high quality and well working product or service. That's what he paid for.

And the whole company's responsibility is to deliver exactly that. Customer service is the basis for customer loyalty. Every great business is built on strong customer relationships. As such, successful and visionary companies always put their customer first, not sales and market shares. They've understood that the latter ones are only a natural consequence of satisfied customers.

In summary: It's not really about customer service, it's about customer obsession!

85. HOW TO BECOME A GREAT NEGOTIATOR

Negotiations are a fact of life. We constantly negotiate both in personal and professional areas of life.

Still, many people don't like negotiating, and as such try avoiding it. As a result it could make resolving and/or progressing problematic.

Others, often success-driven managers and businesspeople, are so competitive that only "winning" would make them a great negotiator in their eyes, causing, of course, the other person to "lose." Helpful? Most likely not!

Applying the below-listed four negotiation principles and executing the outlined three-phased negotiation process will significantly increase the quality of your future negotiations.

Negotiations Principles

Often, negotiations fail when the following 4 key negotiation principles are not being taken into consideration:

Aim At Win-Win Outcomes

Those are the results which satisfy all stakeholders involved. They represent the basis for further business and sustainable relationships.

Always Stay Open-minded

Successful negotiators look at each major aspect from multiple perspectives. They're prepared for anything.

Focus On Long-Term Business Relationships

With this in mind it's rather impossible to fleece the other party.

Show Respect And Appreciation

Honoring the other person as an equal is crucial to any successful negotiation.

Negotiation Process

A professional negotiation process consists of 3 stages: The preparation phase, the negotiation phase, and the follow-up phase. You need to excel in all three of them in order to become a master of negotiation.

Preparation Stage

If you think that negotiating only starts once you meet the other party, then most likely you'll not chalk up the best possible outcome: "By failing to prepare, you are preparing to fail" (Benjamin Franklin).

In this very first phase define your negotiation targets, strategy and objective criteria based on which you later measure the achieved agreement. Be clear about your alternatives and fall back positions; also known as BATNA: Best Alternative To Negotiated Agreement.

It's crucial to collect all accessible information about the other party and your negotiation counterparts: What are their objectives and potential strategy? What might be their perspective, their motivations, and their opinion on relevant topics? Which is their interest and their reservation price (i.e. when would they walk away)?

Negotiation Stage

During the opening phase of the negotiation stage **listen well and frequently ask** (open-ended) questions. As a rule of thumb you should listen more than you talk. **Use silence** as a tactic and **mimic your opponent**. Sooner or later they will talk. Try to **detect commonalities** rather than differences to generate mutual engagement and to establish a first basis of trust. In general it is essential to **separate the people from the issue**. Don't take things personal. Many people consider negotiations as a kind of game. So, stay relaxed and enjoy playing the game!

When you're about to start the actual negotiation be brave and **bring forward the first proposal.** Why should you do that? The opening offer always serves as a reference point. It's what I call an "unconscious anchor." In other words: If you're selling, be first and start the bidding high. And if you're buying, start the bidding low.

Often it might be appropriate **making two to three equivalent, simultaneous offers.** This shows that you understand and respect the other position and possible concerns. Even more importantly, it creates a variety of options and helps avoiding cornering the other side. You should ask for more than what you're actually looking for. That gives you flexibility and room to maneuver.

Don't be afraid to give in first. It's an excellent opportunity to inject an additional layer of trust. When doing it in a pro-active manner you should be able to choose something that has significant meaning to the other party and is of low cost to you. Usually, **whenever you give you should also take.** Every concession you make should involve a trade-off of some kind. By doing so focus on interests rather than positions.

Saying that, and in order to get around cognitive dissonances of your negotiation counterparts, you are well advised to **engage in the theatrics of negotiation:** e.g. when being attacked or confronted with unreasonable proposals and demands you should look visibly put off, or you even might want to flinch.

By the way, that's the only time when you get "emotional."

Experienced negotiators are creative solution seekers, they enjoy thinking outside of the box, and they constantly look for ways to **broaden the pie** instead of haggling over every little detail. However, they also **stand their ground** if the other party is not willing to move or if they were to become (too) aggressive. Temporary confrontations are a normal and stimulating ingredient of serious negotiations. That's life. Consequently, good negotiators **take their time** and let things cool off. They are **not in a hurry** to close the deal. And – when push comes to shove - they might **walk away** as they know that reaching no deal is better than a bad deal.

Follow-Up Stage

After you have closed the deal there is still some final – and very important - work to be taken care of. Write and send out the first draft of the minutes to the other party within 24 hours after the negotiations have finished. Ask the other side for their input and feedback to your minutes and get them finalized by at the latest 3 days after having agreed on the deal. Minutes should be as short and as clear as possible. They contain what was agreed upon, and list what has to be executed by when and by whom. Finally, you need to walk your talk, i.e. you must stick to the agreed points and make sure that the other party does so as well.

Final advice

Try to conduct important negotiations in a face-to-face setting. Sure, an excellent preparation, a clear negotiation strategy, and profound knowledge of key negotiation tactics are required to negotiate well. Of paramount importance, however, is the personality of the negotiator. And that's delivered and reflected best when you can directly look into each other's eyes.

86. HOW TO STRENGTHEN YOUR PERSONAL PRODUCTIVITY

This latest article of our very popular "Rethink for Success" series is also based on a very stimulating business book which has been read and reviewed for you. You don't need to have read the previous articles I wrote, you'll get the messages of this one regardless.

As you know by now, I will not reveal the book's title for the time being in order to fully focus on its unique contents. Let's jump into it with the following article.

In a previous Article I presented the following Ideas & Advices

1. **Go to bed with things that never change:** Don't follow the latest trends and fashion. Advice: Focus on substance, on things that will not change: Quality, good service, affordability, choice, simplicity, etc.

2. **It's not the gear that matters:** Too many people are obsessed with the latest technology, tools and tricks. Advice: There are no sustainable shortcuts in life! It's your head, heart and passion that matter!

Time to move on with today's Thoughts and Tips

Interruption is the Enemy of Productivity

Interruptions break your workday into a series of work moments. You can't get meaningful things done when you're constantly going start, stop, start, stop. Instead, you should get into the alone zone. Getting into that zone takes time and requires avoiding interruptions. It's like REM sleep. And just as REM is when the real sleep magic happens, the alone zone is where the real productivity magic happens. During alone time, give up instant messaging, phone calls, e-mail, and meetings. Just shut it all up and get to work. You'll be surprised how much work you can get done. Your day is under siege by interruptions. It's on you to fight back and create and protect your alone zone.

The worst Interruptions of all are Meetings

Often they are not well-planned, not well-conducted, not followed up and as a consequence not productive and effective. Also, they're bloody expensive. Let's say you schedule a meeting that lasts one hour (most likely it'll last longer anyway...) and you invite ten people to attend. If they all rock-up (and on time...), then that's actually a ten-hour meeting. Minimum! So, if you can't avoid having (another) meeting and you think you really need to get together, stick to simple rules: set a timer, invite as few people as possible (weak managers would do the contrary), have a clear agenda, start with the objective/issue/problem, discuss real things and real solutions, end with a solution, define precise next steps, allocate responsibilities, implement ASAP, and follow up.

87. THROW LESS AT THE PROBLEM

Hot off the press is a new article on how to manage yourself, your business and your team better. It is another one from our series which is based on a very stimulating business book that I read and reviewed especially for you.

The book's title is still not revealed for the time being in order to fully focus on its unique contents. So, let's get started!

In my last Article I presented the following Ideas & Advices

Ignore the details early on: Focusing on details too early means not seeing the whole picture any longer. Stripped Down Advice: Nail the basics first and worry about the specifics later.

Commit to making decisions: Don't wait for the perfect solution. It does not exist.

Stripped Down Advice: Decide and move forward. Get into the flow of making decision after decision.

Time to move on with today's Thoughts & Tips

Be a curator

You don't make a great museum by putting all the art in the world into a single room. That's a warehouse. What makes a museum great is the stuff that's NOT on the walls. In other words: It's the stuff you leave out that matters. Constantly look for things to remove, to simplify, and streamline.

Be a curator and not a warehouse administrator. Stick to what's truly essential.

Throw less at the problem

When things aren't working, the natural inclination is to throw more at the problem. More people, more time, and - of course - more money. All that ends up doing is making the problem bigger. The right way to go is the opposite direction: Cut back! Do less! Your project won't suffer nearly as much as you fear. You'll be forced to make tough calls and sort out what truly matters.

88. LESS IS MORE

Let's move on with part 7 of our "Rethink for Success" series. A series which is based on an insightful and exciting business book that I have found, read and reviewed especially for you.

For the time being, however, we will not reveal the book's title. It's not to annoy you. It's to focus on its words and messages without being distracted by its title and the names of its authors. Vamonos companeros! Some more thought-provoking ideas today!

In a previous Article I presented the following Ideas & Advices

Draw a line in the sand: Great businesses have a point of view, not just a product or service. You have to believe in something. Stripped Down Advice: When you stand for something, decisions are obvious. That's what a successful brand needs!

Start a business, not a start-up: The truth is that every business is governed by the same rules: revenue in, expenses out. Stripped Down Advice: Don't "dream" about a start-up, instead start an actual business!

Time to move on with today's Thoughts & Tips

Less is more (1)

Huge organizations can take years to pivot. They talk instead of act. They meet instead of do. Embrace the idea of having less mass. The more massive an object, the more energy required to change its direction. It's as true in the business world as it is in the physical world. Keep your mass low and you can quickly move and change anything.

Less is more (2)

"I don't have enough time/money/people/experience." Stop whining! Less is a good thing. Constraints are advantages in disguise. Limited resources force you to go to the max to think, to constantly improve, to optimize, to innovate and to be creative. So before you sing the "not enough" blues, see how far you can get with what you have.

89. ABOUT PLANS AND SIZE

Some thoughts on planning and about the importance/non-importance of size. Size matters? Forget about it!

Planning is guessing

Writing a plan makes you feel in control of things you can't actually control. Give up on the guesswork. Save this precious time for doing more value-adding things (my personal advice!). Decide what you're going to do this week, not this year. Figure out the next important thing and do that. Working without a plan may seem scary, but blindly following a plan that has no relationship with reality is even scarier.

Find the right size and stay there

Why is big always good? What is it about growth and business? What's the attraction of big besides ego? What's wrong with finding the right size and staying there? Don't make assumptions about how big you should be ahead of time. Grow slow and see what feels right. Don't be insecure about aiming to be a small business that's sustainable and profitable. Whether your business is big or small, you should be proud of it.

90. READ HOW TO READ 10 BOOKS PER WEEK

Many successful people don't just read. Instead, they sponge up books and articles. They regularly invest dedicated and limited time slots to read books, papers, and blog articles. This gives them an information advantage and stimulates the production of their creative juices. As a result, they become more productive and effective.

Most of them have a reading speed significantly higher than an adult's average of around 250-300 words per minute (wpm). Top readers who apply various speed reading strategies hit around 1,000 to 2,000 wpm with approximately 50-60% comprehension. Anne Jones, who won the Speed Reading World championship six times, reads up to 4,700 wpm with 67% comprehension. She read *Harry Potter and the Deathly Hallows* in just 47 minutes and one second (4251 wpm). Afterwards she reviewed the book for Sky TV.

Also, U.S. president Theodore Roosevelt was known for his impressive reading skills. He was said to have read multiple books per day. Following his footsteps were Kennedy, Carter and other U.S. presidents who made speed reading a priority for themselves and White House staff. They and many others like Tony Buzan – the world-famous proponent of mnemonic systems and mind mapping techniques – were inspired by the American educator and teacher Evelyn Wood who coined the phrase *Speed Reading* in the 1960s. Wood taught the speed reading system Reading Dynamics.

By practicing regularly with one of the speed reading apps and applying some of the straightforward techniques described below, after some weeks you can also increase your reading capabilities to 500-700 wpm while retaining good comprehension. By training 2-3 months on a regular basis you should be able to achieve up to 1,000 wpm.

Recommended Speed Reading Apps

Spritz

Thanks to a smart and big PR campaign, Boston-based startup Spritz momentarily is everywhere in the media. Unfortunately, it is not yet available on many devices. Anyway, first things first: Spritz is focused on text streaming technology which is based on RSVP (Rapid Serial Visual Presentation) to display words one after another using a single focal point. The company stresses the fact that the time consuming part of reading lies mainly in the actual eye movements from word to word and sentence to sentence.

Currently you can spritz in English, Spanish, French, German, Russian and even Korean. They're working on Chinese and a few others right now. The first use of Spritz is an email application for the Samsung Gear 2 and Galaxy S5 smartphone. It's also working on getting the app to customers beyond the Samsung gadgets soon.

Oyster, in cooperation with Spitz, made Stephen Covey's Classic "7 Habits of Highly Effective People, 25th Anniversary Edition" Spritzable on their site. After almost 3 hours – yes I took a couple of breaks - I completed the book; I changed the available speeds from 250 wpm up to 600-700 wpm (and back) to match my reading level. Overall, a satisfying experience for reading a business book.

Fastr

Fastr serves as a book reader for iPhone, iPod, iPad, and the web. It also trains your reading skills. Fastr operates on a comparable principle as Spritz. However, and I like this a lot, you can choose between two ways of reading - classical and speed reading (using word flash). As such you can train your reading skills while reading your favorite book or an article. Fastr lets you add books from Dropbox, Safari, and add files on www.fastr.io website. ePub format is now supported. Unfortunately, due to DRM restrictions you are not able to open books bought on Amazon or iBooks. The launch of Fastr's own book catalog is planned.

A Faster Reader

A Faster Reader uses the same RSVP method as Spritz and is for Android. It is compatible with a variety of reader services such as Pocket, Feedly, etc. You can also share text from Evernote, ColorNote or Google Keep. The in-app purchase to premium provides an interface to the Pebble smart watch (plus many more features). A pretty good app, although the text flow could be made smoother and the text size slightly bigger.

Velocity

Velocity is very easy to use. Its biggest drawback: it's iOS only. Consequently the company's next goal is to bring it to Android. Velocity works with Instapaper, Readability, and Pocket. You can read text, rich text, and word documents from mail and other apps. Velocity is customizable as well, so you can set up your reading preferences.

Reading Trainer

HeKu's reading trainer for $4.99 is not a speed reading tool; it's a sophisticated speed reading course to practice every day for approximately 10 minutes. Luckily it's available for Android, iOS, and even Windows Phone. There are lots of challenging and fun exercises to improve your natural reading rate.

Recommended Reading Strategies

Whilst you can certainly increase your reading speed by using the above-listed speed reading apps, in parallel you should exert some of the following proven techniques (the Reading Trainer covers some of them. By the way, to evaluate your reading speed click here).

Preview

This is particularly helpful for getting a general idea of long and heavy reading material without over-loading you with all the details. Generally you would read in full the first one to two paragraphs of the respective book or article. Afterwards, of each successive paragraph you would read only the first sentence. At the end you would read the complete last one to two paragraphs.

Skimming

An excellent technique to read lighter material or books and articles which you've read before. It is done by forcing your eyes to move faster and to sweep across each line by picking up only a few key words in each line. Skimming often results in lower comprehension rates.

Clustering

Looking at groups of words instead of one at a time is called Clustering. You need to train your eyes to see words in clusters of three to five words at a glance. Try to relax your eyes without concentrating on every word. Instead apply a soft focus like looking at a beautiful picture or painting.

Meta Guiding

By using a finger or a pen as a pointer, the eye can be challenged moving faster along a text. It's like drawing invisible shapes on a page of text in order to broaden the visual span for speed reading.

Suppressing Subvocalization

Subvocalization is a natural process which is defined as the internal speech made when reading a word; allowing the reader to imagine the sound of the word as it is read. It is believed to be a major reason why individuals do not learn speed reading by themselves as they mentally want to pronounce each syllable. An effective exercise that everyone can apply to avoid subvocalizing is to use their inner voice by humming or counting while reading at their normal rate (either in their head or out loud).

Avoiding Regression

Readers should always continue reading forward. Never going backward. Even – and especially – when they feel they have misunderstood or missed something. The brain will automatically fill the gaps.

If you'd like to learn more about various speed reading strategies and extremely powerful exercises I suggest you study Breakthrough Rapid Reading by Peter Kump. It is the best book that I've read on speed reading. After 2 to 3 months of daily practicing I'm sure you'll fly through any book. Go for it!

Summary and final Thoughts

Personally, I've considerably improved my reading speed and comprehension by using the Faster Reader app, practicing 3-4 times per week with the Reading Trainer, and applying the most relevant speed reading strategies. Once Spritz will be available on iOS and Android devices, it should become a compelling alternative.

Certainly, one must be careful not to confuse speed reading with skimming, i.e. finding the right balance between "speed" and "comprehension." This is closely linked with the risk associated with possible misunderstandings due to low comprehension, and the advantages resulting from gaining information quicker than usual.

Of course, also - and especially - the type of reading is relevant. I usually apply speed reading when reading business books, studies, or articles. Or when I re-read already known material, and not when reading great literature like John Williams' splendid and deeply moving novel **Stoner** which is a work of humble perfection and inspiration. In addition, I would only use it on a reduced and limited scale when reading highly complex books and articles. Knowing speed reading gives me the opportunity to choose and adapt my reading speed in a flexible manner. You can always slow down, if you'd like to. Finally, one cannot automatically assume having understood each page and aspect of a book, etc. even when having read it slowly.

Speed Reading takes practice. It's best done, if you'd like to try it, in a comfortable and quiet environment where neither eyes nor mind are distracted. As you increase your speed over time, it is crucial to permanently challenge yourself to read at faster speeds.

Chapter 7

CARE!

TOMORROW'S TOP LEADERS want to support others, to give, to make an impact, and to do good. They care about the well-being of their employees and about broader environmental and social topics. They are aware of the fact that you have to give before you receive. They have integrated values like gratitude and appreciation into their lives and linked them with positive and people-focused thinking and acting to achieve a fulfilled life.

They show a strong interpersonal, day-to-day ability to genuinely and graciously thank other people for what they do. Unfortunately, it's a behavior that's too often forgotten in the heat of the battle. Moreover, outstanding future leaders avoid the common tendency of managers to focus on the shortfalls and misses. Instead they posses the beautiful quality to identify moments of achievement and greatness and to put a spotlight on them. That gives confidence and strength to the teams and often generates innovation and unlocks tremendous organization-wide value.

Clare W Graves – the great explorer of human nature and the father of the famous Gravesian theory – calls them Gold Thinkers. They are people and leaders who do not seek social approval, personal advantage or a sense of absolute truth. More than anything else they seek opportunities to contribute. Their faith in life is such that, even when they screw up, they always come away with a valuable lesson.

Tomorrow's top leaders are also great supporters of cause management, i.e. integrating social issues into their core strategy. For example, they aim at creating shared value, a concept that reflects a desire to generate a profit and support social progress at the same time.

91. GLOBAL CONSUMER VERDICT – BUSINESS FAILS TAKING CARE OF THE PLANET AND SOCIETY

This is the result of a 2014 global study by consultancy Accenture and Havas Media's Re:Purpose. Its survey of 30,000 adults across twenty countries on five continents found that 72 percent of consumers think that business is failing to adequately address, or not address at all, today's environmental and social challenges.

The report From Marketing to Mattering follows a 2013 Accenture report that surveyed CEOs on sustainability and found that two-thirds of CEOs admitted that business is not doing enough to address sustainability issues.

Key Findings

Consumers clearly expect more from companies, from greater honesty and transparency to greater impact on global and local challenges and a more responsible stewardship of natural resources and the environment.

Wide Disparity In Peoples' Optimism

While Western Europe is pessimistic, the outlook in Asia and North America is more positive with the most widespread optimism in Africa and Latin America.

In economies with a large, emerging middle-class, people are less skeptical and public confidence is significantly greater.

People Think Business And Governments Are Accountable

Whether optimistic (Asia, Africa, and Latin America) or despondent about the future (Western Europe and North American markets), people expect brands and companies to impact positively on their lives.

Consumer Consideration Of Sustainability Factors In Their Purchasing Decisions

Countries where respondents are optimistic and express high expectations of business are also more likely to consider sustainability in their purchasing decisions and actively seek information on sustainability performance.

Consumers Want Business To Address Critical Challenges

Job creation, economic growth, pollution, clean energy, and ending corruption to name a few. 81% of consumers expect more from their expenditure than the acquisition of products and services.

Implications

Evidently, many business leaders have failed in embedding sustainability into their core business. Consumers are not engaged, not buying into and believing in superficial sustainability stories which often do not relate to their lives, especially in Western Europe and the US, i.e. in those mature markets where they have been operating the longest. Certainly the trust factor – a crucial key ingredient for any credible sustainability initiative – might still be hampered by the financial crisis of some years ago. Persuading consumers does not do the job. Instead, companies need to convince consumers in an honest and transparent manner.

When only 32% of consumers say they "often" or "always" consider sustainability in their purchasing decisions, quite obviously many companies are not in-sync with consumers' needs and wants. So, how do you earn consumers' confidence and engage with them effectively?

Proposed Actions

Companies should address the following six areas to better engage with consumers:

Business needs to finally understand and accept that people know more about products and companies than ever before.

Today's relevant brands must create products and services that make a visible difference to people's lives while delivering on sustainability criteria.

Companies should promote a holistic and long-lasting commitment to honesty and transparency throughout the whole organization. All departments need to be included. All levels and ranks. Be aware that consumers will actively look for information to validate any company's "claims."

Business should match expectations for responsible business practices while delivering tangible improvements to consumers' lives. It's not enough to be seen as ethical or socially responsible. There has to be a personal benefit.

Companies would need to communicate their purpose and relevance to society in a much clearer way by providing real and specific examples. And not focusing on vague sustainability credentials, prizes, etc.

It all starts at the top. CEOs and senior management need to walk their talk. The times of glossy brochures, flashy presentations, and running after green prizes and awards are over. Fortunately.

Final Thoughts

On the one hand, there still seems to exist this huge sustainability opportunity for companies. On the other hand, and that is sad and disappointing, many companies have not been able to convince (Western) consumers in delivering relevant sustainability results.

What a paradox: Although CEOs consider sustainability as a route to growth and innovation, which eventually will lead to competitive advantage, they do not fulfill consumers' expectations in regards of their sustainability efforts. Although business leaders say they want to do more, reality shows they're not doing enough; especially not enough meaningful things for consumers. Today's citizen consumer has higher expectations of business than ever. She is asking, "What's in it for me?"

92. HOW MANY SLAVES WORK FOR YOU?

"What? Are you serious Andreas? Have you lost your wits? How do you dare asking me how many slaves work for me!

Did you not get that the movie 12 Years A Slave played in the pre-Civil War United States almost 200 years ago? There's no real slavery any longer in modern times. And, for sure, there are no slaves working for me. What a weird question!"

True, what often comes to mind when we think about slavery is captured Africans in chains working on American sugar plantations. And yes, slavery was abolished in the 19th century and it's forbidden by various UN conventions and declarations.

Are you, however, absolutely sure about your idea of a world free of slavery?

SLAVERY IS ALL BUT ABOLISHED!

Yeah, of course you've heard about some questionable working conditions in some far away countries. Sweatshops and the like. Most of them are closed, aren't they? But buying, selling, and trafficking human beings? That can't happen. And if at all, then for sure far away from your influence.

Sorry for having to spoil your dreams by quoting some very real and unpleasant facts, but: The inaugural edition of the Global Slavery Index 2013 estimates that almost 30 million people live in modern slavery today. Yes, 30 million!

The index ranks 162 countries around the world based on a combined measure of three factors: estimated prevalence of modern slavery by population, a measure of child marriage, and a measure of human trafficking in and out of a country. The countries with the highest numbers of enslaved people are India, China, Pakistan, Nigeria, Ethiopia, Russia, Thailand, Democratic Republic of Congo, Myanmar and Bangladesh. Taken together, these countries account for 76% of the total estimate of 29.8 million in modern slavery.

Modern Slavery For Modern Consumerism

Modern slavery takes many forms, and is known by various names: slavery, forced labor or human trafficking. Whatever term is used, the significant characteristic of all forms of modern slavery is that it involves one person depriving another person or people of their freedom: their freedom to leave one job for another, their freedom to leave one workplace for another, their freedom to control their own body, for their own personal or commercial benefit.

Today's slaves are found in the fields, in the brothels, in the sweatshops, in the mines, and in the raw materials processing. It's the supply chain of many consumer goods products, however, that enslaves more people than at any time in history. Those slaves are working for you! They're manufacturing your products, your smartphone, your t-shirt, your toys. That's stuff we buy, and that's stuff that comes from slaves.

Often, companies do not know where all the materials for their great brands are coming from... And yes, you're right – Some of them just do not want to know at all.

39 Slaves Work For Me

In September 2011 Justin Dillon, founder and CEO of Made In A Free World, founded Slavery Footprint. A revolutionary and disturbing website where you can fill-in a survey that asks and responds to the question, "How Many Slaves Work For You?"

The survey allows users to input select data about their consumer spending habits, which then outputs a graphical "footprint" of the user's participation in modern-day slavery (as quantified by their consumption of items created by forced labor and child labor.) The creators of Slavery Footprint researched the supply chains of 400 consumer products to determine the likely number of slaves it takes to make each of those products. They put the information into an online survey where you can determine the number of slaves that are needed to maintain your personal lifestyle.

My shocking survey result – 39 slaves work for me (my wife and children not included).

What We Can Do!

After the survey, the user has the option to share the results and can take action. You can, for example, earn Free World points to counteract your score by spreading the news and asking the brands by mail: "I want to know!" I have sent more than 40 mails asking some of the leading brands where they get their products from and telling them that I care.

We all can support madeinafreeworld.com and similar organizations to closely work with businesses to eradicate slavery from the products we love.

We can also learn more about modern slavery and our own slavery footprint. Ask for more information about the issue, get involved, invite your friends to also take the survey, support adequate organizations, donate, and help to raise awareness and to build the movement. Stop buying questionable products and brands. Why not buy more so-called fair trade products? Why not consume more responsibly, more thoughtfully, and less?

93. SHAME ON US! ONE THIRD OF FOOD IS WASTED!

In October 2013 the head of the United Nations Food and Agriculture Organization (FAO), *Graziano da Silva*, told participants at the Global Green Growth Forum (3GF) in Copenhagen that every year an estimated one-third of all food produced for human consumption is lost or wasted – around 1.3 billion tons. This costs around $750 billion per annum.

According to da Silva this would equal additional food to feed 2 billion people! This is unbelievable, isn't it?

Reality, however, is that per capita food waste is around 100 kilograms in Europe and North America per year. At the same time, FAO estimates that nearly 870 million people of the 7.1 billion people in the world, or one in eight, were suffering from chronic undernourishment in 2010-2012. Almost all the hungry people, 852 million, live in developing countries, representing 15 percent of the population of developing countries. There are 16 million people undernourished in developed countries. In general, children are the most visible victims of undernourishment. Poor nutrition plays a role in at least half of the 10.9 million child deaths each year - five million deaths! Undernourishment magnifies the effect of every disease, including measles and malaria.

Conclusion: The world produces enough food to feed everyone... in theory!

World agriculture produces 17 percent more calories per person today than it did 30 years ago, despite a 70 percent population increase. This is enough to provide everyone in the world with at least 2,720 kilocalories (kcal) per person per day according to FAO. The principal problem is that many people in the world do not have sufficient land to grow, or income to purchase, enough food.

Possible Actions

1. Fighting Food Loss In A Holistic Manner

FAO noted that most food loss takes place in post-production, harvesting, transportation and storage. In developing countries, food waste is mainly related to inadequate infrastructure, while in more developed countries it is largely a problem in the marketing and consumption stages. Consequently, investments in developing countries are needed in areas such as infrastructure, roads, and cold chains. Also, improvement is needed in delivering more and better know-how to farmers on how to properly grow and market their products. In developed countries one priority should be to educate both companies and consumers to apply more responsible consumption patterns.

Fighting food loss and waste is clearly one area in which a strong partnership between governments and various organizations (companies, NGOs) is needed. Developing a global protocol can help provide clear measurements and indicators on which guidance on how to reduce food loss and waste can be based. FAO is working on such a protocol.

2. Stimulating Responsible Economic Growth

Besides climate change, political conflicts and certain political systems, poverty is the main cause of hunger. As a result, economic growth plays a key role in reducing undernourishment. It is most effective in reducing poverty and hunger when it increases employment and income-earning opportunities that the poor can take advantage of. Sustainable agricultural growth is often effective in reaching the poor because most of the poor and hungry live in rural areas and depend on agriculture for a significant part of their livelihoods. However, growth will not necessarily result in better nutrition for all. Policies and programmes are required that will ensure "nutrition-sensitive" growth, including supporting increased dietary diversity, improving access to safe drinking water, sanitation and health services and educating consumers regarding adequate nutrition and child care practices.

Economic growth takes time to reach the poor, and may not reach the poorest of the poor. Therefore, social protection is crucial for eliminating hunger as rapidly as possible. Furthermore, when properly structured, social protection also promotes economic growth by building human capital and helping farmers manage risk so that they can adopt improved technologies. Finally, rapid progress in reducing hunger requires government action to provide key public goods and services within a governance system based on transparency, participation, accountability, rule of law and human rights.

3. Behaving And Acting Responsible Ourselves

Firstly, and most importantly, all of us can and should adjust their consumption behavior, i.e. thinking at least twice when shopping (what is really needed, who will consume it, by when should it be consumed, etc.) and before throwing anything away. We should act as role models and should try to positively influence our environment, our families, friends, colleagues, and others we're interacting with.

No need to blame others if we're not doing what we should be doing.

Have you ever heard of The Food Recovery Network in the US? It's an organization which unites students at colleges and universities across America to fight food waste and hunger by recovering surplus perishable food from their college campuses and surrounding communities that would otherwise go to waste and donating it to people in need. Founded in September of 2011, it has since expanded to reach 23 college campuses and recovered over 160,000 pounds (72.75 metric tons) of food that would otherwise have been wasted.

Very similar, and much more known, is the Food banking system which exists in many countries around the world. Food banks acquire donated food, much of which would otherwise be wasted, from farms, manufacturers, distributors, retail stores, consumers, and other sources, and makes it available to those in need through a network of community agencies. These agencies include school feeding programs, food pantries, soup kitchens, AIDS and TB hospices, substance abuse clinics, after-school programs, and other nonprofit programs that provide food to the hungry.

Have you ever supported your local food bank or any similar institution?

Finally, and from a company perspective, the concept of Corporate Social Responsibility is not new. Still, there is significant room for many more organizations getting involved, donating money, providing know-how, and "walking their talk! in regards to being serious about helping our society and our planet. In other words: How many companies do you know which have teamed up with organizations such as the SAVE FOOD project, WRAP (Waste and Resources Action Programme),Think-Eat-Save, or with any other programme targeted to change wasteful practices, to fight hunger, and to promote responsible consumption habits?

94. IS THE DREAM OF EDUCATION FOR ALL ALREADY OVER?

One Laptop Per Child (OLPC), a non-profit organization that was set up to bring education to the world's poorest children. The organization has impressed and inspired me with its original mission and approach for the last few years. Very recently, however, they have changed their strategy by launching a mass market kids tablet for Western countries. Does that mean the dream of *bringing education and as such a realistic opportunity for a better life to everyone in developing countries* is over?

The Vision of Nicholas Negroponte

OLPC was launched by Nicholas Negroponte, the founder and Chairman Emeritus of Massachusetts Institute of Technology's Media Lab and younger brother of former United States Deputy Secretary of State John Negroponte, technology enthusiast and author of the best seller *Being Digital* (which eventually became the manifesto of the Internet Age). In 2005, Negroponte unveiled the concept of a $100 laptop computer, The Children's Machine, designed for students in the developing world (later the price increased to around US$200). The project was originally funded by member organizations such as eBay, Google, AMD, Red Hat, etc. In 2006 the United Nations Development Program (UNDP) announced it would back the laptop.

The organization has since distributed 2.5 million of its specially designed XO laptops to children in 60 countries. Although far behind its original target, it is still a pretty good figure. The laptops are sold to governments to be distributed through the ministries of education with the goal of distributing "one laptop per child". They are given to students, similar to school uniforms, and ultimately remain the property of the child. The operating system and software is localized to the languages of the participating countries.

Criticism from the Beginning

The OLPC project has received criticism both specific to its mission and which is typical of many such systems, such as support, ease-of-use, security, content-filtering and privacy issues.

In some countries the project has been bashed for its high prices, cultural emphasis and priority as compared to other basic needs of people in third-world settings. It was mentioned that the project was using an overly U.S. mindset that presented solutions not applicable to specific problems of developing countries. The OLPC project has also been attacked for allegedly adopting a "one-shot" deployment approach with little or no technical support or teacher training, and for neglecting pilot programs and formal assessment of outcomes in favor of quick deployment. It was highlighted that the approach needed to become more holistic, combining technology with a prolonged community effort, teacher training and local educational efforts and insights.

Proven Successes

Speaking at the Techonomy Conference in August 2010, Negroponte himself argued that already by then the organization had managed to rebuff one of the biggest critiques of his effort: The idea that you can't just give a kid a laptop connected to the Internet and walk away.

Kids in the remotest places not only teach themselves how to read and write, but most importantly – and we found this in Peru – teach their parents to read or write.

Negroponte said that this is the point of his program. "I don't have a better story."

Afghanistan was another big focus for OLPC where more than half of the children don't go to school, the majority of whom (75 percent) are girls. And even in schools, a quarter of the teachers are illiterate and another quarter have only one more grade of education than their students. In those places, the students need to be a bigger part of the education system. "It's actually using the kids as the agents of change." Negroponte offered a challenge to the U.S. government.

The U.S. government spends $2 billion per week on war and only $2 million per week on education in the U.S. All you have to do is move half of 1 percent from column A to column B and every child in Afghanistan could have a laptop. That's what the U.S. would be remembered for. Why not do it? Everything is ready. That would make transformational change.

An article called "The Miracle of Wenchi - Ethiopian Kids Using Tablets to Teach Themselves" describes how OLPC has handed their XO OLPC tablet computers to children in the remote Ethiopian village of Wenchi in an experiment aimed at enabling them to teach themselves. It is described how the kids have started to genuinely love them and how they have started to learn to read and to write, even though their town is situated in the Ethiopian highlands with the closest school 12 miles away.

Degradation to a Commercial Offer?

Fast forward from 2005 to present times: In 2014, OLPC announced a very different product. A $150 Android-based tablet for kids. Actually, not for children in developing nations in the first place. Instead it has been sold in Walmart stores in the US since the beginning of August. The XO tablet looks a little funky with its green rubber case, but it's actually a fairly straight-forward kids tablet with regards to its hardware and technical specifications. It's a 7-inch tablet manufactured by Vivitar, a maker of affordable cameras and tablets that was bought by a company called Sakar some years ago. Without any doubt, its USP is its learning apps and learning curriculum. Contents and lessons are being provided by leading names in education, including Oxford University and Discovery Communication. Together with a custom-made interface specifically designed for kids it could be well accepted by young children and educational institutions.

Quo Vadis OLPC?

Still, the key issue remains: Why would OLPC bother to introduce a $150 tablet, if their official mission statement is *To Empower the World's Poorest Children through Education*? Whereas the XO-1 laptop was from the very beginning designed for developing nations, the XO tablet clearly targets Western kids. Where is the charitable angle in selling a mid-priced tablet to children who can afford it anyway? Is there any profit OLPC can generate to invest to ship devices to developing nations? Or, and this does not seem to be unrealistic, are margins being eaten up by Vivitar and Walmart? And why have they chosen to launch a Western tablet? Don't get me wrong, there are definitely many poor families and kids both in North America and Europe with no or only limited access to education, but why would you not have launched a charity program together with Wal-Mart and Vivitar/Sakar to donate a certain percentage of profit for each device sold to buy new tablets for US schools and kids?

I understand the value of the currently chosen partnership for Walmart and Vivitar by using OLPC's image and recognized social ambitions. However, I do not see the same benefit for OLPC; except for the risk of possibly and quickly losing its original purpose, mission, and focus.

Marketing the XO tablet in the US seems to be quite a change of pace for OLPC. It's not a real doing-good device any longer. Instead it has been transformed into an affordable and commercialized kids tablet.

OLPC is a not-for-profit organization that planned to change the world by creating education opportunities for the world's poorest children where a laptop means education and equals the realistic hope for a brighter future. This was all provided by easy-to-use laptops with cutting-edge technology, low power need, Internet-enabled connections, and an education-focused software of the highest quality. Education next to water, food, and shelter. All at the same time.

And now it's selling more or less average tablets to middle-class Americans in Walmart stores. Was this the vision of Nicholas Negroponte and OLPC? One Laptop Per Child... Is the dream already over?

95. LANCE ARMSTRONG DISMANTLED HIMSELF FINALLY FOR GOOD

Finally in January 2013, and only after more than 10 years of denials, Lance Armstrong confessed in two interviews with Oprah Winfrey about his use of performance enhancing drugs.

Early reviews were negative, although slightly more positive concerning the second interview when he played the emotional card. Why is the public so Anti-Lance now? Why did we not enjoy the show?

Is it possibly because everyone already "somehow" knew about his cheating whilst he was still lying to himself and to the world? Or is it, because often he rudely attacked people – and even his former colleagues and supporters - who had accused him of being dishonest? Or, because he complained about having lost millions of dollars from his previous sponsors? Or, even more simply, because he has let down his family, friends, fans, and himself?

There also still remains this unanswered question: "Why would you do that?" Is it the money, the pursuit of becoming famous, the urge of wanting to be liked and respected by others? Or was it caused by plain overconfidence of the powerful; this haughty assumption that "no one will ever find out"?

I do not want to judge Armstrong. I'm don't have the right to do so. I would just like to express my disgust and huge disappointment. It is very sad for both the reputation of cycling sports and for Lance Armstrong himself. I do feel sorry that he did fall so far... but I'm not feeling pity for him.

96. THE FALL OF THE BERLIN WALL - FREEDOM!

Twenty-five years ago on November 9, 1989, the world watched in amazement as cheering crowds gathered on both sides of the Berlin Wall around midnight to celebrate the opening of the border crossings between the eastern and western parts of the city.

Back then on that memorable evening I was at a friend's house. We were amazed and moved by the peaceful revolution which had taken part in East Germany for many months. When the people finally cracked the Berlin Wall - this grim symbol of the Cold War – we realized that history was about to change. Forever. I still get goosebumps when remembering those beautiful moments.

The fall of the Berlin Wall signaled the beginning of the end of Germany's postwar division and national unity came less than a year later. November 9, 1989 is an unforgettable day in history that led to Germany's reunification on October 3, 1990. It was a day that changed the direction of world history. A day that changed the lives of all Germans.

Let's have a closer look at how it happened and what it means.

Post War Germany

In 1945, World War II ended with the defeat of the Third Reich. The Allied Powers split Germany into four occupation zones, and its capital Berlin into four sectors. Western Germany (Federal Republic of Germany, FRG) aligned to Capitalist Europe (as part of the European Community and the NATO), and Eastern Germany (German Democratic Republic, GDR) became part of the Communist Soviet Bloc and the Warsaw Pact. Germans lived under the divisions throughout the ensuing Cold War.

The Errection Of The Berlin Wall

Germany had been divided for twelve years already when Eastern Germany border police began building the Berlin Wall (German: Berliner Mauer) on the morning of August 13. It completely cut off (by land) West Berlin from surrounding East Germany and East Berlin. The barrier included guard towers placed along large concrete walls which circumscribed a wide area (later known as the "death strip").

The Eastern Bloc claimed that the wall was erected to protect its population from fascist western elements. In practice, the Wall served to prevent the massive emigration and defection that marked East Germany and the communist Eastern Bloc during the post-World War II period. Along with the separate and much longer Inner German border, which demarcated the border between East and West Germany, it came to symbolize the "Iron Curtain" that separated Western Europe and the Eastern Bloc during the Cold War.

Around 5,000 people attempted to escape over the wall, with an estimated death toll of more than 200 in and around Berlin; a precise figure is not known.

Ich Bin Ein Berliner – I Am A Berliner (John F. Kennedy, 1963)

President John F. Kennedy gave a historic speech on June 26, 1963 in front of the Berlin Wall. The speech was given in response to the Cold War and the tension between the non-Communist countries and the Soviet Union. To an audience of 450,000, he declared in his Ich bin ein Berliner speech the support of the United States for West Germany and the people of West Berlin in particular. The speech stands out as a high point of his presidency.

The people of West Berlin understood that he meant to show his solidarity. It was a great morale boost for West Berliners, who lived in an exclave deep inside East Germany and feared a possible East German occupation. His conclusion linked him eternally to his listeners and to their cause:

"All free men, wherever they may live, are citizens of Berlin, and therefore, as a free man, I take pride in the words Ich bin ein Berliner." (John F. Kennedy)

Mr. Gorbachev – Tear Down This Wall (Ronal Reagan, 1987)

In a speech at the Brandenburg Gate commemorating the 750th anniversary of Berlin on 12 June 1987, U.S. President Ronald Reagan challenged Mikhail Gorbachev, the then General Secretary of the Communist Party of the Soviet Union, to tear down the wall as a symbol of increasing freedom in the Eastern Bloc.

The Fall Of The Berlin Wall

In early 1989, under a new era of Soviet policies of glasnost (openness) and perestroika (economic restructuring) led by Gorbachev, the Solidarity movement took hold in Poland and triggered a wave of revolutions throughout the Eastern Bloc that year. A citizen-led movement emerged in East Germany. At the Monday demonstrations that began in Leipzig, East Germans demanded they be given more rights. In May 1989, Hungary removed their border fence and thousands of East Germans escaped to the West. The turning point in Germany, called "Die Wende", was marked by the "Peaceful Revolution" leading to the removal of the Berlin Wall.

Germany 25 Years Later

Germany has come a long way from those days in 1989. After an initial mood of national euphoria back then, we went through a turbulent phase of disillusion by leading multiple discussions about the relative merits of *Ossis and Wessis* until finally we've started growing more and more together as one nation and one people. It has happened along the lines of former German Chancellor Helmut Kohl when he prophesied: "What belongs together will grow back together."

We've built a safe and stable country with a good economy and relatively low unemployment figures (although the unemployment rate is still higher in the East, the gap between West and East has been significantly reduced). There is solid progress rehabilitating the eastern part of the country. The exodus from the former East Germany has ended.

Still, there is much more work to be done. Not all Germans feel like living in one country. We also need to play a more responsible role in Europe and in the world. Although there is no question about electoral democracy, together with countries like the UK and France, we need to continue stopping racist and far-right political parties which have re-gained momentum across Europe in the last ten to twenty years.

In close alignment with our European partners and the US, we need to find better ways to build closer strategic ties with countries like China, Russia, India, and many more to create a more equal and stable world.

Let's Tear Down All The Walls In The World

The German revolutions of 1989 were part of a revolutionary wave that resulted in the fall of communism in Central and Eastern Europe. The events began in Poland in 1989, and continued in Hungary, East Germany, and many other Eastern European countries.

Soviet Union leader Mikhail Gorbachev didn't want a reunified Germany for a long time. The East European Communist elites didn't want it; the West European leaders like Thatcher and Mitterand opposed it and dreaded its consequences; and the US were unprepared for it. Still, it happened. It was a lucky and beautiful event which after four decades reunified many families and a whole country. It was achieved by the vision of leaders like Helmut Kohl - and most importantly - by the sheer will, borderless courage, and immense passion for freedom of East Germans and East Europeans.

Hundreds of thousands of residents of many Eastern German cities took to the streets under the banner 'We Are the People' and sparked peaceful protests that would finally lead to the fall of the Berlin Wall. It was a victory over totalitarianism - a victory for freedom and the right of self-determination.

Let's continue opposing suppression, injustice, and exploitation. Wherever and whenever we encounter them. Let's tear down all the walls which separate us from liberty and peace. The visible and the invisible ones!

97. CAUSE MARKETING - MAKING A DIFFERENCE

In October 2012, super-storm Sandy blacked out various areas of New York and left behind a trail of flooding, destruction, and death along the East Coast.

It even stopped the presidential race for some time, eight days before Election Day. As a result, President Obama declared New York and New Jersey as disaster regions. Many organizations and companies rushed to help to support the people in need. Fortunately of course, mainly since they wanted to help and to do something good. What else did these companies do? And who are they?

Let's have a look: Coke is doing it, P&G is in it, Heinz loves it, PepsiCo does it, Wal-Mart and many more are also embracing it... Cause Marketing!
Cause marketing, or cause-related marketing, refers to a type of marketing involving the cooperative efforts of a "for profit" business and a non-profit organization for mutual benefit.

In this context I'm recalling an excellent study that I read last year. In the meantime, it has lost not a single bit of its relevance. The contrary is true: I believe that last year's JWT's trend survey of Social Good is more relevant than ever: "A number of macro trends are influencing social good initiatives today, including the call for greater transparency, as well as greater corporate and brand participation, rapid urbanization and advancements in technology," said Ann Mack, director of trendspotting at JWT.

The trend report is the result of quantitative, qualitative and desk research conducted by JWTIntelligence in partnership with EthosJWT. Interviewed were experts and influencers from the nonprofit and corporate social responsibility sectors. Quantitative surveys were also conducted in the U.S., the UK and Canada.

The Report's Four Key Trends

The End of Goodwashing: Today's consumers expect greater accountability from nonprofits as well as brands involved in cause marketing — e.g., exactly where the money is going and what impact it's having. More transparency will mean more focus on effecting real change and less "goodwashing."

The Rise of Shared Value: More corporations are starting to shift their business models, integrating social issues into their core strategies. The aim is to create shared value, a concept that reflects the growing belief that generating a profit and achieving social progress are not mutually exclusive goals.

Creative Urban Renewal: As the global population becomes more urbanized and cities boom, brands are becoming key partners in enabling creative strategies for urban renewal — improving local environments, adding beauty or helping to bring communities together.

Ripping a Page from the For-Profit Handbook: Nonprofit organizations are increasingly adopting for-profit tactics, fusing social consciousness with business acumen and focusing on achieving visible change.

"One of the most interesting developments in the area of social good is the rise of 'shared value' — by putting social issues at the center of their strategy, brands can benefit their business, their customers and society in general," says Tony Pigott, global director of EthosJWT. *"By reconsidering products and target demographics, forging partnerships with local groups and improving productivity in the value chain, companies can become a force for positive change while enhancing their long-term competitiveness."*

Findings From U.S., UK and Canada Surveys

People are cynical about where their donations go: 88% of American, British and Canadian adults said they are "sometimes suspicious about how much of the money I donate actually goes to people in need, as opposed to management and administrative costs." Britons (91%) were more apt to say this than Canadians (87%) and Americans (85%).

Consumers believe corporations should do more good: 9 in 10 respondents felt that "companies need to do more good, not just less bad." More Canadians (95%) felt this way than Britons (91%) and Americans (83%).

Brands have a responsibility toward local communities: 84% of adults across all three markets agreed with the statement, "Brands and large corporations have a responsibility to improve the local communities in which they do business." Those in Canada (87%) and the UK (87%) agreed with this more than respondents in the U.S. (77%).

What do you think about Cause Marketing? Is it needed? If so, how best doing it?

98. WHAT YOU GIVE OUT, YOU GET BACK

The human being and the human mind form a very powerful team. With each thought we think, and with each word we say, we create our own future. Nothing less.

According to Louise L. Hay, the key is "gratitude" to achieve a fulfilled life. Long before it was fashionable to discuss the connection between the mind and the body, Louise had developed a set of healing techniques and the concept of positive thinking.

Her self-healing-focused approach and her belief that "what you give, you get back" is very similar to Byrne's best-selling book The Secret, which itself is based on the law of attraction. Both Hay and Byrne claim that positive thinking can create life-changing results such as increased wealth, health, and happiness.

Their books have been sold millions of times, but at the same time they have also attracted a great deal of controversy. Often, critics were among the so-called academics and representatives of the business world – what a surprise.

Still, myself being a big believer in the concept of "positive thinking" and "what we give out, we get back," I'd like to share some of Louise's key thoughts which I've found very helpful and inspirational:

We are each responsible for all of our experiences
Every thought we think is creating our future
The point of power is always in the present moment
It's only a thought, and a thought can be changed
Resentment, criticism, and guilt are the most damaging patterns
When we really love ourselves, everything in our life works

Now, my dear friends, it's really up to* you what you make of these statements of belief. Do you believe in yourself and in your capabilities and skills? How strongly?

99. GIVING THANKS - EVERY DAY!

In these busy times we often forget the really important things in life. One of them is to express gratitude towards others, like colleagues, neighbors, friends, and family. For example, when did you last say, "Thank you?"

True! Most of the time we miss it even without bad intentions. Why? Because we have so many other "priorities" to think of. That's not an excuse, however. On the contrary, it's a good reminder that "thankfulness" and "appreciation" are important behaviors in life and at work - behaviors that need to be fostered throughout the year, every day, even – and especially – when we are busy.

I would like to share with you a great article from Ron Ashkenas I came across the other day. And guess what? It's exactly about our topic: Thankfulness! Read and enjoy it!

There are actually two kinds of appreciative behaviors that managers need to develop: interpersonal and organizational. Interpersonal appreciation is the day-to-day ability to genuinely and graciously thank other people for what they do. This may sound like Etiquette 101, and we assume it's the basis for most of our interactions in organizations. Unfortunately, it's a behavior that's too often forgotten in the heat of battle, the tension of deadlines, or the routine performance of repetitive tasks. In fact, many managers seem to think that a salary and a steady job are the only thanks that subordinates need.

The reality is that all of us need affirmation and positive feedback, at least occasionally. Without it, it's easy to lose self-confidence ("Did I make the right call?") or become cynical ("Nobody cares whether I work hard or not"). More importantly, without some measure of day-to-day appreciation it's difficult to build relationships and trust, which are essential to a well-functioning workplace.

In fairness to managers, neglecting to give interpersonal thanks is usually unintentional, particularly for the busy and overwhelmed. When someone points out to them that a "thank you" is needed, they usually comply. The challenge, though, is how to make the process of giving thanks more routine, so that it occurs without a reminder.

One way to do this is to build a "thanks step" into your project plans; another is to periodically bring your team together to celebrate and appreciate what's been accomplished. And of course, as some managers do, you can always put a post-it note on your desk as a reminder to say "thank you."

The second type of thanksgiving is appreciating how effectively your organization solves problems and gets things done. Many managers have a tendency to focus on the things that are not working well, the shortfalls and the misses. On the other hand, much of the power and potential in organizations is revealed by its success stories. By identifying these vignettes and shining a spotlight on them, managers can help to tease out important lessons, reinforce innovation, and unlock tremendous value.

The Appreciate Inquiry movement was started by my former colleagues at Case Western Reserve University and has demonstrated that this approach can not only improve corporate functioning, but also facilitate social innovation.

Similarly, an approach called Positive Deviance shows that finding people who succeed, when everyone else is struggling, can be key to large-scale innovation.

It's wonderful to have a holiday dedicated to giving thanks. But perhaps if all of us were more thankful and appreciative throughout the year, we'd have much more to be thankful for.

100. DO YOU DARE EXPRESSING YOUR LOVE?

Some minutes ago I read a truly fascinating article called How to let Your purpose find You by Umair Haque.

He's giving what he calls his "top four admittedly idiosyncratic — yet hopefully pragmatic — tips" about how to have a more fulfilled life. I was moved and inspired by his first tip especially. Let's jointly read the following lines to tip 1 and then please share your thoughts with us.

"Be uncool enough to love. Purpose is a kind of love; it bridges the gap between the individual and the world. Yet, at every turn, in our brain-dead cult of the glacial machine, we're discouraged from even using the word love — unless, of course, when it serves the consumerist purpose of selling diamonds or cheeseburgers or SUVs. So we substitute lower-quality ingredients for it, talking about "passion" or "dreams" or "bucket lists." Yet, just as a McBurger is more of a food-like product than real food, so McLove just gives us the sensation of emotional fullness without the lasting nourishment of sustenance.

Real love, today, is outmoded, passé; it just isn't cool. Love your work? Love your neighborhood? Love your life? Love humanity? Love yourself? See, I just made you roll your eyes with the coolly detached irony of the moustachioed hipster overlord.

In our overly numb culture of icy cool, when we do feel something, we so often feel the opposite of love: hate, anger, fear, and envy. And those can give you drive. But drive isn't purpose — drive is a fury to be slaked, an ambition to be achieved.

Purpose is love, not just little-l love, but Big Love, the grand affair that defines a life — first between you and your better, fuller, truer, worthier self; and then between yourself and the world. And the longer you spend insulated in the armor of ironic detachment, icy cool in your igloo — the longer you're on something like a permanent vacation in the lifeless arctic wastelands of the empty tundras of the human soul."

ACKNOWLEDGEMENTS

THERE ARE MANY people who made this book become a reality. All of them I owe an incredible amount of gratitude.

First and foremost are my beautiful wife Bianca and my gorgeous daughters Jule and Felicity. An incredible source of love, inspiration, and continuous support and tolerance. I'm deeply grateful for every moment I am with you!

Second, there are the tens of thousands who commented my articles and helped me to question my ideas and beliefs. And as such helped me to grow and to develop to become a better leader and manager. Thank you!

Third, I have been very lucky throughout my career having worked with many exceptional teams, colleagues, line managers, business partners, and mentors who have challenged me to accomplish more than I could have done on my own.

ABOUT THE AUTHOR

ANDREAS VON DER Heydt is an Amazon director and the head of Kindle in Germany.

Before that he was the Country Manager of Amazon's flashsales site Amazon BuyVIP for Germany.

His background is in management, sales, marketing, digital and traditional media, branding, team building and development. He has worked in the United States, Europe (West and East), Asia, Australia and New Zealand. Andreas has studied in Germany, the UK, Spain, and Japan and holds an MBA from Henley Business School, UK. He's a passionate and respected leadership expert and keynote speaker with a very broad international working experience in Consumer Goods, Retailing, Digital Media, and Internet/E-Commerce.

Prior to joining Amazon, Andreas was the General Sales Manager for Europe at L'Oréal in Paris, France. Before that he held various senior management positions at L'Oréal, including General Manager in Poland and New Zealand, Marketing Director in Germany, Commercial Director in Australia, and Director of Key Account Management in Germany.

In addition, Andreas is a certified master coach (systemic coaching, executive coaching, leadership coaching). In his spare time he coaches executives, young entrepreneurs, and teenagers.

Andreas wrote two books on Efficient Consumer Response (ECR) and Category Management as well as various popular articles on leadership and management. Some of his articles have been featured in The Business Insider, WSJ blog, and World Economic Forum blog. In October 2012 Andreas was nominated as a founding member in LinkedIn's Influencer program.

Andreas, his wife and their two daughters live with their dog and two birds close to Frankfurt, Germany.

Made in the USA
San Bernardino, CA
20 January 2017